OCT 0 7 2022

D0699296

NO LONGER PROPERTY OF
THE SEATTLE PUBLIC LIBRARY

EXTRAORDINARY VALOR

EXTRAORDINARY VALOR

The Fight for Charlie Hill in Vietnam

WILLIAM REEDER, JR.

LYONS
PRESS

Guilford, Connecticut

An imprint of Globe Pequot, the trade division of
The Rowman & Littlefield Publishing Group, Inc.
4501 Forbes Blvd., Ste. 200
Lanham, MD 20706
www.rowman.com

Distributed by NATIONAL BOOK NETWORK

Copyright © 2022 by William Reeder, Jr.

All rights reserved. No part of this book may be reproduced in any form or by any electronic or
mechanical means, including information storage and retrieval systems, without written permission from
the publisher, except by a reviewer who may quote passages in a review.

British Library Cataloguing in Publication Information available

Library of Congress Cataloging-in-Publication Data
Names: Reeder, William, Jr., author.
Title: Extraordinary valor : the fight for Charlie Hill in Vietnam / William Reeder, Jr.
Description: Guilford, Connecticut : Lyons Press, [2022] | Includes bibliographical references and index.
Identifiers: LCCN 2021050988 (print) | LCCN 2021050989 (ebook) | ISBN 9781493063673 (cloth) |
    ISBN 9781493063680 (epub)
Subjects: LCSH: Duffy, J. J. (John J.) | Lê, Văn Mễ. | Easter Offensive, 1972. | Vietnam War, 1961–
    1975—United States.
Classification: LCC DS557.8.E23 R44 2022 (print) | LCC DS557.8.E23 (ebook) | DDC
    959.704/3373—dc23/eng/20211028
LC record available at https://lccn.loc.gov/2021050988
LC ebook record available at https://lccn.loc.gov/2021050989

♾️™ The paper used in this publication meets the minimum requirements of American National
Standard for Information Sciences—Permanence of Paper for Printed Library Materials, ANSI/NISO
Z39.48-1992.

Người Ở Lại Charlie*

Oh you
The ones who stayed at 'Charlie'.
Oh you
The ones who died in battle.
Yes, you are the nation's newest heroes,
You are the bravest of the brave.
We mourn your passing with sorrow.

---

*"Those Who Stayed at Charlie," written by Trần Thiện Thanh in 1972. A popular song in the Republic of Vietnam (South Vietnam) then, and still today among many in Vietnam and especially in overseas Vietnamese communities.

To Major John Joseph Duffy (United States Army, retired),
Colonel Lê Văn Mẽ (Army of the Republic of Vietnam),
Major Đoàn Phương Hải (Army of the Republic of Vietnam),
and all the brave paratroopers of South Vietnam's 11th Airborne Battalion.

This is the true story of the Battle for Charlie Hill. It is an account of the actual events and the real heroes who fought there. The dialogue used in telling the story has been crafted from the recollections of those involved. The conversations are faithful renditions drawn from their memories. This is their story.

CONTENTS

List of Maps xiii

CHAPTER 1: End of the Road 1

CHAPTER 2: Boy on a Buffalo 7

CHAPTER 3: New York, New York 23

CHAPTER 4: Next Stop Is Vietnam. 39

CHAPTER 5: Soldiering On 55

CHAPTER 6: Brothers in Arms 71

CHAPTER 7: Kontum 85

CHAPTER 8: Rocket Ridge 95

CHAPTER 9: Opening Salvos 109

CHAPTER 10: Interlude. 125

CHAPTER 11: Tuesday 131

CHAPTER 12: Wednesday 139

CHAPTER 13: Thursday. 149

CHAPTER 14: Friday 159

CHAPTER 15: Saturday 179

CHAPTER 16: Aftermath 191

Epilogue 207

Appendix 1: Lessons Learned 219

Appendix 2: Key Personnel. 221

Appendix 3: Historical Note: The ARVN Airborne 223

Contents

Author's Note. 231
Glossary 233
Notes 241
Sources 249
Index 255
About the Author 261

Maps

North and South Vietnam 5

Saigon Area 67

The Central Highlands, Part of South Vietnam's II Corps. 89

The Charlie Hill Battlespace 103

11th Airborne Battalion Positions on Charlie Hill 105

Chapter 1

End of the Road

THE EXPLOSION ROCKED THEM, THE BLAST DEAFENING IN THE night. For an instant, it lit their dirty, blood-smeared faces, their hollow eyes set in hopeless determination. A few more shells crashed around them, none as close as the first. Each blinding flash shone upon the corpses lying across the battlefield, gruesome evidence of the fight that had raged over the past days.

Hundreds lay dead over the hilltop outpost—the bodies of South Vietnamese paratroopers mixed with those of their determined North Vietnamese enemy. The hellacious battle had allowed the paratroopers to recover only some of their fallen comrades. They'd wrapped a number in plastic ponchos and placed them in trenches. That was a while ago, earlier in the fight, when there'd been time to render a modicum of respect. Later, they'd stacked other bodies in rows, as they were able. Most of the dead, though, were strewn where they'd been cut down in the last hours of combat—punctured, torn, dismembered, and shredded; grotesque reflections of their final, violent seconds of life.

The explosions stopped. The dark returned. Only the moans of the wounded pierced the silence of the night. The stench of death filled the nostrils of the last two men fighting. Smoke choked their lungs. They waited in anticipation. They heard orders shouted from across the field. They sensed movement as another attack wave swept toward them.

The American advisor leaned close to his Vietnamese counterpart and exclaimed, "Shit. Here they come again."

The reply, in broken but well-practiced English, was resolute. "I know. We fight. We fight more."

The enemy once again rose from the darkness, tearing through the night, coming at them as vague shapes, screaming and shooting, throwing grenades as they advanced closer, and closer still. Both U.S. Army advisor Special Forces Major John Joseph Duffy and South Vietnamese Major Lê Văn Mễ, the senior surviving battalion officer, knew this was the final assault. Bullets whizzed by them. A grenade exploded, ripping a hole in Major Mễ's chest. He gasped for air.

John Duffy, already wounded several times himself, looked over his left shoulder. He nodded, satisfied, seeing the decimated force, all that was left of the once mighty 11th Airborne Battalion, escaping down the hillside. John and Mễ, the rear guard, were all that stood between the remnants of the battalion and their annihilation.

They'd been out of food for days. They had no water left in their canteens. Their ammunition was nearly gone. But still the American and his South Vietnamese comrade fought, and still the enemy came. There was no talk of surrender. No thought but to kill as many as they could before they were, themselves, cut down where they squatted on the edge of their abandoned positions.

Lê Văn Mễ strained to speak. "Fight, Duffy. Fight."

They battled with everything that remained in their hearts and souls, but the end of their road was only minutes away. They knew they were about to die.

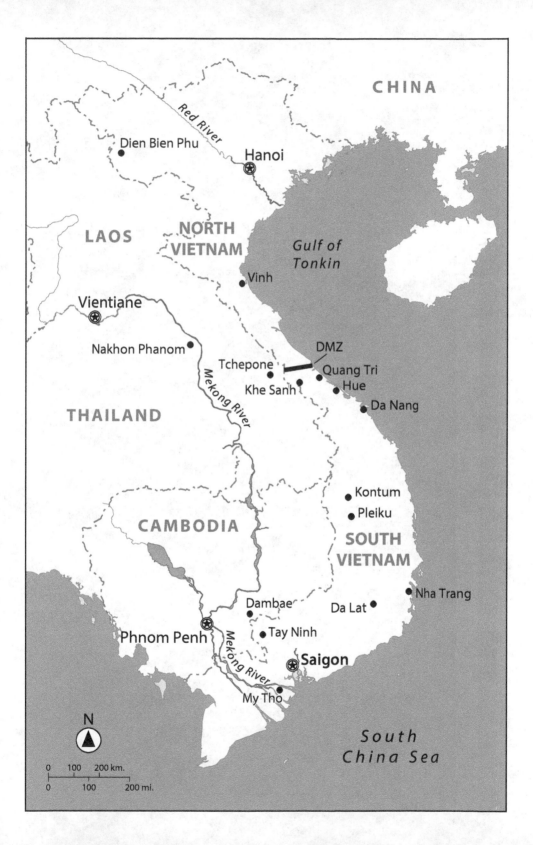

Chapter 2

Boy on a Buffalo

TWENTY YEARS EARLIER, A YOUNG BOY SAT ATOP A WATER BUFFALO, leading another. The animals grazed lazily in a small, muddy field on a simple family farmstead near the village of Mậu Tài in the countryside six miles from the old imperial capital city of Huế, Vietnam. The sun burned in the sky. The day was typically hot, the air heavy with humidity. The boy wore dark cotton shorts and no shirt. His feet were bare. A wide straw hat covered his head. In one hand, he held a wooden switch. He sat on the buffalo quietly, his mind adrift in dreams of fantastic adventure.

From time to time, he'd maneuver the beasts to fresh grass with smacks of the switch, shouts and kicks, and pulls on the single rein that ran from a crudely fashioned rope bridle wrapped around his animal's head and strung through its large, black, rubberlike nostrils. The brute snorted, grudgingly acquiescing to the boy's commands, dragging the other along.

"Mẽ! Mẽ!" his mother shouted from afar. "Time to eat!"

"I'm coming, Momma!" he yelled. He turned his animal and urged it toward home, twisting himself halfway around and pulling the lead rope of the trailing buffalo.

As he neared the farmstead, he leaped to the ground and led the two animals outside a small, open-sided, thatch-roofed pen beside the house. There he drew water from a concrete cistern. He dumped buckets of water over their backs and used a scrub brush to wash the red mud from their hides. Only then did he lead them into the pen and tie them for the night. He washed himself before heading inside to eat.

Lê Văn Mễ was a good boy, hardworking, and respectful. He came into the world in 1942, the second of nine children, the oldest a sister. That left him lots of responsibility as the eldest son in a large family. He'd routinely help his father on the farm. That included chores with the chickens and pigs, tending the garden, and using the buffalo to plow their small fields. He also oversaw much of the work of his siblings, assisting them as they needed help. All the while, he went to school and studied hard.

He graduated from Quốc Học High School in Huế, one of the top schools in the country. Quốc Học attracted students from the elite of Vietnamese society. Mễ did not fit that mold. He came from a poor family, struggling to survive on their small subsistence farm. But Mễ excelled in his village school and gained the attention of his teachers. After scoring high on competitive exams, education officials invited him to attend Nguyễn Tri Phương Middle School and Quốc Học High School, only the second person from his village ever to do so.

Mễ continued to help his father on the farm, herding the buffalo and toiling at innumerable chores. His family couldn't afford to buy his schoolbooks, so Mễ worked odd jobs each summer to earn money, both for school and to help his family at home. He took whatever jobs were available, most often hard labor.

After completing his high school Baccalauréat I examinations in 1961, he took a series of exhaustive tests for advanced education. He scored high, gaining admission to the National Military Academy. He left for the academy without finishing his Baccalauréat II.*

The military school was situated in Đà Lạt, a beautiful resort town and agricultural center, boasting fine coffee, fruits, vegetables, and flowers. Đà Lạt sits beside a picturesque lake on a nearly five-thousand-foot plateau in the southern highlands of the country. The weather is always mild, and springlike days abound throughout the year.

The government had shortened the normal four-year academy program to two years for a brief time because of the demand for young officers in the field. Mễ finished in November 1963, on the same day Lee Harvey Oswald cut down President Kennedy in Dallas, Texas. The radio announced the assassination while Mễ stood in formation for the graduation and

---

*A series of high school achievement tests based on the French education model.

commissioning ceremony. The news brought back memories from his youth. In high school, he spent hours studying at the National Library in Huế. He read a good deal about the American senator and later president. Kennedy inspired him, filling him with deep respect and admiration. News of Kennedy's death shocked and saddened him, dampening Mễ's joy on that special day, but deepening his commitment to service to his country.

The army commissioned Mễ a second lieutenant in the infantry. He asked for immediate assignment to a unit in combat. He wanted to go into the Airborne Brigade, the most elite unit in the Army of the Republic of Vietnam (ARVN). Instead, he got the 7th Infantry Division, fighting in the Mekong Delta region in the southern reaches of Vietnam. It wasn't his top choice, but he'd still see combat. Happily, he set off on his first assignment with gusto.

Mễ reported to the division headquarters in Mỹ Tho, a city just over forty miles southwest of South Vietnam's capital, Saigon. Mỹ Tho functioned as a commercial hub, the gateway to the Mekong Delta. It had been key to French colonial dominance of the region. Its importance was not lost to the government of the Republic of Vietnam, which committed significant resources to its security.

The division assigned newly minted Lieutenant Mễ to the 3rd Battalion, 12th Infantry Regiment. There, Mễ got his wish. After several weeks hanging with Headquarters Company to learn the organizational ropes, he took charge of the 2nd Platoon, 1st Company, a role that thrust him into combat operations. His unit pursued an elusive Việt Cộng[†] enemy that hid in the swamps and forests, terrorized villages, and ambushed patrols at will, then vanished like ghosts back into the tangled, murky maze.

Mễ's first taste of combat came in February 1964. He led his platoon on a chase of enemy soldiers in the swamps of Bến Tre Province, just across the Mekong River from Mỹ Tho. They found their enemy, surprised him, and killed several.

His 3rd Battalion was shuttled by boats through a complex of rivers and canals to a location just outside an area that served as a sanctuary. It

---

[†]Việt Cộng translates to Vietnamese Communist. These were the insurgent fighters of the National Liberation Front (NLF), an organ of the North Vietnamese government and armed forces that carried out the guerrilla war in South Vietnam.

had harbored enemy activity for the past several months. The Việt Cộng accumulated stores of weapons, ammunition, and rice that enabled their insurgent enterprise across the lightly populated region. A series of air-strikes had not been effective in stopping their atrocities. The situation required boots on the ground. Early the next morning, the battalion set out on a series of search-and-destroy missions. Find the enemy and kill him. Capture his weapons and ammunition, and destroy his supplies.

The 1st Company formed the point of the battalion operation. Mễ's 2nd Platoon made up the left side of the spear point and his sister 3rd Platoon the right. The company's 1st Platoon followed as a reserve, ready to reinforce either of the two lead platoons if needed.

The going was tough. Rivers and channels meandered among swamp grasses and groves. Rice paddies surrounded the few sparse clusters of hab-itation. Stately coconut palms grew in abundance. Other sizes and shapes of palm shrubs and trees flourished everywhere. Mễ's platoon tramped through mud and wet sand, sometimes dragging thigh-deep through black water, occasionally finding relief on a dry, sandy rise. As they pushed through palm thickets, Mễ took personal offense as wet fronds slapped him rudely in the face.

Contact! Heavy enemy fire stopped their advance.

The radio cracked with a call from the adjacent platoon. "One-two, one-two, this is one-three. Over."

Mễ grabbed the handset from his radio operator. "One-three, this is one-two. Over."

"One-two, we are pinned down here. Heavy fire. Lots of VC. Maybe a company."

"Roger, one-three. I will try to advance and relieve the pressure on you."

Mễ's soldiers stopped in their tracks. He needed them to advance across an open expanse. His greatest anxiety in pondering his role in com-bat was not fear for his life, but rather, whether soldiers would follow his orders. He knew what was expected of him. He worried he might not be able to deliver.

He spied two soldiers nearby whom he felt could be key to his bud-ding plan. One carried a .30-caliber Browning automatic rifle, known affectionately as the B-A-R. The other held a .45-caliber Thompson sub-machine gun. Both designs dated to World War I. Mễ boasted a more modern weapon, an M-1 Garand carbine that had seen service in World War II.

"Come with me," he called to the pair. "Stay close."

Mễ turned to the platoon, raised his arm, and shouted, "Follow me!"

They moved forward, arcing to the left, circling the enemy's right side. Mễ stayed in the lead, firing his carbine. His two-man assault force made good use of their automatic weapons. The rest of the platoon moved to keep up, placing effective fire as they advanced. They took casualties; individuals fell, wounded, some crying in pain. Still, his soldiers fired and maneuvered behind his lead until he got them into a position to attack directly into the enemy's flank. Mễ led the onslaught. Insurgents fell—dead, dying, and wounded. They broke. They ran. The 2nd Platoon pursued until Mễ called them back to consolidate on the position they'd just overrun. He congratulated them on their victory. They looked at him with the respect and admiration he had earned.

Mễ exhibited extraordinary leadership on that first mission. Within days, the army promoted him to first lieutenant and placed him in command of the 1st Company, routinely the lead company in battalion operations. The action set his reputation as a respected combat leader.

The 7th Division continued combat operations throughout 1964. The battle tempo increased the following spring. In one fight at Chợ Gạo in Gò Công Province, Mễ's company engaged a Viet Cong battalion, a five-to-one disadvantage. During the operation, named Tiền Giang 54, the company attacked a Viet Cong stronghold, routed the enemy, and took control of the position. The enemy re-formed and tried to take it back. In the heat of battle, Mễ pushed the body of a dead machine gunner aside. Manning the weapon himself, he sprayed deadly fire on the enemy, decimating the counterattacking force. The company held, controlling the field of battle, victorious. Mễ had further demonstrated his toughness as a battlefield leader.

In July 1965, Mễ got a brief respite from combat when his command selected him to attend the two-month British Army jungle-warfare training school at Kota Tinggi in Malaysia. There he learned jungle-movement techniques, ambush, and camp fortification and security—all with a good dose of British lessons learned from their own counterguerilla experience in Malaysia. Mễ never forgot that knowledge, putting it to good use over and over in the years of hard fighting that lay ahead.

After finishing jungle school in Malaysia, Mễ headed to Saigon for a day of leave before reporting back to his unit in the 7th Infantry. He went with two military academy classmates who attended the jungle course with him, Nguyễn Lô and Nguyễn Đức Tâm. They were bound for a good time.

They'd kicked around town for a while, when Tâm led them down a narrow street, past rows of stuccoed homes, ranging from one to three stories, some with meticulously constructed clay tile roofs, others with corrugated steel or some form of lightweight roofing material. Tightly closed shutters and locked doors sealed the sanctity of family space from the chaos of the world outside. Still, the small street was alive with people, moving with purpose, busily engaged in their business of the day. Tâm stopped beside one of the houses. He turned to Mễ and smiled as he knocked on the door and hollered, "Hello!"

"My uncle's house," he said, swinging the door open wide. "Come on."

Inside the house, Tâm introduced Mễ to his two cousins. After learning a bit about each other, they sat down to a game of cards, *Tứ Sắc*. They got into the game, winners rejoicing and chiding the losers after each round.

A beautiful young woman passed through the room. She caught Mễ's eye. He didn't say a word. Embarrassed, he turned his eyes back to his cards, then back to her, then to the cards again. She cast a quick a glance and the slightest smile as she moved from the room.

"Who's that?" Mễ asked.

One of Tâm's cousins responded, "Big sister. Her name is Sen."

"She's lovely," Mễ remarked, regretting he'd not at least said hi.

The card game went on. Mễ felt his heart pounding and smiled.

He spent that night at a friend's house nearby. In the morning, before returning to duty at Mỹ Tho, Tâm invited Mễ to breakfast at the *Bún Bò Huế, Quốc Việt* restaurant, a short distance away. He was happy to see Sen there with her cousins. After being introduced, they talked and talked some more. Mễ was taken with her and she with him. Looking into his eyes, she found him the most dashing young man she'd ever seen. At five-foot-nine, Mễ stood taller than most Vietnamese. He was handsome, with a look of confidence mixed with a dash of mystique. And there he stood in the sharp-looking uniform of an army first lieutenant.

Mễ discovered Nguyễn Thị Sen to be a bright twenty-year old woman. She worked in the marketing department of the American CALTEX Oil Company in downtown Saigon. She had just returned from Đà Lạt, where she'd spent a week seeking advice from cousins and friends on whether she should accept a marriage proposal from a schoolteacher, a matchup arranged by her parents. And now there was Mễ.

He fell hopelessly in love with her at that first meeting. In that instant, with that introduction, Mễ's life changed forever. Sen was charming and lovely. Unable to do otherwise, Mễ delayed his return to his unit, extending his one-day leave to two weeks so he could spend time with her. On Mễ's final day in Saigon, they went to dinner at the *My Canh Café*, a glitzy floating restaurant on the Saigon River. It became an evening they'd never forget. The next day, Mễ headed to his unit, catching no small amount of hell for the extended leave.

It was worth it, worth every bit of it, Mễ said to himself with a smile.

❦

Sen called off her arranged engagement to the schoolteacher, rejecting his proposal. She knew, already, that Mễ would be her partner for life. Her father was irate. He wanted his daughter to have the status that came with marriage to a respected teacher from an upstanding family, not suffer the condescending looks she'd get being the wife of a soldier from a poor farming family that had been unable to send him to a proper college. And there was the war. Mễ would always be in danger. Sen would suffer the angst of an army wife.

She told her father, "I can't marry someone I don't love."

At the same time, she thought to herself, *Yes, I'm in love, but life is going to be rough from here on out.*

Over the months ahead, they wrote long, impassioned letters to each other. Mễ returned to Saigon as often as he could. Occasionally, Sen risked a bus ride to Mỹ Tho to see Mễ when he was off duty.

Mễ felt something missing in his military service, though. As interesting as his duty was in the 7th Division, he yearned for something else.

There's got to be more for me in the army than this, he thought.

He needed a new challenge. He knew he had more to give than was being asked of him in the infantry. In November 1965, he got his chance. The Airborne Brigade expanded to become a division-size organization. They needed more officers. When Mễ had graduated from the Military Academy two years earlier, he failed to win the lottery for an airborne assignment. He'd had to settle for combat infantry. Now he had the chance to make his dream come true. He volunteered and was accepted to serve in the Airborne Division. He went off to the army's jump school in Saigon to become a paratrooper.

Parachute training turned out to be the hardest thing he'd ever done in his life. The physical exertion proved intense. The instructional cadre constantly barked degrading slurs while demanding perfection.

"Do it again, you slime-bellied wimp!"

The airborne candidates repeated physical drills and exercises over and over until they got them right. It was tough. Those who made it through that first week of physical pain and verbal harassment went on to learn the needed parachute skills and finally demonstrate their proficiency in a series of jumps during the last week of the course. Mễ stood tall at attention— head high, chin down, shoulders back, and chest out—as a school jumpmaster pinned airborne wings on his uniform at graduation. In this, Mễ earned admittance into the proud brotherhood of the *Angels in Red Hats*, the *Mũ Đỏ*, the moniker by which all of Vietnam knew these warriors who wore red berets and dropped from the sky. The Airborne Division was the most elite unit in the Republic of Vietnam's Army. It was here that Mễ found his place. It was here that he belonged.

Mễ enjoyed a major benefit from being in the airborne. All Vietnam's parachute units were assigned around Saigon. They formed the Army of Vietnam's strategic reserve. They normally deployed only for short periods to deal with a combat crisis and then returned to Saigon. Sen lived in Saigon. Mễ now found himself close by. Their relationship blossomed. They talked of marriage, but the war always held them back. Mễ felt skeptical about bringing Sen into a marriage that could be shattered in an instant with his death in battle, or worse for Sen, his being maimed for life and her burdened with his care.

Nonetheless, the romance continued, and their love grew. They cherished every moment together. But the war went on, as well, its specter haunting them and their dreams for their future together.

After parachute school, Mễ went to the 33rd Company of the 3rd Airborne Battalion. As a first lieutenant, Mễ's rank qualified him to be a platoon leader, responsible for forty paratroopers. However, the company commander wanted first to assess his ability in combat. He dispatched Mễ on a night mission to set up an outpost beyond the unit's perimeter. When the squad returned the next morning, a perimeter guard mistakenly opened fire.

Mễ jumped forward and yelled, "Cease fire! Friendlies. Friendlies. Don't shoot."

The firing stopped. But not before a bullet hit Mễ, knocking him down. He felt moisture down his side. He stood back up to assess the damage. The bullet had hit his canteen and had not gone through his webbed pistol belt. That saved his life. He was okay. It had not been a pretty mission, but he'd kept his cool under fire and reacted as a leader should. The commander immediately made him the platoon leader.

A few weeks later, Mễ led the platoon against a Viet Cong unit in Bình Định Province, an enemy-infested area midway up South Vietnam's coast. Once again, he led from the front. He got shot in the chest, miraculously survived, and went to the military hospital in Saigon for three months. Sen visited daily, spending every minute possible with him, helping with his care. When Mễ returned to duty, he became commander of 33rd Company.

In November 1966, Mễ's battalion returned to Bình Định Province for Operation Đại Bàng 800 (Eagle 800). Mễ put his near-death experience behind him and aggressively led his airborne company in combined operations with units of the U.S. 1st Cavalry Division and Korean Army Tiger Division to rout Viet Cong forces in Bình Định Valley. They destroyed the enemy Yellow Star Division and decimated other local insurgent forces.

Mễ thrived in combat, his confident, aggressive personality serving him well—with one exception. Early in the new year, Mễ had a personal conflict with his battalion commander. It could only end in one way. He'd have to move. Mễ transferred out of the 3rd Airborne Battalion and into the 9th. There, he quickly gained the respect of his new boss, who placed him in command of the 91st Company. He continued to excel as a combat leader.

By the spring of 1967, the Viet Cong grew stronger in the most northern region of South Vietnam, an area the military designated as I Corps. U.S. Marine Corps units engaged in bloody battles at their outpost, Cồn Tiên, on the southern edge of the Demilitarized Zone, or DMZ, that separated North and South Vietnam. In response, Mễ's battalion joined other ARVN and U.S. Marine units in Operation Lam Sơn 54 (known to the Americans as Operation Hickory).

Labeling the operation Lam Sơn had special significance for the Vietnamese. They reserved this title for only the most important ARVN offensives. The name comes from the Lam Sơn Uprising of 1418–1427. Lê Lợi, a wealthy landowner in the village of Lam Sơn, led a rebellion against the occupying forces of the brutal Chinese Ming Empire. It took nearly ten years, but his armies grew and eventually defeated the Chinese, driving them from the country and achieving four centuries of independence, lost only on the arrival of the French in 1858. Lê Lợi became emperor and is regarded as one of the country's greatest heroes. Thus, "Lam Sơn" holds very special meaning.[1]

During Lam Sơn 54, Mễ's unit fought against main force North Vietnamese Army (NVA) units, engaging the 31st and 812th NVA regiments and inflicting heavy casualties.[2] In the follow-on operation, Lam Sơn 60, Mễ's 91st Company relocated northeast of Huế. The company fought bravely to secure a big victory for his 9th Battalion. Immediately afterward, on June 6, 1967, the vice president of the Republic of Vietnam personally promoted Mễ to the rank of captain in a ceremony in the city of Huế, his hometown. Mễ was so proud to have fought for his native land.

All came to a tumultuous head early the next year, with the 1968 Tết Offensive. The war suddenly exploded in a fury that shocked the country and rocked Mễ's and Sen's lives. The year opened with North Vietnamese forces threatening remote border regions and laying siege to the U.S. base at Khe Sanh in the extreme northwest of the Republic of Vietnam. Allied attention focused on defending the base. The siege, in part, was a largely successful diversion. The United States moved additional reinforcing units to the area. The ARVN dispatched a brigade task force to I Corps including the 2nd, 7th, and 9th airborne battalions. Mễ's 9th Airborne Battalion took up positions around Quảng Trị City, the northernmost provincial capital in South Vietnam. His company acted as a defensive force on the south side of city.[3]

On January 30, communist Viet Cong guerrillas, with support from the North Vietnamese Army, rose up in towns and villages across South Vietnam in hopes of sparking a popular uprising that would overwhelm the military, topple the government, and bring the communist National Liberation Front to power in Saigon. The communists staged the attacks during a mutually agreed truce for the annual Tết Lunar New Year holiday. The campaign failed, but not before days, and in a few cases, weeks of hard fighting. Mễ's airborne unit found itself in the midst of some of the toughest battles of the Tet campaign.[4]

In the first hours of the offensive, the NVA attacked the 9th Battalion with a vengeance. They attacked along two axes, one from the north and one from the south. North of Quảng Trị City, the enemy hit the battalion's 94th Company hard. The fighting took the lives of Captain Thừa, the company commander, and his American advisor, Sergeant First Class John Church, a Korean War veteran. Most in the company were killed or wounded.

Attacks on the southern axis slammed headlong into Mễ's 91st Company. His paratroopers fought hard. He utilized available artillery while his advisor, Master Sergeant Mike Smith, called in American airstrikes and coordinated medical evacuation to U.S. 7th Fleet ships offshore. The 91st Company repulsed the attack, counterattacked, and pushed back the multibattalion enemy onslaught. The victory cost them dearly. Casualties brought the company's strength from four platoons down to two. Still, they held the ground they'd gained. In three days of fighting, the 9th Airborne Battalion routed the enemy in Quảng Trị and secured the city.

And so went Tết. Across Vietnam, ARVN and American forces crushed the uprising quickly and decisively. That is, everywhere except for the old imperial capital city of Huế. There, main-force North Vietnamese units fought from well dug-in positions inside the historic walled citadel for over a month, making it one of the longest and costliest battles of the Vietnam War for both the Americans and the Army of the Republic of Vietnam.[5]

Helicopters lifted the 9th Airborne Battalion from Quảng Trị to Huế on February 3, 1968. There they joined the ARVN 1st Infantry Division and the 2nd and 7th airborne battalions, fighting in conjunction with U.S. Marine units in the city. Mể's company, paired with his sister 92nd Company, set out that night, leading an attack to retake the critical Chánh Tây Gate, a key entrance through the citadel's imposing twenty-foot-high west wall.

The two companies moved quietly in the darkness to positions near the gate. At dawn, they attacked with Mể's 91st Company in the lead. A fierce, two-day battle ensued. The paratroopers captured the gate with moderate casualties. They'd succeeded in an important mission in the bloody battle for Huế.

Mể's company continued fighting and taking casualties for two more weeks. Their numbers fell to 25 percent strength. They were no longer an effective combat force. The army ordered the 91st Company, along with the rest of the 9th Airborne Battalion, back to Saigon to receive replacements and train for their next campaign. Mể regretted leaving Huế with the clash still raging, but his unit could no longer remain on the field of battle.

~~~

When Mể returned from Tết, all doubt disappeared. He and Sen would spend their lives together. Nothing could stand in the way. They married on March 17, 1968, before the dust of the Tết battles had fully settled.

Security restrictions following Tết limited their choice of venues. They decided on a simple ceremony at Sen's home with her parents, siblings, a few close friends, and two cousins present. They dressed in the Western style. Mể wore a dark suit and Sen a beautiful white wedding dress with a veil and the new earrings and gold necklace her mother had just given her as a wedding gift. They moved to an altar in the home that had been prepared for the ceremony. There, they lit candles and incense. They bowed first to Sen's parents and then to the ancestors represented at the altar to ask permission for their marriage. They exchanged rings and vows, and kissed. They gazed into each other's eyes for a moment, their smiles the biggest they'd ever been.

"We've done it," Mễ said, the smile broad on his face. "I love you."

Sen looked radiant. "Yes, we have. I love you."

After the ceremony, they chose the *Quốc Tế* international restaurant in the center of Saigon for their reception. Sen's parents, siblings, friends, and other family members attended. Mễ's family could not make the journey from Huế, but he was well-represented by uniformed members of the 9th Airborne Battalion, to include his American advisor, Mike Smith. Mike produced bottles of Martell cognac, and glasses were filled around the room.

Someone loudly asked, "What does *VSOP* stand for?"

VSOP, of course, are the letters on the label of quality cognac. They stand for *Very Superior Old Pale*. The most elite force in the Vietnamese military had another rendition, however.

The airborne officers present all shouted in unison, "Very sexy, old paratrooper!"

Everyone laughed.

After the wedding, Mễ and Sen flew to Đà Lạt for their honeymoon. They spent a week there. Mễ knew the area well from his days at the Military Academy. Sen had visited on vacation. Now they shared the wonderland together, Mễ showing his new bride the beautiful landscapes in and around the city. They dined at the floating restaurant on Hồ Xuân Hương Lake. They walked forested paths to the picturesque Prenn and Cam Ly waterfalls. Mễ took Sen to the famous coffee shop, *Cà Phê Tùng*, where he'd hung out on weekends as a military academy cadet. Now it proved a romantic setting for sitting, talking, and exploring each other's souls. It was a magical time in a place of tranquility. It went by too quickly.

Sen and Mễ flew home to Saigon and got ready to return to work and to war. They were deeply in love and dreamed of starting a family. That would have to wait.

Chapter 3

New York, New York

There is no question where John Joseph Duffy is from. He was born in Manhattan, moved to Queens at a young age, and then Brooklyn. He never lost the accent—or the peppering of profanities he picked up in the public schools and on the streets of the city.

World War II raged during his early years. He was seven years old when it ended. He remembered it well. His father, an Irish immigrant, worked in the Brooklyn Navy Yard, right across the East River from Lower Manhattan. The family looked at the job as a godsend after struggling during the Depression. John visited the navy yard on annual open-house days. The ships fascinated him, as did the uniformed sailors, marines, and officers he saw.

Duffy grew up the younger of two children. He looked up to his big brother, Tom, five years older. However, with that great of an age difference, John often became nothing more than an unwanted tagalong. He spent a good deal of time by himself, and at those times, he put his mind and his imagination to work. He proved to be a smart kid with a natural affinity for numbers. He excelled in math, but he found the pace of school boring. He'd whiz through his in-class assignments, then daydream of great adventures until the rest of the class caught up and they moved on to the next exercise.

John generally kept his nose clean, but he began pushing boundaries in the seventh grade. His behavior in math offers an example. His math teacher, Mrs. Kent, tasked her students at the end of each day: "Class. I've written your math homework problems on the board. Copy them down and do them tonight."

John scratched the problems on his paper and scribbled more numbers on the sheet. On the way out of class, he handed the paper to the teacher.

She asked, "What is this?"

"My homework."

"I want you to work on it tonight, at home."

"I did it. It's done."

"John Duffy, you are being silly. It can't be done. There was only time to write down the problems."

"Take a look. I finished in class."

"You can't do that. You've got to do the problems at home. It's homework."

After a time, she gave up and came to respect John and appreciate his skill with numbers. When he finished his work ahead of the others, Mrs. Kent would have him make runs to the office for her. He'd frequently not return to class, but he'd go to the library instead and read books. He loved to read.

In high school, John took to cutting class and walking to the public library on Saint Edwards Street, a few blocks away. His route took him past the Raymond Street Jail. He looked at the imposing penal fortress as he hurried by, its huge, dark monstrous bricks appearing like something from the Dark Ages. It was a terrible place. Small windows, just above curb level, hid frightening secrets behind three vertical and three horizontal iron bars. He felt a cold wind of dread across the back of his neck as he said to himself, *I hope I never do anything to get locked up in that place*—all the while knowingly cutting school. Still, he relished his petty rebellion. The haunting prison only added to the excitement of his quest. At the library, he'd explore the shelves of books, investigating his curiosities. He'd sit reading for hours.

John acted largely as a loner, deeply introspective, but he showed a certain degree of bravado in his social interactions. One Saturday afternoon, he ran into a group of friends in his largely Sicilian neighborhood. On approaching, John shouted, "Hey, Tony. How's Gina?"

Tony snapped back, "Keep away from my sister, medigan!*

"Fuck you. How about a game of cards?"

"Briscola?"

"No. Gin Rummy."

"No, a game of Briscola first, and then we can play Gin Rummy . . . Hey guys, over here. Cards with Duffy."

The guys in his neighborhood played Briscola, an Italian card game. John was pretty good, but he was better at Gin Rummy. He had an uncanny ability to remember what cards were played and work that into a strategy. As usual, he won and pocketed several dollars. Card games kept him in spending money.

However, John's boredom with school continued. He was lost. No direction in life. No motivation. No channel for his dreams beyond the shelves of the Saint Edwards Street Library. He yearned for something, but he had no idea what.

When he was sixteen, a neighbor, a paratrooper in the 187th Airborne Regimental Combat Team, visited the family. He'd just returned from the Korean War. The war had ended some months earlier, but the soldier was just now being sent home. He stood in the family's living room, his uniform sharp, his pants tucked into his tall, shined leather boots. John was impressed. The stories of war impressed him. The immaculate uniform with its badges and medals impressed him. But the shiny boots impressed John the most, the boots that only paratroopers could wear with their "Class A" service uniform. Those highly polished brown jump boots caught his eye—and his imagination. In that instant, John was hooked.

"Yesss, paratrooper. That's what I want to be!"

As soon as he turned seventeen, he got his parents' permission to enlist. He entered the army as a private two days after his birthday—before finishing his junior year of high school.

He breezed through basic and infantry training. Airborne school at Fort Campbell, Kentucky, proved more of a challenge. John endured the verbal abuse and the physical pain, gutting it out until earning his coveted jump wings at age seventeen and a half. The army assigned him immediately to the 11th Airborne Division in Germany.

---

*"Medigan" is a derogatory label, meaning non-Italian.

He arrived at his military barracks near Munich in the fall of 1955. He settled comfortably into the established army routine. That routine held until late one October evening the following year. His sergeant burst into the platoon bay shouting.

"Paratroopers! Grab your combat gear. We're heading out."

The urgency in the platoon sergeant's voice was clear. John put on his gear and grabbed his ready bag. He drew his M-1 rifle from the arms room and headed out the barracks door. He climbed into the back of a big army truck that rumbled off to the airfield. Supply personnel issued live ammunition. John sat on the tarmac with his fellow soldiers, waiting for the "Go" order, not knowing what was up.

They sat there for three days, ready to jump into combat, their airplanes lined up beside them. Ammunition was issued and turned back in, only to be issued again. They'd later learn that first alert was for potential U.S. intervention in the 1956 Hungarian Revolution. The second, the Suez crisis, to oppose British, French, and Israeli intervention there. In the end, America did not intervene militarily in either, and the paratroopers returned to their barracks. The Russians allowed tens of thousands of Hungarians to flee to the West and escape communist oppression. The Suez crisis ended when the British, French, and Israelis withdrew after President Eisenhower advised them that the U.S. Congress would not fund hundreds of millions of dollars in military aid to them if they insisted on occupying Egypt. But for those three days, John and his fellow paratroopers had been the spear point of any potential U.S. response.[1]

John found the rest of his tour more mundane. His commander selected him as the Information Education Officer. As such, he informed unit soldiers about German customs and appropriate behavior with the young women around the base, emphasizing the dangers of unprotected sex. He occasionally gambled with some of the other paratroopers, winning enough to buy a new Austin Healey sports car. With his new wheels, he headed out most weekends to explore the German countryside. That winter, he learned to ski, quickly mastering the sport.

John came home from Germany at the end of his enlistment in 1958 and was discharged from the army. He'd enjoyed his time in service. He'd been a soldier. He'd earned credit for high school, passing his GED. He'd also learned a bit of German. Still, he itched for different adventures, other things he wanted to explore. Back in the United States as a civilian, he jumped in his Austin Healey and headed out, touring the country. He had enough savings to last for several months. He visited friends in Tennessee, Florida, and California. He headed to Detroit to be the best man in his big brother's wedding. While there, he drove past an Arthur Murray dance studio. A sign in the window read, EXPERIENCED INSTRUCTOR WANTED.

I'd like to learn to dance, he thought, and stepped inside to apply for the job. His gift of gab carried the day. He was hired. He seemed a natural, quickly grasping the different dance styles. He became the studio's star salesmen. The confidence, poise, and charm he developed as a dance instructor stayed with him.

In three months, he hit the road again—this time to make a fortune in Las Vegas. He'd played cards most of his life. He'd most always won. He had no doubt that talent would earn him a fortune at the Sin City gaming tables. He soon lost all his money and his car.

Broke, John headed for the army recruiter. He reenlisted on March 10, 1960, knowing he'd now make a career of military service. The army sent him to Fort Ord, California, for retraining, then right back to Germany. So went the roll of the dice.

Based on his high math scores, the army made him a finance clerk in the 24th Infantry Division in Munich. Because he was airborne qualified, John soon talked himself into a transfer to the 10th Special Forces Group in Bad Tolz. The post, a former Waffen-SS officers' training school during the Second World War, sat next to a small town nestled in the foothills of Germany's Bavarian Alps. Thus opened a whole new chapter in John Duffy's life that carried him through the rest of his military career, his time in the U.S. Army Special Forces.

Before moving to Bad Tolz, John met a young lady working in a dairy store in Munich. The store sold cheese and milk. John wasn't that keen on either, but he found himself frequenting the store often. The young woman working behind the counter caught his eye. She was tall and slender. Her beauty captivated John.

After a few visits, he decided to carry the conversation further than merely thanking her for the change she handed him at the end of his purchase. He took a deep breath and gathered his nerve. He'd learned a little German. Speaking the very best he could muster, John said, "I see you working here often. Do you live nearby?"

She looked away, smiled shyly, and answered in good but strongly accented English, "Yes. Only a few blocks away. With friends."

Again in German, John asked, "What's your name?"

Her eyes came back to meet his. "Inge. What is yours?"

John, feeling a bit bolder, reverted to English and thrust right to the point. "My name is John. Would you ever consider having a cup of coffee with me?"

Her smile broadened. "Why, yes. That would be nice."

With that first cup of coffee, they began dating. After moving to Bad Tolz, he returned to Munich often to see her. They married the next year. John knew if he got promoted to sergeant, they would qualify for government family housing. He volunteered to attend the NCO (noncommissioned officer) academy to increase the likelihood of promotion. There, he received the leadership award and was also the honor graduate. Those distinctions earned him an immediate promotion to sergeant upon graduation. Inge joined him in their first home as a couple, living on the Bad Tolz base.

John and Inge enjoyed life at Bad Tolz. Their stairwell apartment was comfortable, the community welcoming, and the surrounding mountains breathtaking. They were young and in love. Romance beckoned. However, the army demanded most of John's time. He loved his wife, but he also loved military service. Required schools and training frequently took him away from home. After attending a five-week course on demolition and mine warfare, 10th Group assigned Duffy as a demolition specialist on a twelve-man Special Forces A Team. That was the very tip of the Special Forces sword. He had arrived. He'd landed right where he belonged.

John excelled in his duties and demonstrated the potential for much more. His commander recommended him for officer candidate school (OCS), provided he'd enroll in night classes in the University of Maryland's on-base military science program. He did and awaited orders for

OCS. His superiors recognized his skiing abilities during winter ski training in the Bavarian town of Berchtesgaden, close to the Austrian border. They made him a military ski instructor while he waited to depart for officer training.

For the rest of the ski season, Duffy lived in a small chalet that had been occupied by Hitler's SS security team during World War II. He could look down at the site of the Fuhrer's old Berghof residence a few yards away. He relished his duty there. He loved the place. He loved the skiing. In his exuberance on the slopes, though, he broke his left arm. It was a bad break of the humerus, the upper arm bone. OCS would wait.

He took four months to recover. During that time, he attended German language school at Oberammergau, another picturesque Bavarian village. He did well, testing at the "professionally proficient" level. The instructors told John he had a knack for languages.

Once John returned to duty, 10th Group sent him back to Berchtesgaden to help get ready for the 1962 military mountaineering competition. It was a big deal under the auspices of the International Military Sports Council (CISM). A plaster cast still covered his arm, and his orders restricted him to light duty. Nonetheless, John helped prepare the mountainside for the events. While trying to set a rock climbing route with his good right arm, he fell from a cliff and rebroke his left arm in the same place—in addition to acquiring a number of other injuries. He returned to the hospital with his shattered cast to have his arm reset and begin another period of mending. His physician, Dr. McLeod, was not happy. OCS would wait some more.

This time during his recuperation, he cross-trained in other Special Forces skill sets. He completed the required courses for communications/Morse code, medic, weapons, and intelligence. He now met all the requirements for official Special Forces qualification and the right to wear the coveted green beret that had just been authorized that past September. He felt good for what he had accomplished, but he was anxious to get back to unrestricted duty.

The X-rays looked fine in August, so Dr. McLeod removed John's cast and returned him to full duty, certifying him good to go. On his way back to his A-Team, John stopped home to kiss his now seven-months' pregnant wife and give her the good news. His teammates welcomed him back and wished him well, knowing he'd soon have a new date to begin officer training.

He went to the airfield that evening, grabbed a parachute, and placed himself on the manifest of the next jump-flight taking off. As they approached the drop zone, on command from the jumpmaster, John stood and hooked his static line to the cable just above his shoulder that ran the length of the plane. He checked his static line and his gear. He felt excited for his first jump in a long time. He moved toward the door. Out he went, counting, *One one-thousand, two one-thousand, three one-thousand.*[†] His chute opened, but one of the risers had caught under his arm. He heard and felt a *snap.* Pain ripped below his left shoulder. John slowly used his right hand to find, to his relief, that his left arm was still attached. It was only broken—again.

John Duffy returned to the hospital, thinking, *Oh shit, I've got to face the Doc again. Same arm, broken a third time. Not good.*

Irate, Dr. McLeod bellowed, "I return you to duty after you broke your arm twice, and that very same day you put your dumb ass right up on a night parachute jump! What were you thinking?"

John looked at him and smiled dumbly through the pain.

This time the good doctor put a steel rod in John's arm. He did not want to see him again with another fracture. The incident delayed OCS yet again while Duffy healed.

—◆—

John slept soundly next to Inge one warm July night. It was Wednesday, the 25th. Just after midnight, she woke him.

"John. John. Sweetheart. Wake up. My water broke."

John, still in a semiconscious haze, mumbled, "What?"

"My water broke. It's time. We're having a baby."

John lurched awake, sat up, looked at her, and said, "Let's go!"

He leaped out of bed and pulled on his clothes while Inge got dressed and picked up the small bag she had ready. John helped her outside and

---

[†]Counting to four gives the parachutist time to ensure his chute has opened. If it hasn't by "four," then it is time to use his small reserve parachute.

into their small VW Bug. They'd have to drive for an hour to get to the hospital in Munich. Inge's contractions came closer and closer. John still had the cast on his broken arm. He'd had Special Forces medical training, but he still wondered, *What if I've got to deliver this baby with one arm, sitting in a Volkswagen Beetle parked alongside a mountain road in the dark?* He held the steering wheel tighter and drove on.

They made it to the hospital in time. Inside, a nurse placed Inge on a gurney in Labor and Delivery and told John to go relax. It would be a few hours. John walked past the fathers' waiting room and headed to town for a drink. He returned in two hours to find that his son had been born twenty minutes after he left. They named him John Eric Duffy, born on July 26, 1962.

⌣

John Joseph Duffy finally reported to officer candidate school at Fort Benning, Georgia, in March 1963. Inge stayed in Germany with their infant son, moving back to her small village to be with her parents. She had a car and was comfortable while John attended the rigorous five-month officer-training course.

During the months in a cast, only recently removed, John's left arm had atrophied. It looked like a broomstick. He worked hard to regain strength, but he struggled for weeks before he could do decent pushups again. He overcame the harassment of tactical officers by excelling academically and militarily. His Special Forces training put him far ahead of the other officer candidates. His class grades—and his uniform, boots, and tightly made bed—consistently stood among the best. He graduated and was commissioned a second lieutenant in the infantry on September 11, 1963, a little over two months before President Kennedy's assassination.

The army assigned the new lieutenant to Fort Bragg, North Carolina, the stateside home of the Special Forces. Inge flew to the United States with young John Eric and joined him there. They lived in a nice house in the town of Fayetteville, just beside the army post. The design allowed space for a walnut tree between the house and garage. They loved that tree in spite of walnuts randomly banging onto the roof at all hours. Fort Bragg was a happy time, especially for John, because he found himself once again working on an A-Team, this time as the executive officer, the number two in charge.

Twelve Green Berets made up a Special Forces A-Team. A captain commanded, assisted by his XO, a lieutenant. Ten noncommissioned officers filled out the rest of the team, each highly trained in one of five specialties: weapons, engineering/demolitions, communications, intelligence, or medical. Every team member also cross-trained in at least one of the other functions to ensure maximum resilience. All had some degree of foreign language capability. John had served as an engineering/demolitions specialist in Germany. He'd trained in each of the other specialties. He'd already qualified as a paratroop jumpmaster. He was well suited for his duties as executive officer.

The team deployed on a training mission to Ethiopia for ninety days in April 1964. Duffy crammed to learn some of the Amharic language spoken there. On arrival, the team met Haile Selassie, the longtime emperor of the country. Selassie's group demonstrated rappelling skills, going out windows on the palace's second floor. The Green Berets quickly climbed back in when they saw what was below, much embarrassed. Palace security included a squadron of leopards on the grounds. When they saw strangers sliding down ropes, the animals gathered below, waiting to deal with the perceived threat. The soldiers made a hasty ascent back up their ropes to the second floor.

While there, John taught tactics to a group of Ethiopian officers. They deployed into battle against a large insurgent force. John had emphasized the need to fire and maneuver, to shoot and move in order to gain an advantageous position against the enemy, often around a flank. Instead, he found that his pupils led their units straight ahead into the center of the enemy's position. They were slaughtered, suffering 80 percent casualties and losing the battle.

After the fight, Duffy asked the survivors, "Why didn't you fire and maneuver?"

They patiently explained, "The stories you told were very interesting. However, if we did not attack them head-on, that means we are afraid of them. That would be cowardice in our culture. We cannot do that."

John registered an important lesson in his mind: *Others' cultural norms and expectations do matter. Learn them.*

On his return to Fort Bragg in July 1964, the 6th Special Forces Group moved John to a staff position as part of his professional development. He worked in the 801st Military Intelligence Detachment as a counterinsurgency analyst and interrogation officer. As an interrogation officer, he learned a good deal about psychology and human nature. His counterinsurgency work gave him access to information on a simmering situation in a faraway place called Vietnam. He'd known there were a few American advisors there; now he learned a lot more.

While at the 801st, he met Lieutenant Colonel Robert Fleet, who became his most memorable mentor. Fleet had risen to the enlisted rank of First Sergeant in World War II. He spent time as a warrant officer before earning a commission and advancing to his current rank. He knew the army. He could deal with any situation. Fleet helped John draw from his enlisted experience in his approach to being an army officer. Duffy forevermore appreciated the grounding his enlisted service gave him and valued the respect he knew every human is due.

John and Inge had their second child, a daughter, at Fort Bragg on April 30, 1964. They named her Natalie Katherine. They liked the name *Natalie*, and *Katherine* was John's mother's name.

Opening the morning paper before leaving for work on August 4, John saw the headline: "WASHINGTON—Attack in the Gulf of Tonkin." He read on: "North Vietnamese PT boats tonight (August 4) made a 'deliberate attack' on the U.S. destroyers *Maddox* and *C. Turner Joy* in the Gulf of Tonkin and two Communist vessels were believed sunk, the Defense Department announced." John had been following the rising tensions in the Tonkin Gulf for a few days. This slammed it home. The situation in Vietnam had exploded and was now the national headline.[2]

Duffy monitored activities in Vietnam as he continued his duties with the intelligence detachment. He tracked the first American airstrikes, the growing naval presence, the rising number of advisors, and the introduction of regular forces with the landing of U.S. Marines in March 1965. Special Forces had a key role in the counterinsurgency fight there. John wanted to go. He recalled hearing the army chief of staff comment that the war would be over by Christmas. He couldn't sit at Fort Bragg any longer. Within weeks after he received his promotion to first lieutenant in

September 1965, he picked up the phone and called his assignment officer in Washington, D.C.

"I'm requesting assignment to Vietnam."

"But you're a German linguist. We need German linguists in Germany."

"I'm also a Special Forces officer, skilled in counterinsurgency warfare. We're fighting a counterinsurgency in Vietnam, and it may be over soon. That's where I need to be."

"Understood. I'll see what I can do."

A month later John got his orders—to Germany.

He left Inge and the children at Fort Bragg until he could get settled overseas and have them join him later. En route to his new posting, the army sent him to a ten-week vehicle maintenance officer course at Fort Knox, Kentucky. He arrived in Germany on March 3, 1966, to find himself assigned as motor officer in the Berlin Brigade, an elite unit deterring any Soviet moves against West Berlin.

Several lieutenants soon departed, on orders to Vietnam. That opened opportunities and demanded a lot more from fewer officers. John quickly advanced to be the headquarters and service company executive officer. With the departure of the commander, he took command of the company on April 18, a rapid increase in responsibility in a unit with important missions.

His company's tasks ranged from all manner of support to the Berlin Brigade, to patrolling East Berlin (exercising U.S. access rights), to guarding the last three high-level Nazi prisoners from World War II: Albert Speer, Baldur von Schirach, and Rudolf Hess. Speer and von Schirach gained their release at the end of September 1966, just after John received his promotion to captain. For the remainder of Duffy's time in Berlin, only Hess remained, the sole occupant of Spandau prison.

Hess, the deputy leader of Hitler's regime, had been captured during the war after a curious flight to Scotland to supposedly seek peace with Britain. His postwar conviction at Nuremburg put him in Berlin's Spandau prison, where he remained even after the other senior Nazi war criminals had been released. Security duties at the prison rotated among the four occupying powers at the end of World War II—France, Britain, the United States, and the Soviet Union. Those duties continued so long as Hess lived.[3]

When America's Spandau turn came, John's company provided the security personnel. One of his lieutenants acted as "officer of the guard." Checking on his soldiers, John observed Hess, by then nothing more than a lonely old man, gardening in a small plot of sunshine that graced the prison's gray interior yard.

⌐ ⌐

Inge arrived with the children in June 1966. The army assigned John a three-bedroom apartment, as government-provided quarters, in a large six-story complex on the edge of a lovely park. John's duties kept him away much of the time. But Inge had learned to bear that. She enjoyed being back in Germany and anxiously awaited the arrival of their household goods, all their personal possessions being shipped from Fort Bragg. John called one afternoon that October and told her he would be home in time for dinner and had something to discuss with her when he got there. He arrived to find Inge setting the table.

She greeted him as he came through the door. "Hi, honey. I prepared a good meal tonight."

John walked in and saw she'd made a nice dinner and had a bottle of German Spätlese wine open on the table. He hugged her and then stepped back, placing his hands on her shoulders. He looked down for a moment, then into her eyes.

"I have good news and bad news."

Her eyebrows rose.

"The good news is that the household goods have arrived."

"What's the bad news?" she asked.

"I got orders today."

"But you haven't been here a year yet. And I just arrived." She looked at him curiously. "Where is the army sending us?"

John's face tightened. "I'm going to Vietnam."

Inside, he rejoiced, but he dared not show it. He fought a smile. *I'm off to war and back to Special Forces!*

CHAPTER 4

Next Stop Is Vietnam

INGE DECIDED TO RETURN WITH THE KIDS TO HER HOMETOWN OF Bindlach in Bavaria. The army redirected their household goods there. John's orders sent him to Fort Sherman, Panama, for Jungle Warfare School before allowing him to proceed on to Vietnam—not an unusual stop for some bound for Southeast Asia.

The U.S. Army Jungle Operations Training Center taught the techniques of jungle warfare to select soldiers. The program included lessons on jungle living, mines and booby traps, jungle navigation, water obstacles, tactical operations, and first aid. The course ended with a weeklong field training exercise that confirmed the soldiers' mastery of jungle skills. The program was tough and demanded much from the students.

The army selected Fort Sherman, on the Atlantic Coast of Panama, for a reason. The country was a beautiful land of striking white sandy beaches, clear ocean waters, picturesque mountains, scenic rivers, lush rainforests, enchanting coastal islands, and a cultural mix of amazing people—all Panamanian because of their rich diversity. It was also hot and humid, with monkeys, sloths, iguanas, parrots, toucans, crocodiles, venomous snakes, poisonous frogs, mosquitos, and any number of other flying, crawling, and slithering creatures. During the rainy season (May through December), it rains over 130 inches. That's three times as much as Seattle and almost five times more than New York City. John's good fortune brought him there in November 1966.

Duffy ran, fell, and crawled through the jungle to avoid the aggressor force and accomplish all required tasks. He succeeded, receiving the coveted Jungle Expert badge on graduation. He felt miserable the entire time, though. It rained for twenty of the twenty-one days he slogged through the jungle. Mosquitos tormented him throughout.

John Duffy returned to Germany for two weeks of leave with his family before heading to Vietnam. He didn't feel well during the flight home. He ached and felt tired and sick to his stomach. The next day, a rash appeared, his head hurt, and bouts of vomiting began to plague him. Luckily, there was an American base at Bindlach. John grudgingly visited a doctor there late on Thanksgiving Eve. The doctor ordered his immediate medical evacuation by helicopter to the army hospital in Nuremburg, an hour's flight at night through a snowstorm.

John thought he had the flu. Medical tests confirmed dengue fever, a disease that, on occasion, could kill. His fever spiked to 105 three days running. Doctors immersed him in tubs of ice. The fever would abate for a couple of days and then start all over again. More ice. He lost twenty pounds in ten days. He recovered in two weeks, got out of the hospital, and finished his leave with Inge and the kids. Finally, he flew off to Vietnam and war.

Duffy arrived at the army replacement unit at Long Bình, just outside Saigon, on January 15, 1967. Since he was a Green Beret, they sent him directly to the 5th Special Forces Group headquarters at Nha Trang. There, the personnel officer asked him, "Do you have any preference on your assignment?"

John sat straighter, his voice resolute, his gestures animated. "Yes, sir. No swamps! Get me as far away from the Delta* as possible."

"We can do that."

A phone call to one of the group's regional commands confirmed John's fate. He'd go to Khe Sanh, in the extreme northwest corner of the country, as far away from the Delta as was physically possible. He'd command the Special Forces A-Team, Detachment A-101. On landing at Khe Sanh, he found the camp crawling with U.S. Marines, not a Green Beret in sight. In time, he located two Special Forces sergeants.

---

*The Mekong River Delta is a maze of rivers, mangrove swamps, and islands spreading across the southern portion of Vietnam. Much of the area is covered with water-filled rice paddies. Americans referred to the region simply as "The Delta." John had had enough of swamps in Jungle School and wanted nothing to do with this region of the country.

"I'm Captain Duffy, the new Alpha One-Oh-One commander. Where's the team house?"

The two looked at each other and back to John. The senior sergeant answered, "The detachment moved to Lang Vei, sir. Not located here anymore. We're the last of the transition element for the move. We've turned everything over to the marines. Happy to give you a ride to the new camp."

"Guess that makes me the last Special Forces commander at Khe Sanh. I bid the old base *adieu*."

With that, he commanded, "Let's go."

They jumped in a jeep and drove six miles through the village of Khe Sanh and west on the old Route 9 to the new location, much closer to the Laotian border. The camp occupied an old French outpost that had been abandoned twenty years prior. It sat across the road from the tribal village of Lang Vei.

Duffy noted the tactical disadvantages as they approached. The camp sat on a rise on the south side of the road. It had fair visibility in all directions. However, the large indigenous village and the surrounding forests limited the distance they could see. The view to the west, along Route 9, disappeared a short distance from the camp as the road made an abrupt ninety-degree right turn around a blind curve. John did take some comfort, though, in seeing coils of fresh barbed concertina wire surrounding the camp as they drove in.

The jeep stopped, and one of the sergeants hopped off, returning soon with the A-101 executive officer, First Lieutenant Franklin Delano Stallings. Stallings had been with the detachment for several months and quickly brought John up to speed.

"Welcome to Lang Vei, sir. We're settling in, but we've still got a lot to do. We put down new concertina. The old French wire is worthless. It's all rusted and busted. There's an old minefield, but it's unmarked. Good thing is, the villagers are happy to have us here. They're Bru tribesmen."

Lieutenant Stallings started to explain further, but John jumped in. He'd been doing a good deal of reading about Vietnam, including the indigenous populations.

"Yes, I understand the Bru are one of the tribal groups that live in the mountains. I've read that the ethnic Vietnamese displaced them during their early migrations out of China. The French called them *Montagnards*. I believe that translates to "mountain people." The Vietnamese call them *Moi*. That means "savage." I don't think there is much love lost between the Bru and the Vietnamese. Most of the mountain tribes, the Bru included, are reportedly happy to fight for the Americans. They see the North Vietnamese Army and Viet Cong guerrillas as intruders intent on doing them harm."

The lieutenant's eyes widened. "That's amazing, sir. You've done your homework."

John coolly responded, "I like to read."

As was his habit, John asked the lieutenant questions about himself. As Stallings shared the highlights of events that had brought him to that place in time, Duffy looked at him approvingly, fashioned a slight smile, and nodded. Frank Stallings impressed John as a sharp young officer to whom he took an immediate liking.

"Tell me more about our situation here."

"Well, sir. We've got nine assigned plus two officers, now that you're here. We're short a PSYOP† officer, one intel NCO, and one demo sergeant. We've got an inbound on the intelligence sergeant in a couple of weeks, but nothing on a demolitions guy. We get PSYOP support on occasion from Group, but we haven't had anyone permanently assigned since I've been here."

John acknowledged, "Roger."

"Our mission is to watch the border with Laos and look for bad guys coming across. We run recon operations from the DMZ south to just above the A Shau Valley, from Khe Sanh west to the Laotian border. Terrain elevations run from a thousand feet here in the camp to well over three thousand feet in some of the mountains."

Stallings shivered. "It gets cold this time of year. We saw it snow last week on a mountaintop. Amazing. Who'd ever think it snowed in Vietnam?"

He went on, "We recruit local Bru tribesmen to guide us and to form local combat units. The program is called CIDG, Civilian Irregular

---

†PSYOP: Psychological Operations. In Vietnam, many Special Forces teams included a civil affairs/psychological operations officer to assist and befriend civilians and conduct an effective psychological campaign to undermine the enemy.

Defense Groups. The guys are pretty good fighters, but they need more training."

Lieutenant Stallings walked Captain Duffy around the camp, introducing him to his team members. Duffy talked to each at length. He asked their needs and wants and solicited recommendations. He knew that in Special Forces, captains might command, but the sergeants were the brains of the organization.

John Duffy had been in the army for nearly twelve years and had never seen combat. He'd volunteered for Vietnam two years earlier. Now, finally, he was there, anxious to test his mettle and prove to himself what he was made of. That opportunity came soon.

The team sergeant offered the invitation. "Hey, sir. We've got a patrol going out tomorrow. Want to go along?"

"Absolutely."

Twelve Bru tribesman and two U.S. Special Forces sergeants constituted the patrol. Duffy tagged along. It was all business, dead serious. They didn't encounter the enemy, but the mission marked the start of John's Vietnam learning process. He went on patrol often after that, sharpening his skills and gaining an understanding of the environment. They'd find signs of enemy presence, but never made contact. John remained anxious for a firefight. He wanted action.

Intelligence reported a Viet Cong guerrilla force operating south of Lang Vei. Duffy planned a helicopter insertion of a hundred-man Bru force twelve miles south along the bank of the Xepon River. He and four other Green Berets went along. Racing over the treetops, the steady popping of the helicopter rotor blades stirred any number of emotions. The choppers rocked back, flaring to begin a rapid deceleration and descent toward the ground. All eyes scanned the landing zone for any sign of the enemy. John's focus sharpened. His senses bristled.

The choppers hovered a few feet above the ground. The Bru fighters and their Special Forces advisors jumped off. The helicopters climbed quickly, departing to the east. The rotor noise faded. All stood in silence. Duffy stayed close to the Bru commander. They moved off the landing zone and set out. They scoured the immediate area before beginning a three-day sweep northward, back to their camp at Lang Vei.

They had no encounters that first day. But the next morning, they walked into a Viet Cong ambush.

Rata-tat-tat. Enemy fire. The Bru militia leaders shouted orders. The commander turned to Duffy, pointing to his left front. "VC. Ten o'clock. Maybe platoon. Maybe more."

The CIDG force spread out and returned fire. The cacophony of the firefight intensified. Bullets zipped past John. Men dropped, wounded. Others fell dead. A hand grenade landed nearby, shrapnel tearing into Duffy's left knee—a wound that would reward him with his first Purple Heart. Another grenade rolled between his feet. He held his breath.

Oh, Christ, I'm dead.

It didn't detonate. His heart pounded. He took a moment to bandage his wounded knee. Then a calm settled over him. He began to methodically appraise the situation, to try to make sense of what the enemy was doing, to consider the tactics of his fighters, to assess the progress of the battle. He turned to the Bru commander and firmly directed, "Counterattack. Counterattack, now."

In the face of the Bru advance, the Viet Cong withdrew, dragging their wounded with them. Duffy's force followed the blood trail for a while, but their foe had escaped. They resumed the sweep northward toward Lang Vei. No further enemy contact.

John Duffy had seen his first combat. He'd reacted as he'd hoped he would, done what he was trained to do, kept his wits about him. He reflected, *Scary, but better than expected. This is my destiny.*

On March 2, 1967, a clear day, two silver jets screamed down Route 9, flying low from the east. Many in the Special Forces camp waved. The jets popped up, turned, and dropped bombs on Lang Vei village, with some hitting the Special Forces camp. Radio calls went out in vain. No contact with the jets. They returned for another pass, this time with 20-millimeter cannons blazing. The camp opened fire, thinking the jets hostile. They weren't. They were American. They'd made a mistake. It was possibly the worst friendly fire incident of the war, killing 112 Bru villagers and wounding 213.[1]

Duffy's Green Berets entered the village. The devastation appalled them. They dashed through flames and still-exploding ordnance to pull injured families from burning structures. Risking his life time and again, Duffy rescued survivors. Many still hid in underground bunkers. John and his men crawled into several, begging the occupants to leave. Some did. Others didn't. They were so terrorized that they were frozen in place. John went for the village chief. When they returned to the first bunker, it was too late. Everyone had died. The flames and smoke made the air unbreathable.

The Americans treated the wounded while the villagers retrieved their dead. Team members soon used up most of their medical supplies. When proper sutures ran out, they turned to safety pins.

John worked on one young pregnant girl. As he pinned her split belly together, she kept talking to him. One of the team's translators helped out. "She say, 'My toe itchy from where blood dry on it.'"

"Well, scratch it for her."

He did, and she was all smiles. The girl survived to give birth to a healthy baby boy several weeks later.

The team helped bury the dead and arranged for medical evacuation of the wounded. Duffy requested help through channels to make amends, as much as that might be possible. Emergency flights brought food, medicine, clothing, and building materials. U.S. Navy Seabee construction engineers showed up with a backhoe. Together, the tribesmen, Green Berets, and Seabees built a new Lang Vei village a short distance from the old one. The Bru chief demanded the old village site be abandoned. He claimed his people saw it as infested with evil spirits because of the terrible fate that had befallen it. Duffy leveraged circumstances to also have an airstrip built adjacent to the Special Forces camp.

John had commanded A-101 at Lang Vei for a little over three months when he received orders to be the executive officer for A-113, the much larger Special Forces mobile strike force for all of I Corps, the northernmost tactical region of South Vietnam. They called it a Mike Force, *Mike* being a shortened term for *mobile strike*. The unit served as a three hundred-man reaction force, ready to relieve pressure brought by an enemy attack on any of the Special Forces camps in the region, such as Lang Vei.

The army billed the Mike Force as a combined U.S./Australian Special Forces team. In fact, it was an Australian SAS[†] unit commanded by an Australian SAS captain with an American executive officer. The Mike Force led three companies of indigenous fighters (one each from the Rhade and Koho mountain tribes, along with one company of ethnic Chinese Nungs). Headquarters wanted a capable American as executive officer, the second in command. They selected John Duffy.

Duffy's replacement at Lang Vei, Captain William Crenshaw, arrived at the end of April. John prepared a three-day orientation for him. Crenshaw thanked him for his effort, but said he had everything in hand and did not want to hold him back from his next assignment. John wished him good luck, said good-bye to his team members, and caught a helicopter ride to Da Nang. There, he completed the necessary processing through his headquarters, Detachment C-1, before reporting to the Mike Force in the adjacent compound.

Five days later, the North Vietnamese attacked Lang Vei. There was no time to launch the Mike Force. The fight lasted only a short time before the enemy withdrew. The casualties shocked John. Twenty of the indigenous CIDG fighters had been killed and another thirty-nine wounded. The attack also killed two Green Berets—Captain Crenshaw, John's replacement, and Lieutenant Stallings. John grieved the death of Frank Stallings. They had grown close during John's tenure in command, and Stallings only had another week until he was to end his tour of duty and return home to his family.[2]

Duffy focused on his new Mike Force job in earnest. His principal duties centered on affecting the interface between the team and U.S. Army support elements, as well as providing intelligence for the mobile strike force missions. He found the Australians professional and dedicated to the mission. John organized a functioning supply system, including access to special rations and equipment. He opened channels for getting timely close air support. He also developed plans for the Mike Force to assault into each of the remote Special Forces camps in I Corps in case of attack. His only failure was his inability to keep up with the Aussies at the bar.

[†]SAS: Special Air Services, or Special Air Services Regiment, is the Australian equivalent of U.S. Special Forces.

Just as Duffy felt confident he had effectively integrated the Australians into the American combat systems, he received orders once again, this time to 5th Special Forces Group headquarters in Nha Trang for further assignment to Saigon, the capital of South Vietnam. He fell directly under the 5th Group intelligence chief in Nha Trang as his liaison officer to the military and civilian intelligence agencies in Saigon. John was disappointed to leave the SAS, but excited to face new challenges.

He started his work in Saigon in mid-July 1967. He interacted with fifty-one intelligence organizations, attending briefings, taking careful notes, and scouring reams of highly classified intelligence information. He pushed the most relevant insights from what he gleaned each day to his Group headquarters. His labors gave Special Forces commanders an edge in finding the enemy and countering their insurgent efforts.

His tour of duty in Vietnam ended on January 17, 1968, just before the 1968 Tết Offensive. The army assigned him as a student in the Infantry Officers' Advanced Course at Fort Benning, Georgia. The six-month course taught the command and staff skills that would be needed as officers continued their careers at increasing levels of responsibility. It also provided a nice break between combat deployments.

John left Vietnam, picked up a new Chrysler station wagon in San Francisco, and drove across the country. He met Inge and the kids in New York City, then took them to Columbus, Georgia, where they settled into a redbrick house just outside the fort. When he reported for duty, he learned his course would not begin until late April. Not satisfied to while away his time working mundane special projects, he marched to the brigade commander and asked for a command position. After a brief chat, John ended the day as the new commander of an airborne training company, responsible for putting young volunteers through the three-week army parachute school and awarding them their coveted jump wings on graduation.

Duffy relinquished command on Friday, April 19, and began his course the next Monday. He welcomed the academic break, but he was anxious for another turn in Vietnam. That would be delayed several months, however. The army selected him for degree completion at the University of Nebraska at Omaha. He already had accrued a number of college credits.

After one semester and a summer term, he earned his bachelor's degree in economics with a minor in geography.

Regrettably, the family reunification at Fort Benning had been a rocky road. John and Inge had been apart too often, for too long. The demands of John's jobs and the separations had taken their toll. The thought of another upcoming Vietnam deployment proved too much. By the time John headed to degree completion, they knew their marriage was done. Inge returned to Germany with the children. Their divorce was final a short time later.

Captain Duffy landed at Biên Hòa Airbase in Vietnam for his second tour of duty on August 18, 1969. His orders assigned him to the Phoenix Program. He was not happy. The CIA program collected intelligence on the Viet Cong through interrogation and attacked its political infrastructure through assassination. John didn't feel he had the requisite language skill. More to the point, he questioned the ethical and legal standing of the program under the Geneva Conventions.[3]

He took his records, borrowed a jeep, fixed his green beret firmly on his head, and drove to Saigon. He made his way to a large, five-story building on Pasteur Street. A high wall surrounded the complex. He passed through the guarded entry point, noting an innocuous sign that read, MILITARY ASSISTANCE COMMAND VIETNAM—STUDIES AND OBSERVATION GROUP (MACV-SOG). That was a front. The name was supposed to disguise the mission of the supersecret organization housed inside. Most were not fooled. To nearly everyone, MACV-SOG meant "Special Operations Group," and though few knew what they did, speculation abounded about the dark arts practiced behind those doors.

Duffy had learned of MACV-SOG on his previous tour; he knew the organization consisted of mostly Army Special Forces, but that it also included Navy SEALs, Air Force Special Operations, Marine Force Recon, and CIA personnel. He understood they conducted a range of highly classified missions outside the borders of South Vietnam. These included deep reconnaissance, raids, prisoner snatches, and downed pilot rescues. He wanted to be part of it.

John found the office he was looking for, entered, and announced, "I'm here to see the SOG commander."

The young clerk looked up. "I'm sorry, sir. He's not here today."

A colonel walking by asked, "Can I help you, Captain?"

"Possibly, sir. I have an assignment issue. I'm assigned to Phoenix, and I want out."

The colonel kept walking and barked, "Come with me."

They walked down the hall and went into another office. The colonel turned and extended his hand, "I'm Colonel Isler, the OP Thirty-Five chief. We're the guys who do all the classified cross-border SOG operations. What can I do for you?"

John explained his situation. Colonel Isler sat down behind his desk and read through John's military records. They chatted for a while. The colonel made a phone call. He leaned back in his chair and said, "You're no longer assigned to the Phoenix Program. You are now a member of SOG. Welcome aboard. I want you to cut off all the insignia from your uniforms and report back here at 0700 tomorrow with all your stuff."

Duffy responded with a loud, "Yes, sir."

The next morning, two SOG operators drove John to a secluded ramp on Tân Sơn Nhứt Air Base. They pulled up close to a cargo airplane, its propellers already turning. John noted the aircraft was painted black and had no markings. He climbed aboard. He was the only passenger. As he strapped into one of the webbed troop seats, he heard the pilots speaking Chinese. The cargo door shut. The airplane taxied for takeoff. John wondered, *What have I gotten myself into?*

The plane flew for several hours before beginning a descent for landing. A tall young Green Beret met John when he stepped off the airplane.

"Welcome to Nakhon Phanom, Thailand. We call it NKP." Pointing over his shoulder, he gave a quick orientation. "We're close to the border. The town is nine miles that way. It's on the Mekong River. Laos is just on the other side. That's where we run our ops, focusing on the Ho Chi Minh Trail."

He continued, "You see, we've got a lot of air here. All propeller driven. You might have thought some of it long gone."

John looked around and saw big, gutsy A-1 Skyraider and smaller T-28 Trojan close-support airplanes, as well as a number of A-26 Invader attack bombers, all veterans of the Korean War. He also spotted O-2 Skymaster and OV-10 Bronco forward air control aircraft, and several cargo planes, and a variety of helicopters.

"The aircraft run reconnaissance missions, bomb the trail, and strike the rebels in the Laotian civil war to the north. They rescue downed aircrews, and they support us. We're Mobile Launch Team Three, MLT Three for short, code name 'Heavy Hook.' We run MACV-SOG missions onto the Trail, same as the launch sites in South Vietnam, but we are their weather backup. When things are too skosh on that side, we insert or recover teams from here. SOG teams out of Vietnam are normally three U.S. and eight to ten indigenous. Most that we work with are two U.S. and four indigs because of our helicopter limitations."

John asked, "What exactly do they do?"

"Mostly reconnaissance behind enemy lines, watching the trail, gathering intel, and sometimes directing airstrikes on enemy convoys or fuel and supply depots. They'll tap in to communications lines when they find them. They also conduct ground raids to destroy supplies and equipment. They'll mine roads on occasion and snatch prisoners too."

He looked right at John. "All highly classified. We don't exist. We're not here." His expression tightened. "It's dicey. We've lost a number of teams."[4]

He turned and motioned to John. "Let's go meet the commander and get you settled in."

Major Bill Shelton, the MLT 3 commander, made Captain Duffy his executive officer, overseeing operations and intelligence activities. At the same time, Duffy functioned as launch officer, responsible for coordinating individual SOG team missions. He also routinely flew in the OV-10 Broncos as a back seat SOG observer. The front-seat U.S. Air Force pilots were all qualified forward air controllers, or FACs. The aircraft provided an immediately available overhead capability to synchronize support in real time as a team conducted its assigned mission deep in enemy-held territory.

One critical element of that support required John to work with the pilot to control airstrikes and direct extraction helicopters should the team get into trouble, a situation that happened far too often. The pilots used the call sign, "Nail," the back-seat observers "Fat Capper." Most SOG observers learned to fly the airplane should the pilot get wounded. John Duffy got a lot of stick time and became proficient in flying the OV-10.

Duffy most often flew with one particular pilot, Captain William "Wild Bill" Sanders. However, while John was away on his midtour R&R,[§] the scheduler teamed Sanders with Sergeant First Class Albert Mosiello as his observer. On June 30, 1970, just as John returned to base from his leave, he heard radio calls for help. Captain Sanders's aircraft had been shot down.

The unit kept an OV-10 on ramp alert for emergency contingencies. John grabbed his flight gear and shouted he'd be taking the back seat. He climbed in just as the Air Force pilot was ready to start the engines. They dashed to the crash scene. They saw only one parachute, not the two they'd hoped for. That chute had landed in the middle of what they suspected to be a North Vietnamese Army regiment, about five thousand strong. Duffy's OV-10 took heavy fire.

John heard the beeping of a distress beacon on the emergency radio frequency. He keyed his microphone. "Beeper, Beeper, come up voice. This is Fat Capper zero-five. Nail four-four, this is Fat Capper zero-five, over."

The response came not from Sanders, but from Mosiello, who keyed his survival radio and calmly spoke, "Fat Capper zero-five, this is Fat Capper zero-eight. I'm okay. Some minor injuries. Nail four-four did not get out. He was killed when we got hit. He did not eject."

John keyed his mic. "Roger."

Mosiello added, "Be careful. I can see the NVA setting up guns about fifty yards away. They're going to blast anything that tries to get in here."

John maintained contact with Al Mosiello and pounded the area with airstrikes to beat down the antiaircraft machine guns. An Air Force HH-53 rescue helicopter from Udorn, Thailand, call sign "Jolly Green," approached for the pickup. Enemy fire shredded its nose. Barely flyable, the pilot aborted and limped back to base.

A second rescue helo arrived from Udorn. As it hovered down through 150 feet, an enemy soldier fired an RPG (rocket-propelled grenade). It hit the top of the aircraft and exploded. The rotors separated. Fire consumed

---

[§]R&R stands for Rest and Recuperation, a weeklong leave taken in any number of attractive locations, including Australia, Hong Kong, Singapore, and Hawaii.

the helicopter as it rolled onto its back and smashed to the ground, already disintegrating in a ball of flames. Duffy's OV-10 flew low, looking for survivors. There were none.

Mosiello called, "They're all shooting at you. Get out of there."

John saw tracers flying past his canopy. The OV-10 strained to climb to a safer altitude.

More airstrikes battered the enemy. John identified the firing guns to be hit. The bombardment sought not only the rescue of Sergeant Mosiello, but also to avenge the dead rescuers just torn from the sky. Duffy put in thirty-eight flights of both propeller- and jet-attack aircraft.

The third try was the charm. An H-3 helicopter from Da Nang, Vietnam, successfully hovered overhead, lowered a crewmember on a hoist through the thick jungle canopy, and recovered Al Mosiello. Mission complete.

John Duffy saw lots of action during his time at Nakhon Phanom. He received five Air Medals for valor during the missions he flew there. Following a year of challenging and rewarding service, his second combat tour ended, and he got orders back to the United States.

Captain Duffy reported for duty as the Special Operations staff officer at the 5th United States Army headquarters at Fort Sheridan, Illinois, in August 1970. He had oversight of the training for all U.S. Army Reserve and National Guard Special Forces, Ranger, and Airborne units in a sixteen-state region.

John, no fan of what he called "Disneyland Training" for special operators, insisted on the mastery of basic skills. He did away with submarine insertions, rappelling from buildings, and ski adventures until each unit became proficient in communications and the use of firepower. John felt the most important skill for special operators to be their ability to relate to local forces, to communicate, and to utilize firepower (beyond the weapons they carried with them). That firepower included air force and navy fighters and bombers, army attack helicopters, and artillery and naval gunfire.

Unit commanders complained, but the 5th Army commanding general supported Duffy. After nine months, he felt satisfied the special units in his sixteen states were fully trained and combat ready. He made his mark on a significant segment of the U.S. Army special operations forces.

CHAPTER 5

Soldiering On

LÊ VĂN MỄ SAW PLENTY OF ACTION AFTER THE 1968 TẾT OFFENSIVE. Following his wedding in March, division headquarters reassigned Mễ to the 6th Airborne Battalion at the coastal resort city of Vũng Tàu. There, he took command of the 62nd Company. In early April, the unit went north to take part in Operation Pegasus. The mission: to relieve pressure on Khe Sanh Combat Base and rout the enemy from the surrounding area. The 6th Battalion joined the 3rd and the 8th battalions under the 3rd Airborne Brigade. They fought along with U.S. Marines, the U.S. 1st Cavalry Division, and two ARVN ranger battalions. The South Vietnamese called their portion of the operation Lam Sơn 207A.[1]

The plan called for U.S. forces to attack to clear the main highway and secure the Khe Sanh base itself. The ARVN 3rd Airborne Brigade would deploy west of Khe Sanh, in the vicinity of the village of Lang Vei, to block any North Vietnamese retreat into Laos. The NVA had overrun the American Special Forces camp at Lang Vei two months earlier, on February 7. That battle took a heavy toll in dead, captured, and wounded before a rescue force extracted the surviving U.S. and South Vietnamese defenders, leaving the camp to the enemy.[2]

On April 4, helicopters inserted Mễ's 6th Airborne Battalion into landing zone Snake, west and a little southwest of Khe Sanh airfield. They fought alongside the 3rd and 8th parachute battalions, all three under the command of Colonel Nguyễn Khoa Nam. Intelligence intercepted a radio transmission directing an enemy force to occupy a key hilltop that dominated the battle space. The 6th battalion set out immediately to get there first. The NVA were already moving. The race was on. Mễ's 62nd Company led the battalion's uphill charge. Arriving at the top minutes before their foe, they strained to catch their breath, their chests heaving in sweat-soaked uniforms. The rest of the battalion rushed up the hill behind them. Barrage after barrage of enemy artillery and mortars rained down while the paratroopers dug in for protection. Then quiet. The pounding explosions stopped.

"Get ready," Mễ called to his troops.

Screams shrieked from below. North Vietnamese soldiers attacked, firing rifles, rocket-propelled grenades, and machine guns. The paratroopers held. Mễ ordered a counterattack, himself in the lead. The paratroopers fought hard. They'd stopped the enemy advance and pushed back their foe. They had secured their position atop the hill. Nearby, Mễ's old 3rd Battalion, also heavily engaged, lost Captain Nguyễn Đức Cần, killed in action. He had replaced Mễ in command of 33rd Company. *There but for the grace of circumstance*, thought Mễ.

In the end, Operation Pegasus/Lam Sơn 207A succeeded in relieving the pressure on Khe Sanh and routing enemy forces in the area. The cost, 93 Americans and 51 South Vietnamese soldiers killed in action, 667 wounded. The victors found 1,304 NVA bodies with estimates of the total enemy dead ranging from 3,500 to 5,000 and some as high as 15,000.[3]

Later that same month, Mễ saw action in the A Shau Valley, just a short distance south. The valley had been in enemy hands for several years. After the Tết offensive, American and South Vietnamese commanders agreed the situation required action. Mễ's company, along with the rest of the 6th Airborne Battalion, helicoptered in to fight alongside U.S. 1st Cavalry and 101st Airborne Division soldiers in Operation Delaware/Lam Sơn 216, an effort to clear communist forces out of what had become a strategic fortress for launching offensives and funneling personnel and military supplies moving from the Ho Chi Minh Trail into South Vietnam. The operation proved costly in men and equipment, but it was deemed a success. Participating units destroyed large caches of weapons, ammunition, vehicles, and rice. The operation ended on May 17 with the withdrawal of all friendly units. The North Vietnamese Army didn't wait long before returning to the valley.[4]

At the conclusion of the A Shau operation, Mễ flew back to Saigon to a different assignment. He'd been specially selected to create a new unit, the 1st Reconnaissance Company, directly under the Airborne Division Headquarters. It was quite an honor. He worked hard for months manning, equipping, and training the special unit.

The Saigon duty had its benefits, as well. Mễ relished returning home at the end of each day and the time he had with Sen. It was surreal in a most wonderful way. A comfortable routine replaced the chaos of battle. Their tender relationship took him far from the grotesque brutality of war. They laughed and they loved, enjoying every moment they had together.

After forming the recon company, and having had a four-month break from combat, Mễ went back to war. He took command of the 51st Company in the 5th Airborne Battalion located at Biên Hòa, only twenty miles northeast of Saigon. He was not that far from Sen, but visits were few because of his frequent combat deployments, many in the volatile Tây Ninh Province along the Cambodia-Vietnam border.

The new year brought significant change to the situation in Vietnam. Richard Nixon became president on January 20, 1969. Upon taking office, he inaugurated a new approach to the war. It had three components: pacification, Vietnamization, and withdrawal. Pacification required government protection and services to the population. Vietnamization called for passing an ever greater share of combat operations to the South Vietnamese armed forces over time. Withdrawal meant bringing Americans home. The drawdown of U.S. forces in Vietnam would begin soon.[5]

For Mễ, the war went on without any perceptible change. The impact of Nixon's new approach would only be seen over time. In March 1969, Mễ's 5th Airborne Battalion joined with ARVN regular army units and other elements of the Airborne Division in an operation southwest of Tây Ninh City to relieve pressure by the enemy's 7th Division along the Cambodia-Vietnam border. Action had been heavy for Mễ's 51st Company. They'd been operating on a solo mission some distance from the rest of the battalion. A determined Viet Cong unit squared off against them.

On Tuesday afternoon, March 25, the intensity of fighting died down, giving the company the opportunity to conduct a sweeping search for the guerrillas who had fought them that morning before disappearing into the jungle's shadows. So far that afternoon, they'd had no further contact with their adversary. Mễ ordered a halt and had his platoon leaders form the company into a defensive perimeter. He thought he'd give the boys a break. The paratroopers used the time to relieve themselves and get some nourishment.

The radio came to life. The operator shouted, "Captain Mễ! The radio is for you."

"Take the traffic," Mễ hollered back.

"No. They want to talk to you. Only you. It's a relayed message from higher. Just for you."

Annoyed, Mễ strode the few steps to the radio, took the handset, and transmitted. "This is five-five-one, over."

"Is this the commander?"

Breaking normal radio security protocol, Mễ answered, "Yes, this is Captain Mễ. What's your traffic?"

"Captain Mễ, congratulations. You are a father. Your wife, Sen, gave birth to a healthy baby boy this morning. They are both fine."

Mễ's face gleamed with excitement. Tears welled in his eyes. He turned to those around him and shouted, "I have a son. I have a son. We decided his name. It's Vũ. Le Huy Vũ. My son."

Mễ couldn't wait for the operation to end so he could get home to see his firstborn child, hold him, and hold Sen. How he missed them right now. In that moment, he yearned for his family, while at the same time feeling a stronger love for his country than ever before, and more determination to defend it—even to his death.

He gave another order. "Prepare the position. Dig in. We'll bivouac here tonight."

His paratroopers went to work. Noncommissioned officers issued orders, though not much guidance was needed. The boys had this drill down. Mễ leaned back, cradling the back of his head in the palms of his hands as he looked to the sky and smiled.

That night, one-third of the company stayed awake and alert on watch. Two-thirds slept. The watch duty rotated through the night so everyone could get some rest. Exhausted soldiers slept soundly. Mễ dozed off.

An unmistakable deep, whistling sound pierced the still night air.

"Incoming!" someone shouted.

Enemy artillery pounded the position. It was four o'clock in the morning.

Mễ jerked awake. The explosions rocked the men from their sleep. Sergeants barked orders, and platoon leaders passed reports to Mễ. He assessed the situation in his normal calm but intense manner.

He directed, "Stand by for an attack."

They came. Soldiers from the enemy 7th Division, a mixed Viet Cong and NVA force. They threw themselves against the airborne company, but they were slowed then stopped by decimating rifle and machine gun fire, the triggering of Claymore antipersonnel mines emplaced by the defenders, and the devastation of well-placed mortar shells.

As was his habit, Mễ ordered a counterattack. The pursuit lasted two hours, until the enemy finally limped across the border to the sanctuary of Cambodia. The 51st Company returned to their position to pick up their stuff and prepared for the day's operations. Along the way, they found a number of dead bodies, machine guns, rocket launchers, and an array of equipment left on the field. The 51st paid with the lives of the first sergeant, the highest-ranking noncommissioned officer in the company, the company clerk, Mễ's radio operator, and a half dozen young paratroopers. Still, Mễ was pleased with this victory in defense of his country, the Republic of Vietnam, and in defense of his family, his wife, Sen, and their new son, Vũ.

A new battalion commander, Major Nguyễn Chí Hiếu, arrived on October 16, 1969, just in time for Mễ's move to the position of operations officer, known in military parlance as the battalion S-3. The unit went through a period of training before returning to combat rotations in the spring of 1970.

On April 30, 1970, President Nixon ordered U.S. forces to assault the communist sanctuary areas inside Cambodia. In his televised speech to the nation, Nixon said the order was to "protect our men who are in Viet-Nam and to guarantee the continued success of our withdrawal and Vietnamization programs."[6] Both American and South Vietnamese units crossed into Cambodia with the objective of attacking North Vietnamese and Viet Cong combat formations, destroying their headquarters, and capturing or demolishing quantities of enemy weapons, ammunition, vehicles, and other military equipment.[7]

Mễ's 5th Airborne Battalion fought alongside both U.S. and ARVN units throughout the Cambodian campaign, operating in the Parrot's Beak and Fishhook regions until operations ended in July. They saw a lot of action, working with the U.S. 1st Cavalry Division, 11th Armored Cavalry Regiment, and the ARVN 1st Armored Cavalry Regiment as well as other 3rd Airborne Brigade units. The South Vietnamese labeled the campaign Toàn Thắng, "Total Victory." The U.S. command called it "Rock Crusher."[8]

Back home, Americans protested in the streets of every major U.S. city against what they saw as Nixon's widening of the war. However, the campaign went far in meeting the stated goals and cost the enemy dearly: 22,000 weapons, 1,800 tons of ammunition, 8,000 tons of rice, 29 tons of communications equipment, 431 vehicles, and 55 tons of medical supplies. The operation killed more than 12,000 NVA and Viet Cong. However, the allies paid a price: 809 ARVN and 434 American soldiers killed in action.[9]

After serving six months as the 5th Battalion S-3, Mễ received his promotion to the rank of major. A welcome break followed with his selection to attend the advanced infantry course at the staff college in Đà Lạt. Mễ relished returning to the tranquility of the highland city. For three months he studied hard during the week and kicked back on weekends. He reflected and recharged his psyche. He made occasional trips to Saigon for brief visits with Sen and his children—young son, Vũ, and new daughter, Quyên. Sometimes he flew. Sometimes he risked the dangers of the two-hundred-mile bus ride with his academy classmate and longtime friend, Nguyễn Lô. Their paths had crossed once again. They'd both been assigned to the course together. Even with all the distractions, Mễ graduated second in a class of one hundred.

From Đà Lạt, Mễ took an assignment as the operations officer of the 2nd Airborne Brigade. He'd only been in the position for a few weeks when the entire Airborne Division deployed to Khe Sanh to join Operation Lam Sơn 719, the largest and most famous of the Lam Sơn series.

The concept was hastily put together only weeks before execution. The time available did not allow for sufficient planning or adequate preparation. Lam Sơn 719 called for ARVN forces to sweep deep into Laos from just south of the DMZ. The mission: Cut the Ho Chi Minh Trail, destroy enemy supplies, and reduce North Vietnam's capability to conduct offensive operations, then withdraw. However, this would be the first major operation of the Vietnam War without the participation of American ground forces. After the Cambodia invasion the previous year, Congress had passed the Cooper-Church Amendment, barring U.S. ground troops from operating outside South Vietnam. That meant the ARVN would go it alone, at least on the ground. The United States would still deliver long-range artillery, airstrikes, and helicopter lift support. The United States would also provide security and logistics support up to the border. Helicopters could fly across into Laos, but all American ground forces would stay inside South Vietnam.[10]

Mễ worked diligently in crafting the 2nd Airborne Brigade's portion of the OPLAN, or operations plan. The brigade would be the key element of the entire attack, the point of the spear in seizing the final objective of the operation.

The overall plan for Lam Son 719 called for a westward attack along Route 9 by a combined armor-airborne force. The flanks of the advance were to be secured by ARVN infantry and ranger forces. The ARVN 1st Armored Brigade would advance on the roadway while the 1st Airborne Brigade made a series of helicopter assualts on objectives along the route. The attacking South Vietnamse forces were to occupy and destroy the enemy base areas they encountered. The final objective of the operation was to be the destruction of the enemy's logistic and communications hub in the vicinity of the ruins of what had once been the town of Tchepone. Mễ's 2nd Airborne Brigade was the force chosen for that final attack. His planning efforts were key if success was to be achieved, and his plan was sound.[11]

Lam Son 719 began on February 8, 1971. The campaign, however, did not go according to plan. The media had leaked details of the pending operation. The enemy committed more forces than anticipated with reinforcements arriving daily. They fought harder than expected. Intense antiaircraft fire erupted everywhere. The weather turned bad. Route 9 became nearly impassable. The attack westward bogged down as ARVN casualties and American helicopter losses mounted. Orders changed. The ARVN 1st Infantry Division made the assault on Tchepone, not the 2nd Airborne Brigade. As soon as that final objective was taken, the commanding general, in consultation with the president of South Vietnam, ordered the withdrawal of South Vietnamese forces from Laos, beginning on March 9. The North Vietnamese Army tore into the retreating units, bloodying them badly, turning the retreat into a chaotic flight for survival. In the end, Mễ's brigade stood by as an uncommitted reserve at the border until being tasked to protect the ARVN forces rushing back into South Vietnam. It was all over by March 25. Mễ wondered what might come next.[12]

❦

Colonel Lich, the 2nd Airborne Brigade commander, shouted, "Mễ, get your ass into my office!"

Mễ moved quickly, pulling his shirt down as he went, to make his uniform look as smart as possible. He stood straight and tall in front of his commander, his right hand snapped to a salute. "Yes, sir."

The colonel looked him over for a moment, then said, "We're making some changes. You're going to the 11th Battalion. Lieutenant Colonel Tỉnh asked for you by name."

Mễ looked puzzled.

Lich continued. "You know the 1st Battalion commander was killed in Laos. Division moved Tỉnh's XO to take command of the 1st. Tỉnh needs a new executive officer. He wants you. Division supports him. You're the new XO of the 11th Airborne Battalion."

Lich handed him a set of orders. "Get outta here."

Mẽ beamed. *I'm off the brigade staff. Down to an operational battalion. Right where I belong.*

He left with more spring in his step, gathered his stuff, said quick good-byes, and caught a ride to the battalion's headquarters. They'd just moved to Quảng Trị City, over forty miles east. Mẽ reported to the commander, Lieutentant Colonel Ngô Lê Tỉnh. Tỉnh introduced the 11th Battalion staff and commanders. Two staff officers stood out: Captain Đoàn Phương Hải, the operations officer, and Dr. Tô Phạm Liệu, the battalion surgeon.

Mẽ studied Hải for a moment. He was a strapping young officer, tall, lean, and fit. A few minutes of conversation proved he was also intelligent and motivated. He showed the typical "gung-ho" zeal so common among paratroopers, but Mẽ also saw a focused, serious intensity that set him apart from others.

Dr. Liệu approached. He shook Mẽ's hand vigorously. With a broad smile, he said, "Hello, sir. I'm Liệu, the battalion's doc."

Liệu struck Mẽ as a happy, talkative fellow. But there was something about him, something special, a look in his eye that revealed his dedication not only to medicine, but to his country, to the *Mũ Đỏ* paratroopers, to this battalion. Mẽ would soon learn that Liệu had a reputation as a bit of a comedian, always entertaining. However, every member of the battalion also trusted him, implicitly, with his life. On duty, Liệu was competent and hardworking. Off duty, he knew how to unwind. He was loved by all and would soon find a big place in Mẽ's heart.

Within days, the battalion loaded onto U.S. Air Force C-130 cargo planes at the Quảng Trị Airport. The soldiers thought they were headed home to Saigon. Instead, they landed at Kontum in the Central Highlands. There, they joined their sister 5th and 6th parachute battalions, along with the 22nd ARVN Infantry Division, to fight a series of battles in the surrounding hills to relieve mounting enemy pressure. They faced three North Vietnamese regiments—the 28th, 66th, and 31st—that had surrounded Firebases 5 and 6, on a ridgeline twenty-five miles to the northwest.

Mẽ felt comfortable in his new role as second in command of the 11th Battalion. With his American counterpart, Assistant Battalion Advisor Captain Skip Lavine, he helped effectively coordinate the airpower and artillery support necessary to ensure their success. The operation ended on April 17, and the battalion returned to its garrision at Red Hat Hill, just on the outskirts of Saigon.

Mễ settled in. The base sat atop a rise a short distance southwest of the huge American Army headquarters at Long Bình. It measured a half mile square and housed the 2nd Airborne Brigade headquarters, Mễ's 11th Airborne Battalion, the 2nd Airborne Artillery Battalion, the 2nd Airborne Reconnaissance Company, and a small American advisor's compound. Long two-story wooden barracks with metal roofs stood around a central parade field. Smaller concrete headquarters and support buildings nestled close by. A high fence, topped with three strands of barbed wire, enclosed the area. Intimidating soldiers guarded the entrances. Even so, the view from the hill, especially from the 11th Battalion headquarters, was exquisite. One could look east, across the beautiful Đồng Nai River, over farmsteads and settlements. Mễ more often chose the view to the southwest, toward Saigon in the distance, his mind filled with thoughts of home.

On May 28, 1971, Lieutenant Colonel Nguyễn Đình Bảo arrived to replace Tỉnh as the 11th Airborne Battalion's commander. Colonel Bảo was tough but compassionate. Mễ had known him for many years. He respected him. Bảo had a reputation in the airborne community as a battle-savvy paratroop commander who understood warfare and knew how to motivate his men. His nickname, "Grey Tiger," came from his courage and ferocity in battle.

Bảo was born in poverty in North Vietnam. His family emigrated to the South in 1954, after the French defeat and the partitioning of the country into the communist North and noncommunist South Vietnam. He never lost his grounding as a common man who'd become a highly regarded warrior through grit and courage. He hated communists, cherished his country in spite of its flaws and shortcomings, and would willingly die for the land he loved or for those he led.

The army granted Bảo's request for assignment to the airborne upon his graduation from the military academy. There, he honed his leadership, rising through the ranks by his exceptional performance in fight after fight—all the while showing compassion for his paratroopers. He respected his men and felt the pain of their sacrifice in battle. In turn, they

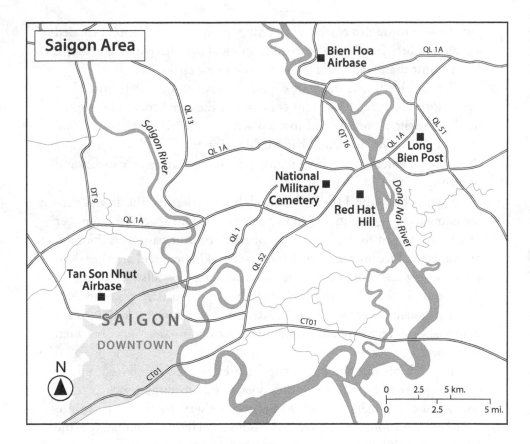

loved him as if he were family. The 11th Airborne Battalion soon came to call him *Anh Năm*,* Big Brother.[13]

With Bảo in command, Mễ and Hải continued their same duties as before, Mễ as the executive officer, the second in command, and Hải as the operations officer. Bảo saw this as a close-knit group of three. He liked Mễ's aggressiveness, and he felt a kinship with Hải because, like himself, Hải had been born in the North, his family fleeing after the country split at the end of French colonial rule. The new leadership team coalesced over the next two months as replacements arrived, and Lieutenant Colonel Bảo

---

Anh Năm literally translates to "Brother Five," in respect for Bảo's rank as a lieutenant colonel, the fifth step in officer ranks (2nd lieutenant, 1st lieutenant, captain, major, and then lieutenant colonel).

put the unit through a rigorous retraining regimen. The train-up included a good number of drills and weapons training, along with parachute jumps. He'd ensure their readiness for their next combat challenge.

While Bảo honed the unit's tactical prowess, he felt it critical to raise esprit and strengthen unit cohesion at the same time. He worked hard to heighten morale and instill a sense of history in the battalion, an appreciation of the proud battlefield victories and selfless sacrifice of those who'd gone before. He encouraged sports, particularly soccer and wrestling.

He also built the 11th Airborne club on Red Hat Hill. It was simple enough, a large room with a bar on one side and space for a number of tables arranged for staff meetings or meals or unit parties. A doorway on the far end led into a smaller room with a kitchen, and another door into the very essential latrine. The club had redbrick walls topped with a metal roof. It shared a similar view to that of the battalion's headquarters, a panorama over the Đồng Nai River to the east and a look into the National Cemetery to the northwest, where so many paratrooper brethren lay buried.

The club became the place where the battalion's few dozen officers came together as family. There they'd gather for meetings, social events, and occasional dinners. The war stories, which always found their way into casual conversation, served to spread lessons from hard-fought battles. The fellowship at the club, sometimes enriched by Martell cognac and other beverages, helped produce a camaraderie that dwelled in their hearts for the rest of their lives. Here they built the emotional ties that would bind them together through all that lay ahead.

The battalion's first test under fire with their new commander came in August 1971. Bảo led the battalion on an operation to relieve enemy pressure on Hưng Đạo Fire Base, which sat along Route 22, connecting Tây Ninh City with neighboring Cambodia. The base had suffered frequent ground attacks and daily artillery shelling. Helicopters lifted the battalion into a landing zone south of the firebase. Mễ, along with his American advisor, led two companies along one axis, while Bảo and Hải took the remainder of the battalion along another.

Mẽ had to continually caution his six-foot-five advisor, "Skip, get head down," as sporadic sniper fire came too close, too often, to taking out the tall American.

In short order, the 11th Airborne decimated two enemy battalions and gave the firebase its first respite in months. The paratroopers returned to Red Hat Hill victorious and filled with confidence, confirming their trust in the new commander. Sadly, this was also the time for the scheduled departure of the battalion's American advisory team. Mẽ bid farewell to his friend, Captain Skip Lavine, but not before Skip treated the leadership of the battalion to a steak dinner at the officers' club on the nearby U.S. Army base at Long Bình. Mẽ had eaten steak before, but on this night he had his first T-bone, a memory he'd never forget.

CHAPTER 6

Brothers in Arms

John Duffy had been making a difference at Fort Sheridan, but he was bored. He wanted to return to Vietnam. He'd been a part of the ultrasecret MACV-SOG mission on his last tour. He wanted more. He called his assignment officer in Washington, D.C.

"Hey, I want to go back to Vietnam."

"You've been there twice already. You don't have to go."

"I know, but I want to. I'll volunteer to go back a third time if you can assign me to MACV-SOG."

"That's a special classified program . . ." the assignment officer started.

John cut him off. "I know what it is. I've done it. That's where I want to go."

The officer stalled. "I'll get back to you."

He called John a week later. "They'll take you. But all I can do is get you to the SOG headquarters in Saigon. It's up to you from there."

John arrived back in Vietnam on May 29, 1971, as a newly promoted major. He found his way back to SOG headquarters in Saigon. It was Saturday. Many of the military headquarters in the city had minimum manning for the weekend. Not so, MACV-SOG. The offices buzzed with activity. John introduced himself to the admin staff, and reported to Colonel John Sadler, chief of SOG.

Colonel Sadler said, "Major Duffy, I'm assigning you to OP-35, Ground Studies Branch."

John beamed. "Great, sir. Back to cross border ops. Which launch site? When do I head out?"

Frowning, Colonel Sadler stilled John's enthusiasm. "You're not going anywhere. You are staying right here to work on the staff. You will be the deputy operations officer in OP-35. You're too senior for any position I have in the field. And things are slowing down, anyway."

"What?" John exclaimed.

"Don't know if you heard. Last month, Special Forces officially went home from Vietnam. We're not here anymore." Colonel Sadler winked and added sarcastically, "Officially."

He paused before explaining, "Of course, SOG's still here. Just no more Green Berets. It's black baseball caps at the launch sites. We still exist, but we're training Vietnamese Special Forces to take over the missions. It's all part of Vietnamization. America's withdrawing. U.S. forces are down to just over two hundred thousand. Down from more than five hundred thirty thousand two years ago. War's about over for us."

John went to work in OP-35. His boss, Colonel Roger Pezzelle, one of the army's original Green Berets, put the best possible spin on things. But still, John found it mundane. He threw himself into work as best he could, but he grew ever more frustrated as weeks became months. He was not happy being in a combat zone with no combat. He did not want to fight the rest of the war from behind a desk.

After four months, he asked to leave SOG and go to MACV's Team 162, the American advisors to the Vietnamese airborne units. They were seeing plenty of action, and John knew it.

On hearing his request, Colonel Pezzelle snapped, "You'll be killed, you ignorant son of a bitch."

"So be it," John tossed back.

Pezzelle approved his transfer. Team 162 had stringent requirements, though, being very selective on whom they accepted. John easily made the cut. On September 13, he got a ride to the ARVN Airborne Division headquarters at Tân Sơn Nhứt Airbase, found the adjacent Team 162 team building, and reported for duty. The team commander, Colonel Jim Vaught, impressed John as a fine officer and gentleman. He'd served during World War II and seen action in Korea and previous combat tours in Vietnam. His heroism had been recognized with two Silver Stars and he'd received a Purple Heart for being wounded. He was tough and demanding, but fair and compassionate. Vaught assigned John as the senior advisor with the Vietnamese 11th Airborne Battalion. The timing was right. The battalion had only recently returned to garrison from its first victory under a new commander.

The next day, John grabbed a jeep and drove the twenty miles to Red Hat Hill. He announced his arrival at the American advisors' compound and made his way to the 11th Battalion. They'd just finished a particularly tough day of training. Colonel Bảo had assembled his company commanders and staff in the battalion clubhouse for a routine weekly meeting.

As business wrapped up, the six-foot-three strapping American strode through the door, his look intense, his movement deliberate. He wore a brand-new camouflage-patterned airborne uniform and red Vietnamese *Mũ Đỏ* beret. He scanned the room, and spotted the ranking officer, Colonel Bảo. He walked over to him. The two spoke. Bảo looked him over before turning to the group.

"This our new senior advisor, Major John Duffy. He is an American Special Forces officer."

All eyes were on John.

After a somewhat awkward pause, Bảo continued, "Why don't you tell us about yourself, Major Duffy."

John briefly recounted his previous tours in Vietnam, highlighting the combat experiences. On concluding, he said, "I'm very glad to be here." His sincerity impressed everyone.

They all greeted him, individually and in small groups. Mễ just stared for a time. He was taken with the fact that John was Special Forces. He knew their work along the border and had heard stories of their covert operations. He'd seen the John Wayne movie at a Saigon theater. The soundtrack tune, Barry Sadler's "Ballad of the Green Berets," played in his head. Finally, he stepped forward.

In his very best English, he said, "Hello. I'm Major Mễ, the XO."

John looked at him, smiled, and said in his best Vietnamese, "I'm Major Duffy. John. I look forward to working with you."

Mễ smiled broadly. He wanted to learn all he could from this American.

As senior advisor, protocol dictated that John work principally with the commander, Lieutenant Colonel Bảo. Normally, his contact with the executive officer, Mễ, would be minimal. The XO was to pair with an assistant advisor. But from the outset, this was no normal relationship. There was no assistant advisor. John was it. Personnel shortages dictated filling the three-man team with only one person. From the outset, the strapping American intrigued Mễ, and John Duffy saw something in Mễ that immediately impressed him. Thereafter, Mễ took every opportunity to talk to John during breaks in training and after unit meetings. Mễ drew from John's Green Beret experience while John learned all he could about ARVN procedures and, most importantly, gaining a better understanding of Vietnamese culture.

Two weeks after Duffy's arrival, the battalion returned to battle in a series of fights in Tây Ninh Province. The new senior advisor quickly demonstrated his worth, though his value proved to be not so much as a mentor, but more as a wizard, wielding flights of U.S. strike aircraft and artillery. He showed himself to also be a jack-of-all-trades, helping in any way he could.

Right away, John found the 11th Battalion to be a deadly fighting machine operated by experienced masters. He might offer a comment now and then based on his Special Forces experience, but as far as maneuvering and fighting light infantry forces, Colonel Bảo, his staff, and his commanders had it down. They knew their stuff and were expert in delivering it mightily in battle. They didn't need his help there. But John could communicate with U.S. Air Force forward air controllers. He could bring in American airstrikes and place American artillery exactly where needed. He could call for U.S. Army Cobra attack helicopters. And he was strong and courageous. He would do anything needed to help in any kind of situation. John Duffy soon established himself as an integral and valued member of the battalion team.

On September 30, helicopters lifted the battalion into a small landing zone in the primordial forest, north of Tây Ninh City, near the Cambodian border. The paratroopers were to fight as one part of a large Airborne Division operation to defeat a substantial NVA force intent on overrunning isolated friendly units and closing Highway 22, the lifeline for ARVN forces deployed inside Cambodia. The South Vietnamese called the operation Toàn Thắng 2-71.

The North Vietnamese 5th and 7th Divisions occupied well-prepared defensive positions and had dug an extensive network of underground tunnels, undetectable under thick jungle canopy. They also employed an array of antiaircraft guns as well as short-, medium-, and long-range artillery. The 11th Airborne had only to find their enemy and destroy him. No one knew what a formidable task that would become.[1]

The battalion searched for their foe for three days without success. But that third night, the NVA probed the battalion's bivouac site. In an instant, the enemy was in the midst of the battalion, wreaking havoc and then vanishing. Paratroopers received fire and suffered casualties, with little time to react. They'd see silhouettes move in the darkness, shoot, and disappear under bushes. The vanishing specters turned out to be enemy soldiers, rising from tunnels for a few moments, then diving back down their holes. The bushes, they found, hid a number of tunnel entrances. What seemed otherworldly phantoms turned out to be nothing more than crafty earthly adversaries.

A North Vietnamese regiment surrounded the battalion and pressed its perimeter ever tighter. Over the next days, they randomly fired AK-47 rounds and shot mortars and B-40 rockets into the position. At night, they'd infiltrate from tunnels and create chaos.

At dawn on October 5, 1971, the North Vietnamese attacked in earnest. A force of over a thousand soldiers hit the battalion hard. Enemy mortars and rockets pounded them. John woke with a start. Officers and sergeants shouted commands, bringing a disciplined response to the madness around them.

John made his way to Bảo. Hải was already there. Mễ ran up in an instant. Bảo calmly passed orders through the radio operator.

Seeing his team assembled, he said, "Ground attack come for sure. Hải. Get us VNAF. Put artillery all around perimeter. Mễ. Go to companies. Coordinate counterattack. Duffy. How 'bout airstrikes? Quick, and real close." Bảo went on in Vietnamese for a moment, providing more detail to his operations officer and XO.

The sound of bugles and whistles and screams filled the air. Small-arms fire intensified. The ground attack had begun.

"Go," Bảo commanded.

They each set about their tasks. John moved a short distance away to a protected spot and got on his radio, attempting to contact an American forward air controller who was airborne in a small propeller-driven spotter plane.

"Any FAC, any FAC. This is Dusty Cyanide, advisor with a Vietnamese airborne battalion. Under attack. Need air badly. Any FAC, any FAC."

"Station calling for a FAC, this is Chico one-two."

"Roger, one-two. This is Dusty Cyanide. Been receiving heavy incoming. Ground attack underway. Multiple enemy battalions. Holding as best we can, but need air."

"Understood, Dusty. Will have fighters for you shortly. What are the friendly locations, and where are the enemy targets?"

John passed the details for the strike to the forward air controller. Bảo approached. As they discussed options for the battle, a rocket blast hit them with the full fury of its shrapnel. Fragments peppered the left side of John's face and tore into Bảo's right eye. It looked bad—blackened and bloody. They wiped their wounds and continued the fight. Bảo headed toward the sound of the most intense fighting.

Duffy looked around and saw several critically wounded nearby. Dismissing his own injuries, he left his protected position, exposing himself to enemy fire, so he could render first aid. He saw the battalion surgeon, Dr. Liệu, doing the same, his uniform torn and dirty, his body bloodied from his own wounds. Once the jet fighters arrived, John moved about wherever necessary to best direct airstrikes, remaining calm and focused, oblivious to the bullets flying around him.

That day, John Duffy put in more than forty flights of fighter aircraft. Those airstrikes, on top of the courageous fighting of the paratroopers, saved the battalion from being overrun. Mễ led a successful counterattack with 114 Company in the lead. In the midst of the fray, Duffy found time to supervise cutting a landing zone so that VNAF medevac helicopters could get in to pick up the wounded. The NVA killed ten 11th Battalion paratroopers and wounded seventy-four. [2]

When it was all over, Duffy, Bảo, Mẽ, and Hải stood facing each other, their uniforms soiled with dirt and blood, their faces smudged with filth, their eyes red from exhaustion. Bảo studied his team, smiled, and nodded in appreciation. Mẽ looked at the intensity on John Duffy's face. John returned his glance, softened his expression, and gave his friend a knowing wink.

The worst seemed over. The battalion anticipated orders back to garrison. Instead, the 2nd Airborne Brigade commander directed them north along Highway 22 to the American Firebase Pace, less than half a mile from the Cambodian border. They had the task of clearing residual enemy forces en route. Bảo sent his most seriously injured soldiers back to Saigon and received a few replacements. He refused evacuation himself, in spite of his torn, blinded eye. He simply had Dr. Liệu bandage it and then pressed on. Bảo would never regain vision in that eye.

At Firebase Pace, the 11th Airborne Battalion formed a joint task force with the ARVN 18th Armored Battalion. Control of the newly formed unit fell to the 3rd Airborne Brigade. The brigade placed Bảo in overall command of the task force. He now had his paratroopers bolstered with tanks and other tracked vehicles from the armored battalion.*

On November 7, 1971, the 3rd Brigade crossed into Cambodia with the 11th Battalion task force in the lead. John Duffy had to stay on the Vietnamese side, though. Congress had passed an act in 1970 that prohibited U.S. forces from operating in Laos or Cambodia.† That included American advisors. Duffy was pissed but had the sense to obey his orders. He headed back to Saigon.

The Brigade column covered ground with little opposition. Upon reaching the intersection of Highways 7 and 72, Mẽ remained with 114 Company and one platoon of armored personnel carriers to defend the critical intersection and the important Hồng Hà firebase located there. The rest of the task force continued northward nearly twenty miles into the Dambae valley, a known stronghold of the 7th NVA Division. Colonel Bảo sat atop an 18th Battalion tank as they reached the final objective of their advance, Dambae Town.

---

*M-48 Patton medium tanks and M-113 armored personnel carriers (APCs).
†Cooper-Church Amendment, Public Law 91-652, passed by Congress on December 22, 1970, and enacted into law on January 5, 1971.

Intelligence reported two NVA regiments in the area, yet engagements were surprisingly light. They encountered few enemy forces. The mood was eerie, though, almost haunting. Earlier that year the ARVN 30th Ranger Battalion, with an accompanying armor unit, had been ambushed in the valley. Both sides suffered heavy casualties. Churned earth, burned tank hulks, abandoned weapons, and twisted vehicles still scarred the landscape.[3]

John Duffy, not being one to cool his heels in the city for long, found employment with the 5th Airborne Battalion. The unit had fought near his 11th Battalion in the Tây Ninh forest battle over the past weeks. They had suffered heavy losses but were now reconstituted and heading out on a new combat mission. Their advisor had gone home on his midtour leave. They needed a replacement. The commander, Lieutenant Colonel Nguyễn Chí Hiếu, asked for John Duffy. Apparently, John had made a name for himself. He was happy to oblige. He found further delight in learning the colonel had a beautiful wife and that his equally beautiful sister-in-law was a famous Vietnamese movie star. Life was good.

John drove a jeep, alone, to join the 5th Battalion for the operation on Núi Bà Đen Mountain (or Black Lady Mountain in translation), just northeast of Tây Ninh City. The Americans called it "Black Virgin Mountain." It is the only high ground for miles, its volcanic cone rising more than three thousand feet above the surrounding, relatively flat, countryside. It is a key piece of terrain that dominates the landscape. Friendly forces occupied an important radio site at the summit, but the Viet Cong and North Vietnamese held the rest of the mountain with well-prepared defenses, including a honeycomb of underground tunnels. The 5th Battalion set out to assault the base, climb to the top, and destroy the enemy and his supplies as they advanced.

The North Vietnamese burrowed deep and remained hidden. The battalion encountered little resistance as they trudged upward. Sporadic fighting and the steep ascent slowed progress, but they reached the summit in a week and declared victory. During the descent, the enemy emerged from their holes to ambush and harass. Casualties mounted, but the battalion successfully withdrew and claimed their task accomplished. They returned to their barracks at Biên Hòa Airbase, not far from Long Bình. John bid *adieu* to Colonel Hiếu and headed over to Red Hat Hill to await the return of his 11th Airborne Battalion.

~

In Cambodia, Bảo, Mẽ, and Hải felt things were going as well as could be expected. The highways were open to resupply. The battalion prevailed in the few limited fights they encountered. Mẽ and his combined Airborne/Armored team at Hồng Hà held fast and conducted a counterattack to repulse the one assault they received, a hundred-man enemy force attempting to sabotage the artillery pieces at the firebase. Every threat had been neutralized. The situation was stable.

With their mission accomplished, the battalion received orders to withdraw. They planned carefully, but history was about to repeat itself. The North Vietnamese lay in wait, ready to spring a large ambush as the task force pulled out. The fight became intense. It turned into a tank battle. Casualties mounted on both sides. One explosion killed the 111 Company commander, Captain Nguyễn Đức Dũng. Dũng had been a bright officer who'd recently transferred from the 5th Airborne Battalion. He bravely led his company in aggressive counterattacks, enabling the successful withdrawal of the battalion task force—at the cost of his own life.

The 11th Battalion's thrust into Cambodia disabled one regiment of the 7th NVA Division. The fighting cost the lives of thirty ARVN paratroopers and tankers killed in action, many wounded, and nearly a dozen tanks and other armored vehicles destroyed. The task force limped back across the border into South Vietnam.

The sound of helicopters chopped the air. The wounded would soon be in hospital, the dead buried, and the rest back at Red Hat Hill to clean up and get ready to go again.

~

The battalion licked its wounds, received replacements, and trained. Everyone soon settled into a familiar garrison routine, though they knew it wouldn't last. One matter needed to be settled immediately, though. Captain Dũng was dead. The 111 Company needed a new commander.

At Mễ's urging, Bảo agreed to replace Dũng with Lieutenant Nguyễn Văn Thinh. Thinh was a young reserve officer with Special Forces experience. He'd not yet reached the rank of captain, a normal requirement for a company commander. It seemed an odd choice to some. But Mễ had been impressed with Thinh's intelligence, judgment, and especially his ability to lead. His recommendation carried the day.

As new recruits came in to replace the casualties of the Cambodian operation, the battalion mounted a focused training program to build their requisite combat skills. They spent a lot of time absorbing the discipline of squad and platoon drills and sharpening their marksmanship on the firing range. Each of the companies had to be ready to go back into battle as quickly as possible.

The battalion's next assignment came soon. In late December, the Airborne Division ordered the 11th Battalion to move to Tao Đàn Garden in the heart of Saigon. They relocated quickly and smoothly. The thirty-acre park was like a dream for the battle-hardened paratroopers and their new recruits. Stone pathways wound magically under the shade of giant Kapok trees, past ferns, shrubs, and colorful flower beds. Expansive lawns beckoned. Sculptures and temples appeared along every walkway. Mễ remembered many romantic strolls here with Sen. Now he was part of an important mission to help secure the capital city of South Vietnam. The 11th Airborne Battalion paratroopers pitched tents in the garden and took charge of securing the adjacent Presidential Palace, the Saigon River Bridge, and several key checkpoints controlling entry into the city.

It was a pleasant time. The world welcomed the arrival of 1972 on January 1. The Tết Lunar New Year followed weeks later. Tết is always a festive celebration in Vietnam, and that year was no exception. The situation in Saigon appeared calm, but intelligence indicated enemy buildups over the border in Cambodia, in Laos, and across the Demilitarized Zone inside North Vietnam. As the Year of the Rat began, some feared it cast an ominous shadow.[4]

The paratroopers took their security duties in Saigon seriously. It wasn't their normal stock and trade, but it was important, and it put them in an idyllic location with plenty of time off. They enjoyed their leisure, not knowing how long it would last or what combat challenges might lie ahead. Some hung around the garden, taking in its tranquility or engaging in friendly sports competitions. Others hit nearby bars. Those with relatives in Saigon spent as much time at home as possible.

Mễ enjoyed visiting his family, Sen and now three children: son, Vũ (two and a half), and daughters, Quyên (one and a half) and Phương (three months). John Duffy read books and wrote poetry, a fact that soon spread across the battalion. He also explored the cultural sites of the city, especially the entertainment establishments along Tự Do Street, the long avenue running southwest of the garden. The French had constructed the wide boulevard early in their colonial rule. They named it *Rue Catinat* and saw it as Saigon's *Champs Élysées*. After they departed, the Vietnamese renamed the street, Tự Do (Liberty). With the arrival of U.S. forces in the 1960s, sections of the street became notorious hangouts for off-duty GIs. The American soldiers had mostly left, but the reputation of the street remained.

Occasionally, Mễ joined John for an evening out at a nearby spot particularly popular with the 11th Battalion officers, the Blue Dragon Bar. It was the opposite direction from Tự Do and only a block from where Mễ and Sen had their wedding reception at the *Quốc Tế* international restaurant. Good music and lovely ladies attracted the younger paratroop officers. John and Mễ enjoyed the unit camaraderie and the opportunity to spend some off-duty time together.

The Vietnamese soldier and the American advisor learned a lot about each other at the Blue Dragon while talking over dinners and drinks. One night a bottle of "very old, sexy paratrooper" Martell cognac appeared. As they drank, Duffy was taken with Mễ's intelligence and charm. Mễ showed John a picture of his wife and kids. He shared some of his dreams and aspirations. *My kind of paratrooper*, John thought. *A romantic with courage.*

A few days later, Lieutenant Colonel Bảo flew to Taipei for two weeks as the honorary guest of the Taiwan military in recognition of his achievements in battle. Mễ acted as battalion commander in his absence. That allowed him to work more closely with John, on duty, as part of his official commander role. That interaction continued after Bảo's return. Bảo, never really comfortable working with Americans, was happy to have his senior advisor teamed principally with his XO. There was no assistant advisor at the moment. John constituted the entire 11th Airborne Battalion advisory group. So Mễ became John's Vietnamese counterpart. They were a team. They'd truly become brothers in arms.

———

Saturday, March 25, began as other days in Tao Đàn Garden. The sun shone through the trees, birds sang, and soldiers set about their duties. Those not working occupied themselves in any number of diversions. A few kicked a soccer ball around on the grass. Others walked the gardens or sat in quiet contemplation. Just next to the command post, Duffy tried his luck at a game of Mahjong with three young officers. He'd been learning this new pastime, but was stymied.

He pleaded to his friend, "Major Mễ, come help me!"

Mễ stopped shuffling through paperwork and walked over. Looking at Duffy's fat, domino-sized tiles, he shook his head.

"What you try to do?"

Ever the competitor, John responded, "Win. What else?"

Mễ leaned over and helped John arrange his tiles into some kind of order. He pondered a strategy. This would not be a winning hand.

Hải rushed out of the command post tent. Seeing Mễ and Duffy, he asked, "You seen *Anh Năm*?"

Mễ pointed to Bảo, talking to a group twenty yards away. He wore sunglasses to hide the black patch over his blinded right eye. Hải went over. They spoke. Hải and Lieutenant Colonel Bảo headed to the command post, motioning for Mễ and Duffy to join them.

Inside, Bảo announced, "We got order. We go Kontum."

CHAPTER 7

Kontum

THE 11TH AIRBORNE BATTALION HEADED TO KONTUM ON MARCH 31, 1972. Conditions there grew more tense each day. For months, intelligence reports had warned of North Vietnamese preparations for a major attack. Two Cobra gunships from the U.S. Army's 361st Aerial Weapons Company spotted enemy tanks in late January. Subsequent sightings by other American helicopters and the Vietnamese Air Force followed. ARVN ground patrols encountered ever-larger NVA units as the weeks progressed. Prisoners and documents seized in February confirmed the presence of ten to twenty thousand NVA soldiers along with tanks, artillery, and large numbers of antiaircraft weapons—all poised in the tri-border area of western Kontum Province.* Analysts identified the NVA 320th "Steel" Division with its 48th, 52nd, and 64th Infantry Regiments. Additionally, the division included the 54th Artillery Regiment with 122mm and 130mm guns that could range up to seventeen miles. Intelligence also located the 2nd NVA Division just north. The 203rd Armor Regiment from Hanoi's High Command reinforced both divisions.[1]

The situation worried the South Vietnamese government. It reworked defensive plans for the Central Highlands and postured military forces accordingly. American military leaders felt the need to support those efforts with eighty B-52 strikes in the area during the first three weeks of February alone. Those B-52 missions continued throughout March. Lieutenant

---

*That portion of the Central Highlands of Vietnam lying in the vicinity of the juncture of the borders of Vietnam, Laos, and Cambodia—three borders, tri-border.

General Ngô Dzu, the senior ARVN commander in II Corps†, directed the 22nd ARVN Division to deploy a forward command post along with the 47th Infantry Regiment to Tan Canh to join its 42nd Infantry and 14th Cavalry regiments, already there. He also ordered elements of the independent 19th Cavalry Regiment to reinforce the 14th.[2]

General Dzu requested additional support from Saigon. In response, the Joint General Staff sent a good chunk of their strategic reserve, the 2nd Airborne Brigade. The brigade headquarters and several airborne battalions deployed to the Highlands before the 11th left Saigon.[3]

The 11th Battalion paratroopers boarded vintage Vietnamese Air Force C-123 transport aircraft at Tân Sơn Nhứt Air Base in Saigon. They sat in the webbed troop seats along both sides of the cargo bays. Pallets of equipment filled the center. The men were pumped, ready for action. They would join their sister airborne battalions already fighting in Kontum Province. Their move took them first to Pleiku, the largest city and airbase in the Central Highlands. Duffy sat next to Mễ on the two-hour flight, lost in his thoughts as the drone of the airplane's two big radial engines made conversation difficult.

Once they landed, the paratroopers found rooms in the barracks on the airbase. Mễ stayed on the flight line with the S-4, the battalion logistics officer. They oversaw the aircraft unloading and ensured all was set for the next morning's ground convoy to Kontum.

That evening, the battalion cooks set up the field kitchen and prepared a meal. Several of the officers headed to the Vietnamese Air Force club afterward. At the bar, they met pilots from the VNAF 530th Fighter Squadron, the Jupiters. These guys flew propeller-driven A-1 Skyraider attack airplanes, vestiges of the Korean War. Nonetheless, the A-1 remained the best close air support platform in Southeast Asia. Both the U.S. Air Force and the Republic of Vietnam Air Force used the aircraft effectively in support of ground forces and for the rescue of downed aircrews.[4]

---

†The South Vietnamese government divided the country into four military regions during the war. They designated the regions from north to south, I Corps, II Corps, III Corps, and IV Corps. Twelve provinces in the center of South Vietnam made up II Corps, Kontum being the farthest in the northwest corner.

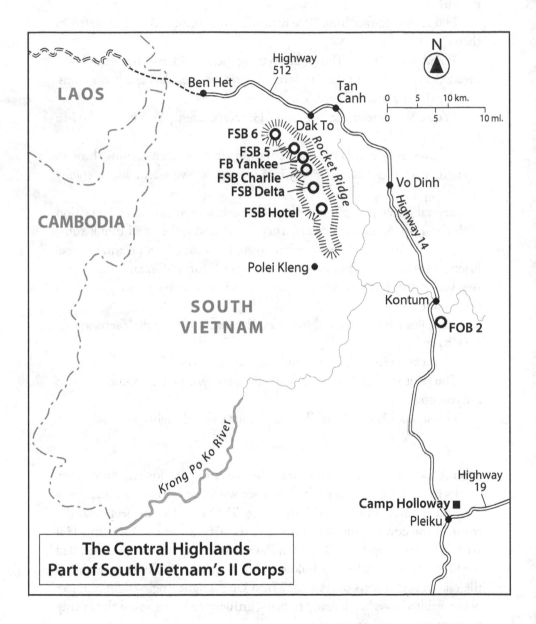

N

LAOS

Ben Het

Highway
512

Tan
Canh

0   5   10 km.
0   5   10 mi.

Dak To

FSB 6

FSB 5

FB Yankee

FSB Charlie

FSB Delta

FSB Hotel

Rocket Ridge

Vo Dinh

Highway 14

CAMBODIA

Polei Kleng

SOUTH
VIETNAM

Kontum

FOB 2

Krong Po Ko River

Highway
19

Camp Holloway

Pleiku

**The Central Highlands
Part of South Vietnam's II Corps**

One of the Jupiter pilots approached. "What brings you guys to Pleiku?"

Hải turned to face him. "We're headed to Kontum to beef up defenses there."

"Glad you're here. Things are getting dicey. Did you hear the NVA invaded across the DMZ in force yesterday? Regular army divisions. They're ripping into I Corps."

"Yeah. We'll hold the line here," Hải responded. "You've got the Mũ Đỏ in town now."

"I know. A bunch of red beret paratroopers have been coming through over the past weeks on their way to Kontum. We've seen a lot of enemy activity up there."

Several other A-1 pilots gathered around and joined in conversation with the 11th Airborne officers. They drank and talked and drank some more. Doc Lieu's humor was in rare form. He kept everyone entertained. Friendships formed. They exchanged contact information and shared stories. Good people, all around, loving life with an intensity only possible in the madness of war.

The pilot who'd been talking to Hai looked at his watch. "Getting late, time to go."

Hai acknowledged, "Yeah, late. Big day tomorrow."

The pilot smiled. "Good luck to you guys. We may fly some missions for you up there.

Hải shook his hand. "It's been a pleasure. Good night."

⌁

After breakfast the next morning, the paratroopers loaded onto army trucks for the drive to Kontum. Bảo rode with the convoy commander, a local army officer familiar with the route. They traveled in a jeep near the front of the convoy, just behind a lead security element. Duffy and Hải sat in the next jeep back. The 11th Battalion's men and equipment filled the long line of vehicles that followed. Mẽ, as executive officer, brought up the rear of the procession. An L-19 Bird Dog, a light single-engine spotter plane, orbited overhead, ready to bring artillery to bear should the enemy attempt to impede progress.

The convoy left Pleiku airbase, moving through the chaotic north end of town, rolling by simple homes and wretched hovels before breaking into the countryside on Highway 14. Picking up speed as they moved steadily toward the mountains in the distance, the trucks slammed into potholes along the sorry road. They passed small farmsteads with little gardens, orchards, and cultivated fields scarred with the pockmarks of war. Anxious farmers, fearing the Viet Cong only slightly more than the terror wrought by government operations, toiled to scrape out enough crops to feed their families and hopefully bring a bit of cash at market.

The trucks rounded a big curve and rumbled over a damaged bridge across the small Ia Ro'al River. There, they came to the first hill of the journey. Drivers downshifted. Diesel engines whined as the vehicles climbed the short grade. At the top, they dropped to a throaty hum with the shift to higher gears. The convoy rolled along the roadway toward a pass, eight miles ahead.

The vehicles strained once again, up the final climb. The paratroopers sat vigilant. The hillsides pressed close. Jungle trees loomed like giants, their dark limbs and scraggly branches spread menacingly. The danger was real. The Viet Cong often staged ambushes here. A mountain loomed on the left as they crossed the summit. They'd weathered Chu' Pao Pass[†] and entered Kontum Province.

The line of trucks descended into a broad green valley, dotted with tribal villages, each with a high-roofed communal house in its center, surrounded by family homes on stilts. Hải, familiar with the area from previous operations in the province, explained to Duffy, "This Montagnard country, land of many tribes."

Duffy nodded. "I know a bit. I did some reading and worked with Bru and Rhadé fighters on my first tour in I Corps. What do you know of the people here?"

"The name *Kontum* come from two native words, mean 'pool of villages.' More Montagnards here than any other place in Vietnam. Nine tribe groups in Central Highlands. They live off the jungle. Small gardens and some fishing and hunting. Many problems, though. Too many VC now."

[†]Americans referred to this as Kontum Pass.

He paused before continuing. "Rhadé tribe important, but in south of Highlands. Jarai all around Pleiku. In Kontum, mostly Bahnar and Sedang villages. They like Americans. Sorry you leave."

John watched native villagers along the road, some dressed in tattered clothing, others in colorful tribal outfits sporting attractive headpieces. They stared back at him. *How their lives must have been changed by this war*, he thought. *What'll happen to them when this is all done?*[5]

Two Cobra attack helicopters flew low overhead, landing in a small military compound just beside the road. John thought it must be Forward Operating Base 2, the home of Command and Control Central, or CCC, one of the launch sites for MACV-SOG's cross-border missions into Cambodia and Laos. South Vietnamese Special Forces had taken over the mission, and the remaining American Green Berets were now mainly trainers. Still, it was a highly classified operation. John simply nodded and smiled as they drove by.

"*Thành phố Kon Tum*," the driver exclaimed as they approached the bridge across the Dak Bla River.

"Kontum City," Hải translated for Duffy. "It is capital of Kontum Province. City have maybe thirty thousand. MACV compound. Airfield. Catholic cathedral. Military hospital. And civilian hospital run by American woman, Dr. Pat Smith. She treat everyone, especially Montagnard."

He pointed ahead. "We head fifteen clicks more north, to Võ Định. We report to brigade headquarters there."

The convoy rolled through the little town of Võ Định and turned into a large, open field half a mile outside of town. The vehicles came to a stop beside a group of fortified bunkers. Previous convoys had pressed the dirt into a hard surface. Still, clouds of dust rose around them as they pulled to a stop. The largest bunkers were made of wood beams supporting the same metal planking used for combat airstrips. Soldiers had stacked multiple layers of sandbags up the inside and outside of the metal walls and layered them across the top of the roof. Many smaller bunkers had been crafted from metal cargo containers similarly covered with sandbags. Electric wires ran from nearby power poles, but generators stood ready in small, sandbagged revetments if needed. The largest bunker served as the command post.

The 2nd Airborne Brigade commander stood outside to meet them. It was Mễ's old boss from Lam Son 719, Colonel Trần Quốc Lịch, still commanding the brigade. By his side stood his senior American advisor, Major Peter Kama, a tall, broad-shouldered Hawaiian who'd just arrived after serving as aide to General Frederick Weyand, the Deputy MACV Commander in Saigon.

John knew Kama's reputation. He was on his third tour of duty in Vietnam. He had served in combat at all levels, from infantry platoon leader to company command and battalion staff. The army had recently selected him for advancement to lieutenant colonel, but he'd not been promoted yet. He'd asked for this combat assignment. He was a tough, no-nonsense officer.

Bảo saluted Lịch, who welcomed him warmly. Lịch then greeted Mễ, Hải, and Duffy before leading Bảo and the others into the command post. Duffy brought up the rear, chatting with Peter Kama. Just before going inside, he looked off, impressed by the ridge of mountains to the west. The rest of the battalion busied themselves unloading trucks and setting up camp.

The brigade staff briefed the situation. It was not good. Each delivered remarks in English, followed by a detailed explanation in Vietnamese to ensure a full understanding by all. The presentations emphasized that enemy numbers increased daily, flowing in from sanctuaries across the border in Laos and Cambodia. The tempo of NVA operations inside South Vietnam had picked up. They shelled military outposts and even major installations. That included the vital airfield in Kontum City. The North Vietnamese brought large numbers of antiaircraft machine guns with them and shot at every aircraft in range. They appeared to be on the cusp of something big.

Colonel Lịch stood up to give his personal appraisal in English. "The enemy will come from Laos, on Route 512, and move east to Tân Cảnh. They come from Cambodia on new road they build along old French route. That set up attack on Kontum City from both west and north. Once take Kontum, they move to Pleiku, then turn east and attack through An Khê to coast. They cut our country in half, just like they do to beat French in 1954."

John looked questioningly at Mễ.

"I tell you more about that later," Mễ whispered.

Lịch summed up. "The 22nd Division defend north of here at Tân Cảnh with two infantry regiments and reinforced tank squadron. Rangers occupy at Ben Het, right on Tri-Border, and at Polei Kleng, west from Kontum to defend both places. Airborne battalions in firebases along the ridgeline just to the west. The 2nd Battalion at Firebase Delta. The 7th Battalion at Firebase Hotel. The 3rd Battalion at Firebase 5 with one airborne company with artillery on Firebase Yankee. Our 2nd Airborne Recon Company operate as 'eyes and ears' in area collecting intel."

He looked squarely at those who stood before him, his face firm. "Situation tense. Big U.S. cargo helicopter, CH-47 Chinook, shoot down yesterday at Delta. Helicopter crash. Crew survive and get inside firebase. Another helicopter come for pickup crew. Cannot. Too many VC. No aircraft can get close to Delta. Too many machine gun."

Finally, he gave their orders. "You, the 11th Airborne Battalion, go onto Firebase Charlie, just north of Delta, tomorrow. Bảo, you are strongest battalion. I know you only fifty-six percent strength. You should be eight hundred thirty-six paratroopers, officer and enlisted. You have only four hundred seventy-one. Still, you my strongest. I put you in most critical place. Your mission: Occupy positions on old firebase and defend it— at all costs."

Peter Kama turned to John. "That string of hilltop firebases, it's known as Rocket Ridge. It is key to the defense of Kontum and therefore all of central Vietnam."

CHAPTER 8

Rocket Ridge

AFTER THE BRIEFING, KAMA AND DUFFY TALKED OUTSIDE. JOHN asked, "Why do they call it Rocket Ridge?"

Peter explained, "The Americans named it Rocket Ridge years ago. The enemy used to fire 122-millimeter rockets from its heights down onto the highway and villages below. The U.S. Army built a series of firebases to control the ridgeline, denying it to the NVA. Now the communists want it back. They need it for their invasion plans."

He went on, "It's April Fools' Day, but this is no joke. Rocket Ridge is vulnerable. Hell, the whole region is vulnerable. We're facing the better part of two NVA divisions plus reinforcements. Friendly forces are grossly outnumbered. Seventeen kilometers north, the South Vietnamese Twenty-Second Division is not well regarded. Their new commander, Colonel Dat, doesn't have a good reputation. He's not an effective leader. Seventeen kilometers southwest, who knows how long the ARVN rangers at Polei Kleng can hold out against a major attack? In between is over twenty kilometers of Rocket Ridge. And I know the bad guys want it. ARVN artillery along that ridgeline impedes their maneuver against Tan Canh and will disrupt any movement south along Highway Fourteen toward Kontum. The firebases also block his direct path eastward should he choose to advance over those hills. The direction of such an attack would likely go right over the top of Charlie."

"Understood," Duffy said.

Kama continued, "NVA divisions pushed across the DMZ two days ago. Looks like they're planning something just as big here. Intel warns that a thrust out of Cambodia toward Saigon is also possible. We're looking at an all-out invasion of the South by North Vietnam. And we've got no American troops in the Highlands. We've pulled most of our units out of Vietnam. Here in II Corps, there are no American ground forces left at all. They are all gone. We've got only a few U.S. Army helicopter companies and some U.S. Air Force tac-air available—and the B-52s out of Guam or Thailand when we can get them. That's it. Winning the fight on the ground is now up to the ARVN."

Peter's brow lowered. "This brigade was a strategic reserve for the nation. It's now been committed. The 11th Airborne Battalion was our reserve within the brigade. You're now being committed. That leaves nothing. There's nobody else. No one to come in behind you. No reinforcements. You're it. You've got to hold at Charlie and stop the NVA from crossing Rocket Ridge. They cannot take that high ground and gain access along Highway Fourteen straight into Kontum and then Pleiku."

Kama promised, "I'll get you all the air support I can. I'll pull every string possible. John Paul Vann is the senior U.S. advisor in II Corps. He's got some clout. But know that this is the second of two fronts, and there may be a third. It could be tough getting everything we need."

Peter Kama studied John and noted, "You're the lone advisor with the battalion. That's usually a team of three, two officers and an NCO. You'll need a backup in case you get wounded. Only an American can call in U.S. airstrikes and helicopters. That includes medevac. I've got a Special Forces lieutenant I'll give you. He's away on midtour leave right now, but he'll be back in a few days. He can join you then."

John thought a moment. "No thanks. I've got it. I don't plan on getting wounded. And I've been working alone with these guys for a while now. Not a problem."

"Okay. But if you change your mind, let me know."

Kama's assessment of Duffy? He thought he was nuts. But he took him to be confident and brave, very much up to the task at hand. Peter would do all he could to get him the support he knew he'd need to defend Charlie.

As an afterthought, Kama added, "Tomorrow's Easter Sunday. God be with you."

Duffy smiled. "Thanks. Happy Easter."*

The battalion leadership spent the night planning. After careful map study and discussions with local ARVN officials, Lieutenant Colonel Bảo solidified the plan in his mind. Early the next morning, he assembled the battalion and talked to his staff and company commanders.

"It is a single-ship landing zone. One Twelve Company will go in first. Have your artillery observer team ready to call fire support should we need it. One Thirteen Company goes next, followed by One Eleven and One Fourteen. Commanders, be in the lead ship for each company. I'll be in the first aircraft. Captain Hải and Major Duffy in the second. Major Mẽ will come in with One Thirteen. Split the headquarters personnel amongst the last two companies.

"The Brigade's Reconnaissance Company has been in the area for a couple of weeks, giving us a good feel for the situation. The LZ† is expected to be cold, but be prepared. The NVA are moving east from Cambodia. Hill Ten Twenty is the best crossing point. That's where we are going. They must not get across that ridge.

"The flight time is only ten minutes. The insertion should take around three hours. Get in, offload, and prepare defenses. Expect an attack. Be prepared.

"Are there any questions?"

He waited but a second. "If not, check your men, check your commo, prepare your loading order. Be ready to go by noon. We will do battle. Fight like a paratrooper!"[1]

Mẽ gave Duffy a summary of Colonel Bảo's comments in English.

The commanders went to their companies and finished preparations for the air assault. Mẽ tended to his executive officer duties, double-checking company preparations and ensuring the loads were correctly positioned, ready to go. Hải confirmed he had the necessary communications gear and grabbed an acetate-covered map sheet for the area.

---

*It is interesting to note that the 11th Airborne Battalion's assault on Firebase Charlie took place on Easter Sunday, April 2, 1972. Of significance is that the major North Vietnamese campaign, which this battle was to become a part, became known as the 1972 Easter Offensive, the largest enemy offensive of the war.
†Landing Zone.

Each paratrooper carried an M-16 rifle, seven magazines of ammunition, hand grenades, a small entrenching tool, a canteen, and combat rations, both Vietnamese and American C-rations. The officers also carried .45-caliber pistols. Each company took two M-60 machine guns, nine M-79 grenade launchers, and a number of LAW light antitank weapons, Claymore mines, and 60mm mortars. The headquarters company weapons platoon brought the heavier 81mm mortars and 90mm recoilless rifles. Piles of ammo, water cans, and medical supplies, along with food provisions sat ready to be hauled to Charlie on later lifts after the paratroopers were in place.

Duffy brought what many thought was overkill, but he knew was not. He had a carbine and the standard army backpack radio, known affectionately as the Prick 25 (official nomenclature PRC-25, FM radio). His assigned radiotelephone operator, or RTO, carried that. In Duffy's rucksack, he had a long, folding whip antenna for the radio, three extra batteries, and a commercial long-range AM/FM radio to monitor American Forces Vietnam Network (AFVN) news broadcasts. He filled the remainder of the space in the pack with LRP rations, a few cans of C-ration fruit, extra socks, a poncho liner, four fragmentary grenades, and four smoke grenades.[†]

He stuffed his uniform pockets, as well. He filled the four large shirt pockets and cargo pants pockets with two signal panels, compass, signal mirror, strobe light, small flashlight, knife, P-38 can opener, map, notebook wrapped in plastic, and pens for writing, plus markers for his map. On his web belt and harness, he'd fastened eight twenty-round ammo magazines, four smoke grenades, two fragmentary grenades, flares, snap links, a sharp killing knife, two water canteens, and a medical kit that included compress bandages, Band-Aids, tourniquets, morphine, and a self-injection blood-volume expander. He also clipped on two emergency aircrew survival radios (AN/URC-10).

A little after noon, eight VNAF UH-1 Huey helicopters landed beside the troops and shut down. Hải greeted the crews and gave them a rundown on the plan for the air assault.

[†]LRP Ration: Lightweight Long Range Patrol ration of freeze-dried food.

C-ration: A small box of canned food items. The standard army ration at the time.

A "poncho liner" is a lightweight military blanket made of quilted nylon with a polyester fill.

Captain Hoàng Ngọc Hùng, the 112 Company commander, loaded the first of his paratroopers onto four of the Hueys. The rest would follow in the four remaining helicopters several minutes behind. All but the crew chief and door-gunner seats had been removed, so the soldiers sat on the floor. Captain Hùng climbed into the lead aircraft, saving a space for Colonel Bảo. He had been given the name "Skinny" Hùng to help differentiate him from the other Captain Hùng, Phạm Đức Hùng, commander of 113 Company, who became "Big" Hùng.

As Bảo, Hải, and Duffy approached, the pilots cranked their engines. The starter motors whined, the sound increasing in pitch until a burp of black smoke belched from the exhausts as rotor blades began to turn. The starter noise gave way to the *whoosh-whoosh* of the rotors as they gained speed and engines came to life in a steady turbine hum. The smell of warm jet fuel exhaust filled the paratroopers' nostrils. Once Bảo was onboard the lead helicopter, and Hải and Duffy securely loaded on number two, the pilots increased rotor speed and manipulated their cockpit controls, pulling the workhorses from the ground. The first lift was in the air.

Bảo looked over his shoulder at his paratroopers. Determination marked the faces of the veterans. The new recruits looked scared. Lieutenant Colonel Bảo gave a reassuring glance before turning back to his own thoughts, watching the green jungle canopy race beneath the speeding helicopters. As they crossed the Krong Poko River, he raised his eyes to the vista of the Central Highlands that opened before him. *Beautiful*, he thought. *This is a beautiful land. Damned Communists. They've got to be stopped.*

He felt the pilots increase power as they pulled the aircraft upward toward the top of the ridge. He imagined the ridge as a giant elephant, pressed on all sides by thick forest, dominated by the high, rugged mountains to the northwest and a lesser ridge to the southeast. Bảo saw the elephant's head as a hill on his right, the body a larger grass-covered mass to the left. They headed between the two. They'd land atop the nape of the elephant's short neck.

There was nothing there. It had not served as a fire support base for a long while. Artillery pieces no longer roared. No soldiers held the ground.

The old trenchworks had long ago been swallowed back into the earth. Only tall grass, brush, and jungle remained.

The four helicopters spread out. The lead Huey began its approach. It came to a low hover about a foot off the ground. Bảo stepped off first. The others jumped out behind him. The chopper lifted off. The next took its spot on the small landing zone. In moments, dozens of paratroopers from the first four aircraft filled the LZ. They executed a well-practiced battle drill, fanning out to form a defensive perimeter. The 112 Company commander stuck close to Bảo. Hải and Duffy soon joined them.

Bảo surveyed the situation, confirming his vision of how the 11th might occupy the terrain. He spoke to the three officers by his side. "Must deal with what we have, not what we wish we had. I don't like ground here. But this where we are. We deal with it."

Bảo told Skinny Hùng, "You get the rest of your company landed and strengthen the perimeter here, around the LZ. I'll pass the other companies through your line as I put them in positions around the firebase."

He turned to Duffy and Hải. "Get FO.[§] Get communication. Be ready with artillery and airstrike if NVA attack."

John Duffy surveyed the terrain, trying to visualize how the enemy commander would think, trying to put himself inside the mind of his foe. What was his battle plan? What approaches would he use to advance his troops? Where would he put his observation posts to adjust artillery? How would he position his air defense weapons? Duffy had to understand what the NVA might do in order to plan the airstrikes needed to stop them.

The next flight of Hueys arrived in minutes, the distinctive *whop-whop* of the rotor blades chopping the afternoon air as they approached. It was a sound that could not be missed, by friend or foe. The helicopters continued to shuttle paratroopers from Võ Định, coming in flights of four choppers every ten to fifteen minutes.

When Big Hùng arrived next, with 113 Company, Bảo pointed to the high hills to the west and the terrain rising to the northwest. "I am concerned with that high ground dominating this position. Work your way up the ridgeline to the northwest. I saw a defensible place there about five hundred meters out. It has good overwatch of the rest of Charlie."

[§]Artillery forward observer.

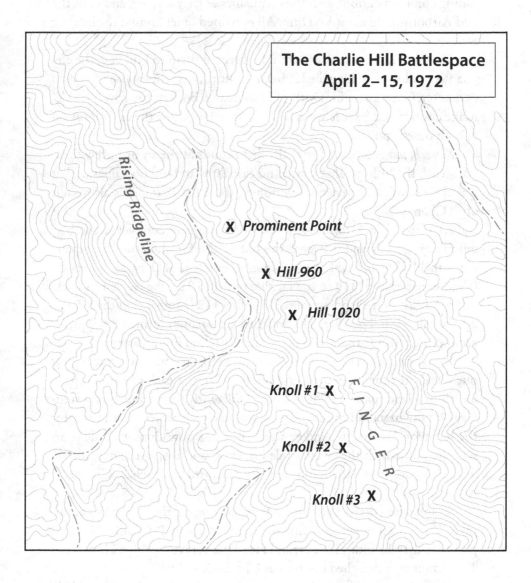

The Charlie Hill Battlespace
April 2–15, 1972

Rising Ridgeline

X Prominent Point

X Hill 960

X Hill 1020

Knoll #1 X

FINGER

Knoll #2 X

Knoll #3 X

Mễ and Dọc Liệu got off the next helicopter behind Big Hùng's. Finding Hải and Duffy, they formed a mobile battalion command post, establishing communications with the companies as they arrived, and with the 2nd Airborne Brigade at Võ Định. All remained quiet around the landing zone.

The 111 Company came next. Bảo directed them to Hill 960, the elephant's head, overlooking the LZ from the northwest. "Establish your own perimeter. Coordinate fires with 112 Company. Both of you cover the LZ. Make contact and be sure you and 113 Company know the exact location of each other's positions."

Swoosh, bang! Swoosh, bang! The first rounds of enemy fire, a few rockets, struck the hilltop. They caused no casualties and did no damage. That was the extent of the enemy reaction to the 11th Battalion's air assault onto Charlie.

At three o'clock that afternoon, 114 Company completed the battalion's air assault and delivered the last of the Headquarters Company personnel.⁕ That brought the battalion strength to 471 paratroopers on Charlie. Bảo moved 114 to the far side of Hill 1020, the elephant's back, just southeast of the landing zone. He pulled 112 Company off the LZ and up the hill a bit. Together, 112 and 114 Companies formed a perimeter around the hilltop. There, Bảo placed his battalion headquarters.

Everyone spent the rest of the afternoon digging in. The paratroopers burrowed into the ground around the perimeter at each of the company locations. Headquarters soldiers worked diligently to excavate spaces sufficient for the battalion command post and to create protective enclaves for the battalion leadership and key staff. They began fashioning crude roofs with logs on which they would pile layers of sandbags in the days ahead. The 11th Airborne Battalion had set its footprint on Firebase Charlie. It would do.

Colonel Bảo drew circles around the locations of the companies on his map. The 111 Company on Hill 960 became Charlie 1. Charlie 2 encompassed Hill 1020 with 112, 114, and Headquarters companies. He marked 113 Company's detached position as Charlie 3.

"Get an overlay of this to the company commanders," he ordered Hải.

⁕Headquarters Company was numbered as 110 Company, with Captain Nguyễn Tấn Nho commanding.

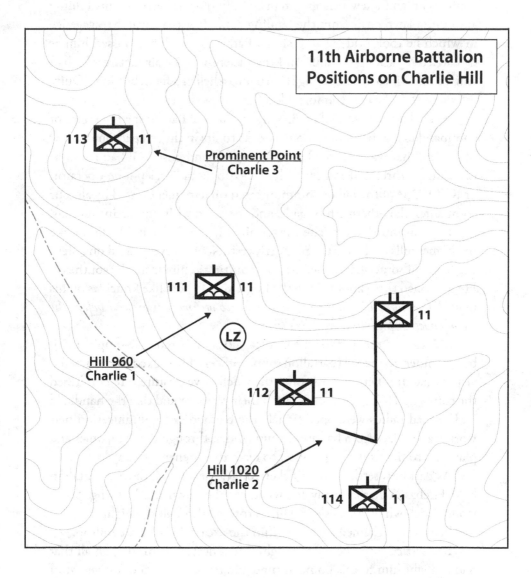

11th Airborne Battalion Positions on Charlie Hill

113 11

Prominent Point
Charlie 3

111 11

LZ

Hill 960
Charlie 1

11

112 11

Hill 1020
Charlie 2

114 11

Follow-on helicopter lifts brought shovels, sandbags, additional ammunition, water, and food, as well as medical supplies, headquarters equipment, and a few personal items. Duffy quickly retrieved his folding aluminum lawn chair from the landing zone. It was a small extravagance in which he took pride having along. Paratroopers duly harassed him as he carried it back up the hill. And then there was the air mattress he had stuffed into his rucksack. It might turn into a hell of a fight, but John Duffy intended to make it as comfortable a fight as possible.

As the battalion settled in, digging continued. Bảo grasped the reins of command as Hải brought radio networks to life in the scraped-out hollow of ground that was now the battalion's command post. Hải had communication on three FM radios, each carried by a radiotelephone operator, or RTO. One of the radios communicated on a frequency used by all four companies, the other with brigade, and the third with supporting aircraft.

Bảo continued to evaluate the terrain. He didn't like it. He didn't like the higher hills to the north and northwest. Now his eyes settled on a slender finger of somewhat higher ground pointing at him from the southeast. He identified three knolls along the finger that looked like knuckles on his map. *I'll get something out there tomorrow to occupy that ground before the enemy does, or push him off if he's there.*

Mễ selected the spot for the medical aid station and gave supply distribution orders to the S-4 (battalion supply officer). He walked the perimeter, visiting paratroopers and assessing their defensive posture. He confirmed the companies had radio contact with their platoons and that the handheld VHF squad radios were operational. The battalion's communication network was in place from battalion commander, through the companies and platoons, to the fighting squads set to react to any enemy threat.

As darkness settled over Rocket Ridge, the 11th Airborne Battalion held Firebase Charlie, ready for whatever the dawn would bring. Some stood watch while others slept. Duties rotated through the night.

Each leader claimed a space within the excavations on the hilltop.

Bảo settled into one for the night. He reflected on his life, on all that had brought him to this point in time. He felt the tremendous weight of leadership, the responsibility for his men and this mission. He'd bear the burden just as he always had. He was, after all, the commander, a good commander, one of the best commanders in the elite Vietnamese airborne. He was ready to lead his men in battle once again.

Hải remained in the hollow he'd been using for the command post. He examined the maps and log entries. He checked that the radio operators had the correct frequencies set. After speaking with the operations sergeant, he spread out his poncho in a corner, lay down, and pulled his poncho liner up over his shoulders. Thoughts swirled in his head as he anticipated surprises that might come in the night and wondered what challenges the next day held.

Mẽ and Duffy each selected separate locations, several yards away. Bảo had wanted the command group dispersed, so if a position got hit, not all the leaders would die at once.

Mẽ sat in his own hollow, fidgeting with his helmet. It had felt tight all day. As he turned it in his hands, he looked at the major's leaf painted on the front and reflected on how far he'd come from that young boy sitting atop a water buffalo tending his family's meager farm. He loosened the headband a bit, noticing his name marked on the inside. He put the helmet back on. *There, that's much better*. He thought of Sen and his three children, how much he missed them.

In his dugout, John Duffy grabbed a ration from his pack, sat in his lawn chair, and had dinner. He retired early to his air mattress. He lay there, eyes open, fixed somewhere in the darkness with thoughts of the defense of Charlie spinning in his head, his radio and weapon by his side. He loved that weapon, an automatic carbine, a CAR-15. As his hand rested on the stock, he thought about how it had come to be his.

Several months ago, working at MACV-SOG Headquarters in Saigon, Duffy encountered a longtime Special Forces friend, Captain Jim Butler. Jim had come to Saigon after leading one of SOG's elite recon teams, RT Python. He'd seen intense combat. One fight pitted his fourteen-man special operations team against a North Vietnamese regiment in the A Shau Valley. He was to harass the regiment as part of a deception operation designed to divert enemy forces away from the ARVN's Lam Son 719 thrust into Laos. The plan succeeded when the two-thousand-man regiment paused to send battalion-sized attacks against Butler's small group. They fought a hellacious two-day battle until extracted by helicopters. He had several wounded, but no one killed. His CAR-15 got a workout, helping to save his life and the lives of his men.[2] When Duffy left MACV-SOG for his duties as advisor to the 11th Airborne Battalion, Jim Butler gave him his beloved CAR-15.

"You may have use for this," Jim said as he handed the weapon to Duffy.

"Yes, I might. Thanks."

"Just be sure that you pass it along to another brave warrior when you leave."

"I will. Meanwhile, I'll take good care of it and keep it close."

With those memories, John's eyes closed, and dreams formed in the hollows of his mind as he fell soundly asleep.

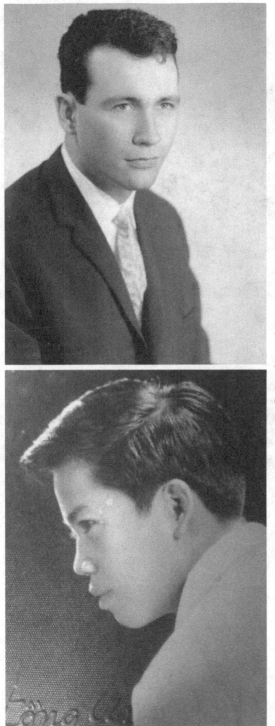

John Duffy and Lê Văn Mễ—
two young men growing
up on opposite sides of the
world.
SOURCE: (TOP) JOHN DUFFY PHOTO
COLLECTION; (BOTTOM) ME VAN LE
PHOTO COLLECTION.

Boy on a buffalo.
SOURCE: GETTY IMAGES/ITTIPON NAMPOCHAI.

Officer Candidate School
graduate, 2nd Lieutenant
Duffy, September 11, 1963.
SOURCE: JOHN DUFFY PHOTO
COLLECTION.

1st Lieutenant Duffy (walking, in helmet) trooping the line. Berlin Brigade, May 1966.

SOURCE: JOHN DUFFY PHOTO COLLECTION.

1968 Tet Offensive, Battle for Hue Citadel, the old imperial capital of Vietnam.

SOURCE: AP PHOTO/EDDIE ADAMS.

Beautiful Nguyễn Thị Sen.
SOURCE: ME VAN LE PHOTO COLLECTION.

Wedding Day, March 17, 1968.
SOURCE: ME VAN LE PHOTO COLLECTION.

Captain Duffy, Commander Special Forces A-Team, Det A-101, Lang Vei, Vietnam—February 1967.

SOURCE: JOHN DUFFY PHOTO COLLECTION.

Second tour of duty. Mobile Launch Team 3, Nakhon Phanom, Thailand—August 1969. Duffy kneeling, third from right. To his right is Major Bill Shelton, MLT 3 commander.

SOURCE: JOHN DUFFY PHOTO COLLECTION.

Lieutenant Colonel Nguyễn Đình Bảo, 11th Airborne Battalion commander—November 1971.

SOURCE: ME VAN LE PHOTO COLLECTION.

Major Duffy at Võ Định—April 1, 1972. On the eve of the assault onto Charlie Hill.

SOURCE: JOHN DUFFY PHOTO COLLECTION.

WARBIRDS OVER CHARLIE

A-1 Skyraider piloted by Lieutenant Phạm Minh Xuân, VNAF 503rd Fighter Squadron, "Jupiters."
SOURCE: TRUNG NGUYEN PHOTO COLLECTION.

U.S. Army AH-1G Cobra attack helicopter.
SOURCE: *AH-1G COBRA ATTACK HELICOPTER IN VIETNAM*, PAINTING BY RON COLE, RONCOLE.NET.

U.S. Air Force support to the fight on Charlie Hill.
From the top: O-2 "Covey" forward air controller, F-4 Phantom II
fighter/bomber, AC-130 "Specter" gunship, B-52 heavy bomber.
SOURCE: U.S. AIR FORCE

A-1 pilot Dương Hùynh Ky
(killed in action at Charlie).
SOURCE: TRUNG NGUYEN PHOTO
COLLECTION

A-1 pilot Phạm Văn Thặng
(later killed in action).
SOURCE: TRUNG NGUYEN PHOTO COLLECTION

A-1 pilot Nguyễn Đình Xanh
(shot down at Charlie—
later shot down again and
captured).
SOURCE: TRUNG NGUYEN PHOTO
COLLECTION

South Vietnamese Air Force A-1 Skyraider pilots of the 530th "Jupiter" Squadron that flew heroic missions at Charlie.

Standing: Phạm Minh Xuân, Nguyễn Hữu Hiếu, Phan Đắc Huề, Nguyễn Văn Mười, Nguyễn Văn Bá, Nguyễn Văn Hai, Lê Bình Liêu, Hoàng Mạnh Dũng, Nguyễn Văn Đệ. Kneeling: Trần Kim Long, Nguyễn Hữu Lạc, Vĩnh Thuận, Trương Minh Ẩn, Nguyễn Thành Trung, Đinh Bá Hùng, Nguyễn Quang Hải.

SOURCE: TRUNG NGUYEN PHOTO COLLECTION.

Đoàn Phương Hải promoted to major after the Charlie fight.
SOURCE: HAI PHUONG DOAN PHOTO COLLECTION

Major Lê Văn Mễ back into battle at Quang Tri.
SOURCE: ME VAN LE PHOTO COLLECTION.

Cobra pilot Lieutenant Dave Messa after a day at Charlie Hill, with the
.51-caliber hit that went through the armor plate inches from his head.
SOURCE: DAVID MESSA PHOTO COLLECTION.

Chief Warrant Officer Dan Jones and the author beside their bullet-riddled
gunship, April 1972.
SOURCE: AUTHOR'S PHOTO COLLECTION

South Vietnamese President Nguyễn Văn Thiệu visiting the Quang Tri battlefield in July 1972. Major Mễ is farthest left, then General Luong (Airborne Division Commander), President Thieu, and Colonel Ngoc (1st Airborne Brigade Commander).
SOURCE: ME VAN LE PHOTO COLLECTION.

11th Airborne Battalion command post during the Quang Tri battle. From left: Major John Howard, Colonel Barrow (MACV staff), Captain Dickson (Team 162), and Major Mễ. Major Howard would replace Captain Furrow as the 11th Airborne Battalion advisor on September 19, 1972.
SOURCE: ME VAN LE PHOTO COLLECTION.

11th Airborne Battalion surgeon Dr. (Captain) Tô Phạm Liệu in military medical school.
SOURCE: THAI TO PHOTO COLLECTION.

Doc Lieu safely settled in the United States.
SOURCE: THAI TO PHOTO COLLECTION.

Artillery Forward Observer
Lieutenant Nguyễn Văn Lập,
during training, 1968.
SOURCE: LAP VAN NGUYEN PHOTO
COLLECTION.

Lập at a *Mũ Đỏ* reunion,
Washington, D.C., 2005.
SOURCE: LAP VAN NGUYEN PHOTO
COLLECTION.

The Me Van Le family, 1979. New beginnings in the United States of America.
Me, Sen, then Phuong, Quyen, Vu. Ozark in front.

SOURCE: ME VAN LE PHOTO COLLECTION.

John Joseph Duffy, 1979, Major, U.S. Army (retired).
SOURCE: JOHN DUFFY PHOTO COLLECTION.

Three *amigos*: Mễ, Duffy, and Hải, 2016.
SOURCE: CHARLIE WITMER.

Memorial to the South Vietnamese Airborne and their American advisors, Arlington National Cemetery, Section 47.

SOURCE: TIM 1965, WIKIMEDIA COMMONS.

DEDICATED TO THE MEMORY
OF THE PARATROOPERS (MŨ ĐỎ) OF THE VIETNAMESE AIRBORNE DIVISION
(SƯ ĐOÀN NHẢY DÙ) AND THEIR ADVISORS (CỐ VẤN),
THE RED HATS AND RED MARKERS
OF
ADVISORY TEAM 162, MILITARY ASSISTANCE COMMAND VIETNAM (MAC-V)
WHO FOUGHT FOR FREEDOM AND DEMOCRACY
IN VIETNAM

1960 - 1975

"AIRBORNE ALL THE WAY"
"NHẢY DÙ CỐ GẮNG"

CHAPTER 9

Opening Salvos

THE RADIOS CAME ALIVE AT DAWN. THE TENSE CHATTER WOKE MỄ. He grabbed his gear and headed to the command post bunker. He found Bảo already there, intently listening to the radios with Hải. Duffy soon bent his tall frame through the sandbagged entrance and joined them. Firebase Delta, only two miles south of Charlie, was under attack. It was Monday, April 3, the day after Easter.

At least two North Vietnamese battalions had launched human wave assaults against the 2nd Airborne Battalion there. That might well have explained the lack of resistance to the 11th Battalion's landing at Charlie the day before. The enemy had postured for the Delta attack. The 11th's arrival surprised them, but the NVA would not allow it to unhinge their plan for the first-light attack against Delta the next day. However, a strange twist of circumstance would.[1]

Three days earlier, a U.S. Army Chinook resupply helicopter had been shot down at Delta. The crew survived and made their way inside the firebase. Colonel Lich had addressed the incident in his briefing to the 11th Battalion leadership at Võ Định. The enemy repulsed every effort to land a helicopter to extract the crew. The U.S. Army aviation headquarters at Camp Holloway, near Pleiku, put together a plan to rescue them at first light on the third day. The rescuers included every available Cobra attack helicopter in the Central Highlands. Captain Lynn Carlson of the Army's 361st Aerial Weapons Company led the mission.[2]

Just as the enemy unleashed his assault, the Cobras arrived on station. The 2nd Battalion's senior advisor, Captain O'Brien, adjusted the Cobra

111

fires to devastating effect. The Cobra crews mauled the enemy, ripping their formations with destructive fire. The Cobra strikes in conjunction with well-placed ARVN artillery stopped the onslaught in its tracks and pushed the attackers into a hasty retreat. The 2nd Airborne suffered twenty men killed and fifty-four wounded. Their opponent, however, was decimated. Of the estimated thousand-man NVA force, the defenders counted three hundred bodies in the wire at the end of the fight, with an unknown number having been dragged from the battlefield. Firebase Delta was secure, and the CH-47 crew later recovered. The attack got the attention of the 2nd Battalion's sister unit at Charlie, though.[3]

Bảo turned to Mê. "Form an assault force of One Twelve and One Fourteen Companies. Leave the headquarters, One Ten Company, here to defend Charlie Two. Lead Task Force Mê along that fingerlike ridge to the southeast. If the enemy is there, push him off and kill him. The ridge has three knolls, like knuckles on a finger. Advance all the way to the third knuckle and secure it. We need to control that high ground. It should also take some pressure off Second Battalion."

Mê acknowledged in his usual positive tone. "Yes, sir." He added a request. "Can I take Major Duffy with me?"

"No. We've got only one advisor. I have to have him with me. You can call VNAF airstrikes. And artillery is immediately available. Duffy can coordinate U.S. airpower from here."

Major Mê headed out with 150 men at nine o'clock that morning. The tip of the finger ridge pointed menacingly at the assembled attackers as if to say, "Dare you try." Mê swung his right arm overhead in a big arc and shouted, "Let's go!" He went forward, leading the assault down and across a wide saddle before moving uphill toward the first knuckle. That's where trouble began.

The enemy was there. They'd come in the night. The force had likely positioned in response to the 11th Battalion landing on Charlie the day before. They might have intended to block any potential interference with the NVA's planned dawn attack against Firebase Delta. Regardless, they occupied the high ground, ready for anything the 11th might send their way.

Mê had placed a platoon of 112 Company in the vanguard of the assault while positioning himself beside the 112 commander, Captain

Skinny Hùng. Enemy fire erupted as soon as they started up the hill. Three paratroopers fell, one killed, two wounded.

Hùng shouted orders. "First Platoon, fall back on the company. Second and Third Platoons, return fire. Weapons Platoon, get some mortar fire on that knoll."

Meanwhile, Mễ radioed Lieutenant Cho, the 114 Company commander. "Slide to the left of One Twelve. We'll try to flank these bastards. Use your mortars as you wish. I've got the FO working artillery fire."

Lieutenant Nguyễn Văn Lập, acting as the task force's forward observer, pounded the hillside with mortars and artillery. Mễ ordered a coordinated attack by his two companies. They moved up the hill, shooting and maneuvering to gain an advantage against their foe. They got close enough to see hastily constructed enemy fortifications with overhead cover. Mễ called in a strike of VNAF A-1 Skyraiders. The airplanes carried an awesome load of ordnance, including rockets, bombs, napalm, and machine guns.

Before the dust settled, Mễ ordered 114 Company to renew the attack. Cho led with a reinforced platoon. They overran the bunkers with the loss of one paratrooper killed and another wounded. Four North Vietnamese soldiers lay dead. The mangled remains of a .51-caliber machine gun sat nearby.

Mễ consolidated his task force around the site and prepared to continue the attack to the top of the hill. The NVA didn't give him time. They shot 75-millimeter recoilless rifle rounds. They swept down from the heights, firing and screaming. More paratroopers fell, but they held their ground. Mễ organized a counterattack of his own and soon pushed the enemy back up the hill, only to run out of steam as the force encountered stiff resistance. The morning turned to afternoon as the battle waxed and waned.

Bảo, Hải, and John tracked the fight from Charlie 2, but a little after 1:00 p.m. they heard something that turned their attention northward. *Bam-bam.* A minute later, *Bam-bam.* Then again.

NVA gunners adjusted their artillery onto Hill 1314, the high peak southeast of Firebase Yankee. Once they'd confirmed the accuracy of their plotting, they shifted fires to pepper Charlie 1 and 2 with a few rounds. They'd got it right, hitting ammunition boxes and getting a pretty good fire going.

Duffy suspected the NVA had placed artillery observers at strategic positions high on the surrounding ridges. He immediately set to work identifying the most probable locations, though it took him some time to get U.S. airstrikes because of the heavy combat at Firebase Delta. He finally persuaded an Air Force forward air controller, Covey 532, to put in two pairs of F-4 Phantoms and one set of A-37 Dragonflies. Covey orbited overhead in his small O-2 Cessna spotter plane, ready to deliver more U.S. Air Force strike jets wherever John needed them. Duffy also worked a team of Army Cobras in support of Task Force Mễ, six hundred yards away.

Mễ struggled to complete his mission. So far, he'd moved only partway up the first of three knolls and overrun a group of bunkers. He'd resisted enemy counterattacks and launched several of his own. But he'd been unable to push the enemy off the first objective, let alone move on to the second and third. There were simply too many NVA forces to allow his two companies to prevail.

Just before sunset, the enemy threw a fresh infantry company into the fight. They slammed the western flank of the paratroopers, causing them to bend, but not break. Task Force Mễ held, but would advance no further that day. The progress they'd made had cost a dozen casualties, killed and wounded.

Colonel Bảo faced a decision: leave the task force in place with hopes of at least securing the first knoll the next day, or bring them back to Charlie 2. The shorthanded battalion spread its limited manpower thinly across Firebase Charlie. Bảo had three separate locations to defend along the ridge, stretching over half a mile end to end. He had further deployed a huge chunk of his force almost half a mile to the southeast attempting to gain yet more real estate in an increasingly costly fight. The sun set, and all he had left to defend Charlie 2 was 110 Company, consisting of the headquarters personnel and weapons platoon.

Bảo issued his order after dark. "Task Force Mễ disengage, recover your dead and wounded, and return to Charlie Two."

With as much stealth as possible, Mễ brought his force off the knoll and across the wide saddle. He led his exhausted men back onto Charlie 2 a little after 9:00 p.m. One Twelve and 114 Companies returned to their previous positions on the perimeter. Almost immediately, the 114 sector came under attack from the southeast. The enemy had detected the withdrawal and followed with a platoon-sized force, which now probed the perimeter with small-arms fire, and many B-40 rocket-propelled grenades. They quickly withdrew once the paratroopers opened fire and sent a few mortars their way. But the battle for Firebase Charlie had begun.

That night, Mễ scratched out a letter to his wife, Sen, by the light of a small, flickering candle. He hoped he'd get it out on one of the resupply helos.

This may be my last letter for a while. The situation is approaching critical. The colonel is doing all that is possible. The NVA will surely push forward and we will do battle. I may soon fight in a ferocious fight. The commanders and paratroopers are ready. Perhaps, all will not return from this fight. That is the fate of soldiers serving their country.

My thoughts will always be with you. My heart will always belong to you. My strength is a tribute to your love. Our children are a testament to our love. Do not worry when you hear reports of the battle. I am ready and I know how to survive in combat. I will come back home to you, my precious love. I will fight the dragons and return to your arms.[4]

John Duffy awoke early on the 4th, intent on putting airstrikes on the enemy positions to the southeast. He requested hard bombs. They had penetrating power. He was certain the NVA were well dug in. That was their habit. That's how they survived the massive U.S. and South Vietnamese airstrikes and artillery barrages. They found refuge underground, or they took the fight so close to their foe that firepower could not be brought to bear without endangering the very forces it was trying to protect. John knew this and hoped hard bombs, rather than fragmentary or napalm, would get them in their underground hollows. He knew the limitations, though. Tunnels and caves were tough targets.

As the sun rose on Firebase Charlie, a thick fog shrouded Rocket Ridge. There would be no air support until it lifted, and that could be a while. John would have to wait. That would take patience, and John Duffy was not a patient man. That put him in a cranky mood as he strode from one side of the hilltop to the other, his planned enemy targets reeling in his head, ready to go to work to do what he did best for his battalion, deliver devastating attacks from the air.

Mẽ, stiff and tired from yesterday's fight, moved among the companies, ensuring the defenses of Charlie 1 and Charlie 2 were as Bảo had directed. The 113 Company, at Charlie 3, was too far to risk a solo trek. Mẽ couldn't see their position through the fog. He knew their location gave them good oversight on the rest of the battalion—when they weren't cloaked in the thick mist. Still, he worried about their detached site.

Bảo worried too. His concern, though, went far beyond the morning's fog. He didn't like the mission, the static assignment. Aggressive paratroopers, used to moving forward in combat, taking the fight to the enemy, had now been directed to dig in and defend a piece of ground from attack by an overwhelming enemy force. A sense of dread crept into the veins of South Vietnam's most courageous airborne commander. Bảo remembered the fate of the French and their loyal Vietnamese allies at Dien Bien Phu in 1954, when the Communist Viet Minh gained the surrounding high ground and stunned a far more substantial adversary, defeating a combined allied force of nearly fifteen thousand and ultimately forcing the French to give up their prized colony.[5] Yesterday's near disaster at Firebase Delta reinforced his anxiety, as did Mẽ's inability to push the enemy off the southeast finger. Here Bảo sat, with less than five hundred men to defend Charlie against the elements of two North Vietnamese divisions, with supporting tanks, artillery, and air defenses.

Around 9:00 a.m., the fog started to lift. A short time later, John Duffy got a call on the radio from forward air controller, Captain Rod Lennard.

"Dusty Cyanide, this is Covey Five Three Seven."

"Roger, Covey. This is Dusty Cyanide."

"This is Five Three Seven. I'm on station. What can I do for you?"

"Covey, this is Dusty Cyanide. Got some targets for you this morning. Enemy bunker complex and estimated battalion-sized enemy force, dug in, about five hundred meters southeast of my position on Firebase Charlie.

You will see a fingerlike ridge pointing at Charlie with three knolls, like knuckles."

"Roger, Dusty. I've got it."

"Hit the first knuckle, the northernmost knuckle."

"Wilco. I've got a pair of F-4s inbound with hard bombs, as you requested."

"Roger that. Thanks."

Ten minutes later, John saw Covey's small Air Force spotter plane roll onto its side, allowing its nose to fall toward the ground. The FAC fired a pair of smoke rockets onto the knoll to mark it for the strike. Seconds later, the paratroopers heard the screech of fighter jets as they screamed down from altitude, one behind the other, releasing their bombs. The knoll erupted in violent explosions. The two jets climbed, turned, and did it again. John smiled. *Take that, you sorry bastards.*

The paratroopers atop Charlie cheered. Mễ beamed as he stood beside Lieutenant Cho, knowing the price just paid by those who'd frustrated his task force's advance the day before. Bảo's spirits lifted. Captain Hải found only temporary joy, though, as he turned his gaze to the west. His eyes cut through the thinning haze. There he saw a road, many kilometers away, on the far side of the Đak Sir Valley. He peered through his binoculars. Fresh reddish dirt revealed new construction, possibly an old French highway from Cambodia, refurbished. Whatever, it now stood as a major jungle throughway headed straight for Rocket Ridge.

Hải relayed his sighting to the others. The reality of their situation settled back on them. A bomb run by two F-4s had not substantially changed their condition, a small band of paratroopers standing before the onslaught of a formidable chunk of the North Vietnamese Army.

Duffy saw a flash on a distant hillside to the south of the newly discovered road. Twenty seconds later, a huge explosion rocked Charlie.

Duffy exclaimed to himself, *Oh, shit. That's a 130-millimeter gun.*

The Soviets made the 130mm artillery piece, an extraordinary weapon. It fired its explosive shells more than seventeen miles. That was twice the range of any American furnished artillery that remained in the Highlands. The 130 could pound South Vietnamese positions with devastating fire, all the while staying well beyond the range of anything they could throw back at it. Such big guns had never been seen in these parts before. Duffy would have some convincing to do before anyone above him would believe any were there now.

Lieutenant Lập, the 114 Company forward observer, put his artillery expertise to work. He made an analysis of the large crater left by the explosion. Luckily, no one had been injured. He determined the direction back to the gun position and retrieved a fragment of the shell casing, proving the round was a Soviet-made 130mm projectile. He'd send that off to brigade headquarters as proof that the big guns were indeed now in play.

"Dusty Cyanide, this is Covey Five Three Seven. I've got some guys and what appears to be a camouflaged tank a little over a click to your east, northeast. Do you have any friendlies out there? Do you want me to hit it?"

"Covey, this is Dusty Cyanide. Not ours. We have nothing there. If you've got more air, blow 'em to hell." After a short pause, John added, "I've also got a probable one-hundred-thirty-millimeter gun position in grid square nine-three-zero-six, just northwest of Big Mama.* Keep a lookout."

The result of the strike: one enemy tank destroyed and an unknown number of enemy soldiers killed. Like the 130-millimeter gun, it would be a while before higher echelons would believe the NVA had tanks that far south in Vietnam.

Throughout the afternoon, Mễ worked A-1 Skyraiders while Hải had his forward observers lob artillery onto the known and suspected enemy positions around Charlie. John Duffy went back to work developing more potential targets. That included more accurately fixing the position of those distant 130 guns. His mind stirred. *They're probably well dug in. Maybe even hidden in tunnels or caves with rails to roll them out for firing. Tough nut, but I've got to get them.*

That night, several hundred enemy attacked the Charlie 2 perimeter. The NVA pressed hard. A small shell fragment tore into John's cheek, covering the left side of his face in blood. The 11th countered with small-arms fire, mortars, and artillery. A Vietnamese Air Force AC-47, "Spooky,"

---

*Chu' Mom Ray, or "Big Mama" to the Americans. The highest mountain in the region situated nearly ten miles southwest of Charlie and towering above the surrounding terrain at nearly 6,000 feet.

gunship[†] arrived to fire on the enemy as he withdrew. The paratroopers delighted in the fireworks display, knowing the punishment that was being wreaked upon their enemy. The whole thing lasted less than an hour.

Bảo concluded it was a probing attack, designed to gain information. "Our enemy is examining us, gauging the response of our paratroopers to his actions, determining our strength and locations on this hill. Tomorrow, we've got to start making him pay more dearly."

In the morning, Mễ, Hải, and Duffy rounded up every available fire support asset and pounded their foe. Shortly after dawn, John Duffy raised Covey 531, who put in three sets of jet fighters. Mễ directed airstrikes by VNAF A-1s and the small but effective jet-powered A-37 "Dragonflies." Hải coordinated artillery fires and also worked additional A-1 and A-37 strikes.

Something caught Hải's attention far to the west. Columns of dust rose from the road he'd spotted the day before. He raised his binoculars and then summoned Mễ and Duffy. He handed the binoculars to each in turn. "Look. Look there. On road I find yesterday. You see the trucks? Soviet-made trucks. They drive from Campuchia. Even in daytime. Very bold. Bring supply. Bring more soldier."

Not a good omen, Duffy thought to himself. With no words spoken, he knew the others felt the same.

Hải added, "I bomb with VNAF."

John knew they'd need more. He got on his radio and started pushing requests for heavy B-52 "Arc Light" strikes[†] to his boss, Peter Kama, the 2nd Airborne Brigade advisor. He knew chances were slim with everything else going on against the mounting NVA offensive. Nonetheless, he persisted. John Duffy was never one to shrink from arguing a just cause.

[†] The AC-47 was an aerial weapons platform developed by modifying a C-47 (DC-3) cargo airplane to mount a number of 7.62 mini-guns and .30-caliber machine guns in the left-side windows and cargo door along with the capability to dispense illumination flares. The aircraft was often affectionately referred to as "Puff the Magic Dragon."

[†] A B-52 strike, called an "Arc Light" during the Vietnam War, normally consisted of three heavy B-52 bombers, flying in formation at high altitude, each with a mixed load of up to 108 500- and 750-pound bombs. Each Arc Light strike could demolish over three hundred football fields of ground, a rectangle 1.2 miles long by .6 miles wide, destroying and killing nearly everything on it. The NVA suffered debilitating losses due to these strikes. John T. Correll, "Arc Light," *Air Force Magazine*, January 2009.

A call for help shifted attention in another direction. The brigade's reconnaissance company, operating northeast of Charlie, made contact with enemy forces shortly before noon. Mế put in A-1 strikes to support them. The aircraft received .51-caliber antiaircraft machine gun fire. The recon company fought a running battle through the afternoon, only able to break contact after Duffy found a set of Cobra attack helicopters to join the fight. The Cobras took heavy .51 fire, as well. Late in the day, the Recon Company found refuge inside Charlie 2.

John heard shouting as their guests came through the perimeter defenses. The voices, at first sternly barking orders, turned to joyful greetings. John started down the hill to investigate.

He found the Recon Company commander engaged in animated conversation with Skinny Hùng. His advisor, a U.S. Army first lieutenant, on seeing Duffy, walked up the hill to meet him. A very odd-looking individual scampered behind. The lieutenant wore the same camouflage-patterned uniform of the Vietnamese airborne as John. The other man, a tall European in civilian clothes—khaki pants with bountiful, large pockets, and a short-sleeved casual shirt—wore dark glasses and sported a floppy military "boonie" hat. Perspiration soaked his clothing, and rivulets of sweat ran down his face. A 35mm camera hung from a strap around his neck.

The lieutenant pulled his helmet off and greeted Duffy. "Major Duffy? Good morning, sir. I'm Lieutenant Mitchell with the brigade Second Reconnaissance Company."

"Good morning, Lieutenant. What the hell are you doing here, and who is that?"

"He's a French reporter. He'd like to do an interview."

"Well, I'll be damned."

John talked to the guy for a few minutes. The Frenchman recorded onto a small battery-powered tape machine, feverously took notes, snapped a few photos, and then was gone.

The recon paratroopers bandaged their wounds, slept for several hours, and then slipped into the jungle during the darkness of night to continue their mission. Duffy hoped to hell they'd avoid the enemy and return safely to friendly lines. He never learned the fate of the soldiers or anything about the article that might have resulted. The whole thing struck him as very strange.

Thursday, April 6, arrived with Charlie once again shrouded in fog. Eeriness settled over the hilltop. All wondered what the enemy was up to behind the mist. They could only imagine.

Anh Năm ("Big Brother"), Lieutenant Colonel Bảo, assembled his officers and staff, save Big Hùng, because of 113 Company's distance from the rest of the battalion. He summarized their situation and issued an order that he'd relay to Hùng by radio: "The NVA have us surrounded. They hold the mountaintops. They've positioned their guns to shoot down the helicopters. It is here we must do battle. It is here we must bleed them. Do not let them take our positions. This battle is to the end. Tell the paratroopers to fight bravely. Tell them to aim all their bullets well, for we may lose the ability to resupply. Dig in deep and prepare for combat. Any trooper not ready to fight, I want him off the mountain. I'll not have him die with us. I'll not have him share in our glory."[6]

Mẽ translated for Duffy. The weather that morning precluded John from running any airstrikes, so after the meeting he turned on his AM/FM radio for some news. He'd followed the deteriorating situation in I Corps over the past days. The North Vietnamese had achieved rapid success, overrunning the key base at Camp Carroll and gaining control of most of western Quảng Trị Province. John heard more bad news this morning. The communists had launched the feared third prong of their spring offensive. They struck from Cambodia, aimed toward the South Vietnamese capital, Saigon. Heavy fighting raged in Lộc Ninh, a small border town. An Lộc, the provincial capital, would likely be next, opening the path to Saigon itself. John knew air support would now be more difficult to get, and that any chance for a B-52 strike was probably gone. "Just what we needed," he whispered sarcastically to himself.

The fog lifted shortly before noon. Duffy went back to work running airstrikes. He teamed with Mẽ and Hải to integrate all available fire support onto the most lucrative targets. With the priority of air support going against the NVA offensives far to the north and the south, little could be allocated to Charlie. John developed a technique of constantly badgering forward air controllers to divert airstrikes that were not able to hit their primary targets because of weather or situational changes. He got a number of much needed missions that way.

Big Hùng sent out a twelve-man patrol from his company that afternoon. Like the rest of the paratroopers, he didn't like sitting blindly in a defensive position, waiting for the enemy to attack. The 113 Company patrol scouted to the southeast of Charlie 3 with no encounters. Just before sunset, as they headed back toward their company perimeter, the patrol made contact with a group of about thirty enemy soldiers. Company mortars helped them break contact and get back inside the company position. They took a few casualties, but they'd confirmed enemy presence around Charlie 3.

The next morning dawned without fog. Instead, the rising sun glistened on low, soft, wispy clouds, floating gently in valleys below. Patches of jungle showed deeply green through several breaks in the mist. The Krong Poko River curved as a small silver ribbon far to the east. Above, nothing but blue sky. The paratroopers took pause at the beauty surrounding them. Then Mẽ, Hải, and Duffy got to work, taking advantage of the good weather to put in all the artillery and airstrikes they could get. A busy day.

The following day, Saturday the eighth, began much the same. The first airstrikes hit the ridge to the northwest and the gully running along its base. The resulting secondary explosions pleased Lieutenant Colonel Bảo. They showed the attacks hit some of the NVA machine gun, mortar, and rocket positions, and likely a good number of enemy soldiers, as well. Still, he worried about the finger of high ground to the southeast and directed that airstrikes be concentrated there.

For the rest of the day, Duffy worked with forward air controllers Covey 507, 531, and 546 putting in Air Force F-4 Phantoms and Navy A-7 Corsairs on the finger. Mẽ and Hải added VNAF A-1 Skyraiders and A-37 Dragonflies to the mix along with a number of artillery barrages. The effort produced good effects with the destruction of bunkers and mortars and two dozen secondary explosions. They'd inflicted pain on their enemy.

Midafternoon, Mẽ radioed for resupply, and Duffy added a request for his reassignment orders. He had less than a month remaining on this third tour of duty in Vietnam and was anxious to get a copy of his new orders to see where the army was sending him. A Huey arrived within an hour. The pilot landed in a hail of enemy fire. The crew kicked off the load of ammunition, water, and rations, and put several wounded onboard. The chopper rose, turned, and was gone. No orders yet for John.

The day's good weather ended. Clouds billowed around Charlie, and airstrikes ceased for the day. The paratroopers faced the evening with an ominous feeling that conditions were developing for a big fight on Charlie.

Disturbing radio calls at eight o'clock that night confirmed those suspicions. John received the message in English over his advisor channel at the same time the 2nd Brigade transmitted it on the ARVN network in Vietnamese. "Intelligence indicates the NVA plan to overrun Charlie. Repeat, intelligence believes the NVA intend to overrun your positions."

Bảo grabbed the handset from Hai's radio operator. "This is Grey Tiger. Request to maneuver on offensive operations to take the fight to the enemy. I don't want to sit in place on Charlie and wait to absorb the attack the enemy has designed. Airborne doesn't sit and wait. It attacks. I'll consolidate, leave one company on Charlie Two and launch an attack with the rest of the battalion."

The reply came back immediately from the brigade commander, Colonel Lich, himself. "Negative. Defend in place. Block any potential crossing of the ridge. Fight to the death on Charlie. Those are your orders. Fight to the death."

Bảo could only believe that order had been placed on Lich by higher authority.

CHAPTER 10

Interlude

SUNDAY MARKED A WEEK SINCE THE 11TH AIRBORNE BATTALION'S air assault onto Charlie. It also marked a new conviction among the paratroopers. The line had been drawn in the sand. They would fight until victory or until death. The day, though, was bereft of enemy activity—no shelling and no ground attacks. Nonetheless, the defenders worked hard to improve their positions. Mẽ, Hải, and Duffy packed the day with airstrikes and artillery on every potential enemy assault position, headquarters, observation post, and machine gun site they could divine from what they had seen over the past days. They knew the enemy was posturing for an all-out assault against the 11th Battalion. The strikes caused a lot of secondary explosions, but no enemy reaction.

Monday, April 10, remained eerily calm. Low clouds rested along the ridge top, precluding any air support. John tuned his commercial radio to the Armed Forces Vietnam Network for the news. He learned the NVA continued to roll up victories below the Demilitarized Zone in I Corps. They had also advanced rapidly in their southern assault out of Cambodia, now beginning to close the roads around An Lộc, preparing to lay siege and likely attack the city before marching on toward Saigon. The government of South Vietnam reinforced the ARVN garrison at An Lộc with the elite 81st Ranger Battalion and the 1st Airborne Brigade in addition to pounding the enemy with wave after wave of devastating airstrikes including B-52, AC-130, and every other fighter and attack aircraft in the allied inventory. It was going to be a hell of a fight.[1]

Bảo, frustrated by the weather and not knowing what his foe was up to, had 114 Company send patrols to the southeast of Charlie 2 and 112 Company to the northwest. He directed each company, "Send a squad. Locate the enemy. Don't engage. Assess the damage of our strikes against them, and get back here with that information."

The reconnaissance confirmed enemy forces had moved to positions within a few hundred yards of the Charlie 2 perimeter. The airstrikes had caused visible damage, but the soldiers saw no bodies left behind. The information gained influenced the airstrike and artillery-planning decisions for the afternoon.

The weather cleared by noon. Helicopters arrived with more ammunition, water, and rations, including some live chickens for roasting. They also brought mail, to the delight of the beleaguered paratroopers. Peter Kama even put some candy bars on the aircraft for John. He shared them with the others.

The helicopters didn't take any fire. The enemy didn't hit Charlie with any mortars, rockets, or artillery. He didn't come at them with any ground attacks. All was strangely quiet—like the calm before the storm. Still, the defenders improved their positions, digging their trenches deeper. Still, they put in more airstrikes and artillery, hoping to defang the expected communist assault.

Duffy's radio crackled with a transmission coming in. John recognized Peter Kama's voice. "Dusty Cyanide, this is Cellar five one. Give me a target for a B-52 strike. I may have one coming your way later on. Over."

"You son of a bitch. You did it. How?"

"Pulled some strings at MACV. I've got connections. Get me a target. I need it soon. Out."

Young Major Duffy put his mind into that of the senior NVA commander opposing the 11th Airborne. He tried to think of how the enemy's attack plan might unfold. *All the approaches to the Charlie defensive positions are difficult and require an uphill approach—except one. There is the long finger ridge pointing at the main position from the southeast. It is higher terrain, at least five hundred meters long, relatively flat, and wide enough to form multiple battalions in preparation for an attack. If I were the NVA commander, and if I had a full regiment, I would charge a battalion out of the gully to the northwest of Charlie as a feint, causing the paratroopers to shift their forces to prevent a penetration of their defenses there. About thirty minutes later I would unleash my main two-battalion attack off the finger. I would precede the operation with heavy artillery fire beginning forty-five minutes prior. I'd add mortars, recoilless rifles, and B-40 rockets ten minutes prior to the main attack.*

Duffy had his target. He consulted with Hải and Mễ and Bảo, who shared his assessment. He radioed Peter Kama. "Cellar Five One, this is Dusty Cyanide. Target grid follows. Zulu Bravo zero-one-one-five, one-zero-four-zero. Start it there and run it southeast down the ridge as far as it will go. Better give the boys at Delta a heads-up. Over."

"Does that give you five hundred meters separation? Over."

John bit his tongue. "That gives us five hundred meters separation. Barely. We'll hunker down and hold on to our helmets. We know the drill. Over."

"Roger. More to follow. Out."

— ⁍ —

Sen sat in her home in Saigon, listening to news reports of the intensifying combat in the Central Highlands and the dramatic losses elsewhere in South Vietnam. She was a stalwart army wife. Now, for the first time, she felt dread on top of the ever-present fear she always had for her husband.

CHAPTER 11

Tuesday

April 11, 1972

This day, hell unleashed its fury at a place called Charlie.

At midnight, John Duffy's radio came to life. "Dusty Cyanide, this is Covey Five Five Five. Following message relayed from Blue Chip through Carbon Outlaw.* Arc Light inbound to target location per your request. Estimated drop in thirty minutes."

John rousted Bảo and Hải in the operations bunker. Mễ joined them there. Hải radioed the companies. Commanders alerted their paratroopers. As the drop time approached, each crouched down in a foxhole, trench, or bunker, held his helmet on his head, and opened his mouth, hoping to equalize the pressure of the coming blasts that he'd been told would be very close.

Terror rained from the sky. Hundreds of 500- and 750-pound bombs fell from the highflying B-52s. The closest hit only three hundred yards from 114 Company, blasting the nearest knoll of the finger ridge, exploding its shoulders, and smashing a swath of obliteration along the ridgeline

---

*"Carbon Outlaw" was the call sign of the Air Force Direct Air Support Center (DASC), collocated with the ARVN II Corps Headquarters in Pleiku, in communication with both the American senior advisor, John Paul Vann, and the 7th Air Force command post, "Blue Chip," at Tan Son Nhut Airbase in Saigon where a Strategic Air Command liaison officer sat. The system facilitated the diversion of in-flight B-52 strikes to lucrative targets of opportunity, using ground radar sites, known as Combat Skyspot, to vector the Arc Lights onto target locations with precision accuracy in all types of weather, day or night. See Elizabeth H. Hartsook and Stuart Slade, *Air War: Vietnam Plans and Operations, 1969–1975* (Fort Pierce, FL: Defense Lion Publications, 2013), 241–80.

to the southeast. The earth shook. The destruction was horrific and lethal. Debris rained down even on nearby friendlies.

The NVA answered the blow with barrages of artillery, mortars, and recoilless rifle fire while they licked their wounds and rethought their attack plans.[1] Their shells blasted the hill, but they did little to the paratroopers still lying low in their trenches after the B-52 strike. The shelling continued, sporadically, through the night. Even so, those not standing watch were able to fall back to sleep for some moments of rest, fitful as it might have been.

No one saw the sun rise. Dawn came only as a dull glow in the east. A dim light filtered through layers of explosive residue, dust, and floating debris that obscured the sky. Everything appeared in unearthly, colorless, stark gray tones: uniforms covered in dirt and ash, soldiers breathing thick nasty air, their nostrils filled with the acrid smell of the explosions that lingered in the atmosphere. Random shelling threw yet more chunks of earth about the place, now looking much like an old-time sepia-tone photograph.

Ka-boom! Ka-boom!

Huge explosions crashed onto Charlie. The ground trembled. John Duffy knew exactly what it was. *Those damned 130-millimeter guns. I've got to get them. They'll kill us all. They'll blow us to hell.*

As he shuffled down the trench line toward the operations bunker, a round hit nearby. John was fine, but he looked back and saw shell fragments had torn into his air mattress, killing it dead.

He arrived late to Bảo's morning leadership huddle. Mễ noticed his sad expression and caught his eye with sympathy. John melodramatically announced, "Shit, guys. The assholes got my air mattress."

The sound of rotor blades lifted their spirits. They climbed out of the bunker. Looking east, they saw a string of four Hueys inbound with badly needed food, water, and ammunition. Mễ sent orders to have wounded paratroopers moved from the battalion aid station to the LZ, ready for transport to the hospital in Kontum.

Small arms and antiaircraft machine gun fire met the lead chopper on approach to the landing zone. Still, it touched down, quickly discharging cargo and loading wounded paratroopers before rising, turning, and skimming down the mountainside. Mortar rounds greeted the second helo, and the fire became so intense that the last two aircraft, taking several hits, abandoned their approaches. One pilot tried again, took more hits, and limped away. The helicopter crashed on the way back to Võ Định, killing the crew.

Twenty more 130mm shells smashed into Charlie that morning. Big explosions. Big craters. Five paratroopers seriously wounded. The NVA pounded the 11th while they reshuffled units. The 114 Company reported movement southeast. The enemy appeared to be removing bodies from the B-52 strike and replacing them with fresh troops. Hải directed Lieutenant Lập to execute a fire mission, pounding them with a three-hundred-round artillery barrage.

Reports came in of more NVA soldiers only a few hundred yards to the southwest. John worked a flight of F-4 Phantoms with Covey 533. Oblivious to the antiaircraft threat, the gutsy forward air controller rocked onto a wing and swooped down for a low pass over the target after the strike.

"Dusty Cyanide, this is Covey Five Three Three. Lots of bodies down there. Estimate a hundred killed by air."

More helos came to resupply the beleaguered 11th Battalion, both VNAF and American. The .51-caliber machine guns fired relentlessly. The few choppers that braved an approach took debilitating hits before turning away. None were able to get through the deadly wall of bullets. NVA machine guns blazed away at any helicopter that came in range. At least ten .51 positions now ringed Charlie.

Duffy turned to Mẽ. "Those machine guns are out there to kill. They're doing their job. They're good."

"Yes. Big problem for us. Problem for resupply and evacuate wounded."

John nodded. "I'm worried the fire is too intense. They can't get in. All we're going to do is get more helicopters shot down. I'm closing the LZ. Tell me if you or Colonel Bảo have a problem with that."

Duffy took the radio handset from his RTO. "Cellar Five One, this is Dusty Cyanide. I am closing the LZ to Huey resupply and medical evacuation helicopters. They will not survive the gunfire from ridgelines above. I repeat, the LZ is closed. There is no reason attempting the impossible. I've got to get rid of some of those .51-cals before we can get any more helos in here."

He put in more sets of F-4s on the surrounding machine gun positions and asked Covey to hit the suspected 130mm gun positions with anything else he had available. John Duffy had two problems he must resolve if the 11th Airborne Battalion was to survive: kill the antiaircraft machine guns and eliminate the 130mm guns.

Later that afternoon, Duffy asked Mễ, "You remember at Vo Dinh, the brigade commander talked about the North Vietnamese Army cutting South Vietnam in half, just like they did against the French in 1954? You promised to tell me more later. What was that all about?"

Mễ's brow lowered. "In 1954, French have trouble in Vietnam, in all Indochina. Hồ Chí Minh and his communists, called Việt Minh, fight against French. French fight to keep their colony. Big defeat at Điện Biên Phủ, far away in the northwest of Vietnam. After battle, French forces still control much of country. To make final defeat, Việt Minh focus on Central Highlands. They attack, attack, attack in Highlands. They try to cut the south portion of Vietnam in half, from mountains to coast. French decide to pull back army to Pleiku."

He looked at Duffy. "That is where we land at airfield when we come from Saigon."

John nodded. Mễ continued. "French Group Mobile One Hundred withdraw from An Khê, fifty miles east from Pleiku. French have very strong force, more than three thousand soldier. Korean War veteran, Cambodia and loyal Vietnam soldier, armor vehicle, artillery, air support. They die in ambushes near Mang Yang Pass between An Khê and Pleiku. Việt Minh attack. Big fight for days. Two thousand casualty. Lose all vehicle and artillery, most of weapons and equipment. Việt Minh destroy Group Mobile One Hundred. Communist cut southern Vietnam in half.

"French leave Vietnam. Geneva Convention divide country into North and South. Now look like communist try to do again. NVA attack Highlands from west. Try to take Kontum and Pleiku and march to coast. First, try to come over Rocket Ridge. We stop them. We stop them here on Charlie Hill."[2]

At dusk, 114 Company sent out a twenty-man patrol to sweep to the southwest to assess what damage the day's air and artillery strikes had inflicted to their front.

John Duffy munched an army ration and looked sadly at his deflated air mattress. He tuned his AM/FM radio to catch up on developments elsewhere in the war. He found out that, in the north, the enemy had taken most of South Vietnam's northern province and nearly surrounded the provincial capital, Quảng Trị City. Nonetheless, the Allies worked to develop a counterattack strategy. John knew that would pull even more air support north, away from him. In the south, he learned fierce fighting continued around An Lộc, with an NVA drive directly into the city considered imminent. The government of South Vietnam sent more reinforcements there. The Central Highlands remained the third priority in what had become the largest North Vietnamese offensive of the entire war.[3]

CHAPTER 12

Wednesday

April 12, 1972

Exploding artillery shells shook the 11th Battalion paratroopers awake. The 111 Company took the brunt. Heavy artillery, mortar, rocket, and recoilless rifle fire rained down on Hill 960, Charlie 1. Seventy-five big 130mm shells slammed onto the hilltop. First Lieutenant Nguyễn Văn Thinh and his paratroopers pressed their heads tightly against the sides of their trenches, glad they'd dug them deeper each day. Still, young men died.

Khuất Duy Tiến, the NVA 64th Regiment commander, had positioned his force to overwhelm Charlie that morning and win a great victory. He'd ordered battalions 7, 8, and 9 into battle. Battalion 9 would take Hill 960 to begin the fight. A massive artillery barrage preceded the communist assault.[1]

The artillery stopped. The first NVA company rose from the steep gully less than one hundred yards to the west of the Charlie 1 trench line. Scores of enemy soldiers raced forward. The fight was on.

The 111th paratroopers reacted in well-practiced battle drill. Lieutenant Thinh, the company commander, quickly assessed the situation. Claymore mines had bloodied the lead elements of the attack. His soldiers thinned the advancing enemy ranks with disciplined, well-aimed rifle fire. They threw hand grenades in close combat. Thinh repositioned some of his machine guns, grenade launchers, and recoilless rifles. He shifted a rifle platoon to bolster the western trench. He ordered his company mortars into action while his forward observer adjusted artillery fire. Thinh reported the situation to Hải. Hải, in turn, radioed a report to 2nd Brigade. He'd continue to give them periodic updates. Battalion mortars joined the fight while Hải and Duffy set to work bringing strike aircraft into the fray.

A VNAF flight checked in with Hải. "Eleven Battalion, this is Jupiter Two-One. I have a flight of three A-1E Skyraiders for you. We've got rockets and napalm. Where would you like us?"

Hải answered, "Jupiter flight, this is Zero Zero Six. Enemy troops attacking out of the gully, west side of Hill 960. Hit the enemy with rockets and put napalm in the gully. Take care with friendlies. They are danger close. Lot's of VC* machine guns. Watch yourself."

The first Skyraider banked low from the south, the throaty roar of its big radial Wright Cyclone engine and swirling propeller so different from the high-pitched whine of fighter jets screeching down from altitude. Thinh watched the A-1 smack the attacking communists with salvos of rockets. Enemy antiaircraft machine guns spit fire from the ridge, their deep *rata-tat-tat* sounds audible even above the cacophony of battle.

The next Skyraider approached. Braving enemy fire, the pilot descended just above the treetops and released two napalm canisters. Thinh watched them tumble, almost in slow motion, before hitting the ground and exploding in convulsive orange and red fireballs, incinerating the gully. A plume of thick black smoke rose from the carnage. Nothing could survive that inferno. The third A-1 came in with more rockets. The aircraft made a second pass, and were gone.

Mễ and Duffy watched from Hill 1020. The fight looked intense.

Duffy asked, "How do you think Lieutenant Thinh is holding up? This is a tough fight for a young officer."

Mễ didn't hesitate. "Thinh very tough soldier, sharp, brave in battle. He take responsibility to defend Charlie with pride. Great pride, same as me. He one of our best leaders in this fight."

More flights of A-1s hit the attackers. Duffy brought in fast jets and Cobra attack helicopters. The 111 Company held, but the fight had been close.

---

*VC or Việt Cộng, Vietnamese Communist. The term refers to the irregular guerrilla forces drawn from the local population inside South Vietnam. However, the ARVN often used the term indiscriminately to refer to regular North Vietnamese Army forces as well as the guerrillas.

A FAC's radio call shifted John Duffy's attention to the southwest. "Dusty Cyanide, this is Covey Five Eight Zero. I spotted large muzzle flashes west southwest off Big Mama."

"Covey Five Eight Zero, this is Dusty Cyanide. Roger. That's those big fucking 130mm guns. Blow them to shit. Repeat, blow them to shit."

"Roger, Dusty. I've got six sets of air on order. We've got 'em. Will blow them to hell."

"Roger, Covey. I love you."

Duffy watched the distant dance with glee. Flight after flight of jet fighters unloaded bombs on the faraway hillside where he'd seen the big guns' muzzle flashes. *That'll get 'em*, he told himself, smiling.

John Duffy also worked with forward air controllers to run a number of F-4 Phantoms against forces reoccupying the southeast finger ridge, demolished after yesterday's midnight B-52 bombardment. Whatever damage had been done, it did not deter the NVA from reoccupying that natural approach onto Charlie.

Duffy called strikes along the ridge to the northwest and other targets to the south, east, and west. He got plenty of air that morning. They destroyed enemy observation posts, along with recoilless rifle and machine gun positions. The strikes produced a dozen secondary explosions, mostly from hitting ammunition supplies.

The action at Charlie 1 turned out to be but the opening crescendo in a day of artillery bombardment and ground attacks. The NVA shifted their artillery onto Charlie 2 late in the morning. The shelling included some big stuff.

Ka-boom! Ka-boom! Duffy was pissed. *Still those damned 130 guns. What the hell? Can't kill those fuckers.*

Lieutenant Colonel Bảo surveyed the battlefield. Disgruntled by the deteriorating situation on Charlie, he strode back toward his bunker, his shoulders uncharacteristically stooped. The courageous Grey Tiger moved as a big cat wounded, grasping the magnitude of the devastation around him, the desperation his paratroopers faced. Hải followed at a distance and tried to cheer him up, to no avail. Mẽ shouted after him. "We will prevail!" Bảo didn't give them a glance.

A heavy artillery barrage hit Charlie 2 at 11:30. The 130mm shells pummeled the hill. One slammed into Bảo's bunker with a deafening explosion. It turned the place to rubble. Broken timbers and shredded sandbags covered the commander.

Hải got there first. He'd been only several yards away. Mẽ joined in seconds. They began pulling debris off their *Anh Năm*. They summoned Doc Liệu, who came running with Duffy close behind. With the help of nearby paratroopers, they pulled Bảo clear. Doc Liệu went to work, but immediately looked up and shook his head. Their beloved commander was dead. Hải took the loss hardest of all. Mẽ didn't have time to grieve. He was now the commander. All responsibility rested on his shoulders.

John Duffy looked at the lifeless body, sad that Bảo had not been able to utter his final words in death. A feeling overcame John. He sensed what Colonel Bảo's last thoughts must have been. He had no doubt. He shared his notion with the others. "I know what Colonel Bảo wanted to say before he died. I hear his voice in my heart."

> *Tell my wife I loved her true.*
> *Tell my children to remember me.*
> *Tell my paratroopers to never surrender.*
> *To you, my officers, one final salute.*[2]

No one had a dry eye. Hải tended to the body in the Buddhist tradition. He cleaned Bảo's corpse as best he could under the conditions. He and Doc Liệu ceremoniously wrapped *Anh Năm* in a poncho and reverently laid him in the trench near his demolished bunker. They'd evacuate the body as soon as they got helos in again.[3]

Mẽ's eyes met John's in a look of mutual trust and respect. John, his lips tightened in a small, reassuring smile, gave a confident nod. Major Lê Văn Mẽ took immediate action as the new commander. He directed Hải to move the command post away from the battalion command bunkers. Hải sent his radio operators two hundred yards away to locate with 110 Company, the Headquarters Company. Hải would henceforth operate from there when he wasn't out and about coordinating artillery or conducting airstrikes.

The heavy enemy shelling continued all day long.

A flight of VNAF A-1s came on station. Mễ worked them to the northwest, destroying mortar positions and killing more of the North Vietnamese soldiers threatening 111 Company's perimeter.

Major Duffy got back to work. He had Covey 565 put in more jet fighters to the southeast. That finger ridge pointing at Charlie still seemed to be the most likely avenue for major enemy attacks. John kept pounding it. North Vietnamese officials later acknowledged the strikes had decimated the 64th Regiment's 8th Battalion. A bomb, dropped directly on the command post, killed the battalion commander, Đàm Vũ Hiệp, and the political officer, Nguyễn Văn The. The regimental executive officer had to take command of the battalion. He was badly wounded later in the day.[4] Duffy continued to hit the area with jet fighters and attack helicopters throughout the afternoon.

Covey brought in a flight of A-7 Corsairs off the navy carrier, *Coral Sea*.[5] Their first pass on the south perimeter went terribly wrong. They dropped short of the target. Their bombs hit the 114 Company trenches, killing three and wounding seven. Frustrated and angry, John moved the strike well to the southwest, where they could expend their remaining ordnance before heading back to the ship. He targeted 75mm recoilless rifle and antiaircraft gun positions.

Duffy also had forward air controllers continue to place strikes on the 130mm gun positions in the hills far to the southwest. He firmly believed those big guns were on rails that backed them into tunnels after they fired. He figured that's how they had survived all the airstrikes. That made them tough targets, but they had to be killed. With that thought, he headed to his bunker to make a report to 2nd Brigade. Always close to his side, his radio operator was right there with him. They found five young paratroopers sheltering inside from the artillery raining on the hilltop.

At 4:00 p.m., a 130mm round hit the entrance to Duffy's bunker, knocking him unconscious. He regained his senses, but felt warm, wet blood covering his head and chest. His back hurt too, where more shrapnel had torn into him. His ears rang. He couldn't hear. His head throbbed from a horrendous concussion. Rubble and bodies surrounded him. John shoved the closest guy and said, "Come on. Let's go."

The guy lay still. He didn't move. He was dead. John couldn't believe it. All of them dead, save his RTO. Yet John had lived. How could that be? How, in the same space and time, could five men die and he live? He stared at the carnage in shock. Finally, he grabbed his CAR-15 and dragged himself from the rubble, not at all appreciating the seriousness of his own injuries.

His radio operator followed, stunned, without the radio. He was severely wounded and badly dazed. He wandered off, stumbling and babbling incoherently. John called after him. He started to run after him—hobble after him, actually. He'd only taken a few steps when an artillery round exploded nearby, shredding the young man who'd served John so faithfully.

With no time to grieve, Major Duffy returned to his crumpled bunker to retrieve his radios. Amazingly, the PRC-25 survived the blast, banged up but still working. *Thank God.* His commercial AM/FM radio did not fare so well. *Damn. No more news updates.* He pulled on the backpack PRC-25 radio, grabbed his rucksack, and headed to the north side trench line.

"Cellar five one, this is Dusty Cyanide. We are being crushed by heavy artillery. I need another B-52 strike to get those big guns. Over."

"Dusty, this is Cellar five one. I'll see what I can do. Send target location, over."

"Roger, Cellar. Also, I got hurt a bit. My bunker destroyed. Repositioning to perimeter trench line. Will be moving about frequently."

Peter Kama queried John about his wounds. John gave some detail. Kama wanted him evacuated.

"Dusty, I'm getting you out of there. If I can't get a helo in, I'll get the Recon Company up there to carry you out."

"Negative, Cellar. I'm staying. These guys are dead without me. My tie to U.S. air support is the only chance we have. I'm not coming out. That's a negative."

"Roger, out."

Major Mễ assessed the situation on Hill 960. The 111 Company was holding on by a thread. They'd suffered heavy casualties that morning. The enemy continued pressure on their position. He knew they couldn't hold much longer. He decided to give up Charlie 1.

Mễ radioed his order to Lieutenant Thinh. "Four Zero One. This is Zero Zero Seven. Come to Papa. Bring your family and come join us inside our house."

Thinh withdrew, still in heavy contact, carrying the most seriously wounded and dragging his dead. The men on Charlie 2 helped wrap the bodies and lay them in rows with the other poncho-covered corpses of those already fallen on Hill 1020. Thinh integrated those of his paratroopers who could still fight into the defense of Charlie 2.

The NVA pursued their withdrawal, quickly overrunning the saddle, occupying the landing zone. Captain Hải, in frustration, picked up an M-79 launcher and started lobbing 40mm grenades. He killed a few NVA and felt better for it. He then shifted his energies to the more productive task of coordinating artillery missions with the battalion forward observer, Lieutenant Lưu Văn Đúng. In seconds, they had shells blasting the saddle, keeping the enemy at bay. Mễ followed with an A-1 sortie, and Duffy put more Cobra gunships on request.

Soon after, the 64th Regiment launched a large ground attack from both the southwest and southeast with its 7th Battalion coming up out of the gully and the 8th Battalion spilling off the finger.[6] The 114 Company faced two NVA battalions. Hải gave the company priority of fires and immediately shifted the artillery to the company's front. Major Duffy was hard at work, as well—dried, dirty blood caked on his head, back, and chest like a grotesque frosting. In short order, Covey 531 had jet fighters on station, hitting the first knoll, the base of the finger, and the gully. Cougar 36 reported with a team of three Cobras. John had them engage enemy troops coming off the finger. Mễ placed more A-1 sorties there, as well. The mass of firepower turned the tide. The attack culminated short of 112's trench line, and the NVA battalions withdrew.

Meanwhile, the enemy to the north reoccupied the saddle, harassing 112 Company's trench line with AK-47 small-arms fire and occasional B-40 rockets. Captain Dennis Trigg, leading a team of Cobras from the 361st Aerial Weapons Company, made several low passes, firing on the enemy troops, all the while taking .51-caliber fire from the ridges. The Cobras killed at least twenty-five and drove the foe off the saddle once again.

As darkness approached, Duffy had an idea. He asked Mễ to have a tall radio antenna erected on one of the abandoned battalion bunkers.

"It'll serve as a decoy to make the enemy observation posts believe that's where the key leaders still bed down."

John hoped they'd aim much of their artillery there. It worked. The communists pounded Charlie Hill through the night, but much of it fell harmlessly on that vacant target.

John lay down on top of a sandbag, radio in hand, still transmitting, and passed out.

———

But what of 113 Company, now even further separated from the rest of the 11th Battalion, now more isolated than ever?

Chapter 13

Thursday

April 13, 1972

Hải shook John Duffy awake in the middle of the night.

"VC surround 113. They attack. Big Hùng need help."

John raised up on an elbow. His head still pounded from his concussion. He felt groggy and disoriented, his thoughts not yet totally clear. He ached in every inch of his being. *Need to focus.*

Hải went on. "Hùng hear many hundred soldier move in dark. Then attack. He think big attack. Maybe whole battalion."

Duffy asked, "What time is it?"

"Zero one hundred."

"Christ. One o'clock in the fucking morning. Do you really think they're coming at him with a major attack in the middle of the night?"

"We hurt them yesterday in daytime. Maybe try different tonight. Maybe so."

"Okay, let me see what I can do. Can you request artillery flares be ready to go in case I'm able to get some tac air?"

John got on his radio. "Any Covey, any Covey, this is Dusty Cyanide. Need some help. Any Covey, any Covey."

He was surprised by an immediate reply. "Hello, Dusty Cyanide, this is Covey Five Two One."

"Roger, Five Two One. Our northern element is surrounded and under attack. Troops in contact. Possible NVA battalion. Request any available air."

"No fighters, Dusty. Weather Delta Sierra.* I know Spectre is work-ing several miles northwest. Let me check his status. But cloud cover here might be a no-go."

Duffy, always confident, came right back. "You get him overhead, and I'll make it work. The weather is clearing. Looks like a break in the clouds right where I need him. Get him over that hole, and I'll take it from there."

John wiped the dry blood and mud from his eyes and gave his head a slight shake to clear it. That only made the throbbing pain worse. The AC-130 gunship came up on his frequency.

"Dusty Cyanide, this is Spectre. You got work for me?"

"Roger, Spectre. Friendly element surrounded and under attack. Lots of triple A. Need your piss and vinegar. Give me a short burst through the hole in the clouds, and I'll adjust your fire from there."

"Roger. I'm over a good-sized break in the clouds. Will put rounds on the extreme west side of that hole."

"Got your rounds, Spectre. My element is about two hundred yards directly east."

"Roger, Dusty. We've got a good tally of your friendlies on our sys-tems. We'll hit what's moving around them. Clear to go hot?"

"Roger, clear to continue firing. Hit everything around those guys. Next nearest friendlies are two kilometers north of that position and five hundred meters south. Nothing east or west."

"Roger. Here we go."

The big, lumbering AC-130 gunship opened up with the row of guns running down its left side. The roar of Gatling guns harmonized with the drone of its four hefty turbo-prop engines. Spectre circled above 113 Com-pany for half an hour, dropping flares and spewing streams of 20mm cannon, mini-gun, and 40mm grenades on the NVA. As the clouds broke up, John moved the huge gunship to engage other targets around Charlie 2, as well.

"Dusty, Spectre. Counted twenty-five bodies, confirmed KIA. Sure there's lots more. We're returning to base. Good luck to you guys."

Covey 521 stayed on station, dropping flares and firing rockets before heading home himself. John closed his eyes, but he didn't sleep.

---

*Delta Sierra is military slang for "dog shit"—in this case meaning lousy weather.

Sporadic enemy artillery continued all night. No one slept more than a wink. Thirst parched their mouths. Dust clogged their throats. Cracked lips bled. Hunger gnawed their insides. Red eyes burned in dry sockets. Mud caked their soaked, foul uniforms. They didn't know what would come next. The stench of death hung heavy in the air. Worse, ammunition now ran dangerously low. These tough men had become a desperate band at the end of their tether. They would fight. They were warriors. But they needed resupply, and they needed it badly.

Once again, the sun didn't rise. The still air was thick with lingering smoke from enemy artillery bombardments, dirt churned by many thousands of exploding rounds fired by Spectre, and the incessant parachute flares. Dawn came only as a brightening yellow hue in the toxic vapors suffocating Charlie.

All expected a major attack that morning. It didn't come. The NVA did pound the hill with artillery, unmercifully, all day long.

Mẽ had an urgent priority. He summoned Skinny Hùng and ordered, "Keep a minimum force in defense. Take the rest of 112 Company and clear the LZ. We've got to get helos in here today. Take that LZ back!"

Captain Hùng saluted and went to form his company for the attack. Mẽ picked up his radio handset and called to Big Hùng up on Charlie 3.

"Four Zero Three, this is Zero Zero Seven. Send a force into the flat just below your position. Secure an LZ for your resupply and medevac. We're going to get some helicopters in here today."

The 113 Company still reeled from almost being overrun a few hours earlier. Their mission to gain an LZ didn't last long. Big Hùng radioed with the bad news. He called Hai, the S-3, not the commander.

"Zero Zero Six, Zero Zero Six, this is Four Zero Three. Mission aborted. We encountered enemy and withdrew. We are back inside our position. We cannot establish landing zone. Repeat. We can not establish landing zone."

Mẽ was irate.

Meanwhile, Duffy was on his radio. Once 112 Company recaptured the battalion's landing zone in the saddle, it would be critical that he reduce the antiaircraft machine gun threat so helicopters could use it.

"Any Covey, any Covey, this is Dusty Cyanide on Firebase Charlie. We need some air this morning. Badly. Any Covey, any Covey."

"Roger, Dusty. This is Covey Five One Eight. I'll have fast movers inbound shortly for you."

"Roger, Covey. I've got fifty-one-caliber machine guns all around. Need to knock them down so we can get some helicopters in here. Desperate need for resupply and medevac. Will appreciate your help."

"Roger, Dusty. Should have a flight of F-4s shortly."

The fighter jets arrived, looking to inflict pain. John Duffy couldn't work the air from where he was. He couldn't see the machine guns. He had to get above ground. Had to move. The hilltop erupted as enemy artillery shells hit, again and again. Nonetheless, Duffy lifted himself out of the trench and headed across the exploding landscape. He cleared his mind of everything except the task at hand—spotting enemy machine guns and radioing that information to Covey so the guns could be destroyed.

Duffy moved about the hilltop with what many saw as reckless abandon. The long radio antenna swaying over his head marked him as a target. For Major John Joseph Duffy, though, he was a man on a mission. He had one purpose in life, and that was to direct airstrikes, trying to save this battalion, his battalion. That was his task, his duty. Nothing else mattered.

He'd jump in a trench, work a target, watch the fighters roll in and release their ordnance, then pick up and run to another trench for a better view of his next target. Enemy gunners caught on to his strategy and opened up on him as he ran, shells bursting all around him.

"Covey Five One Eight, this is Dusty Cyanide. Hit the ridge four hundred yards west and running north. I've had fifty-ones there every day."

The first jet rolled in, dropping two five-hundred-pound bombs. Nearby machine guns opened up as the pilot pulled out and climbed to altitude.

John called Covey, "Still along the ridge. Two fifty cals firing now. You can see the tracers. Hit those guns."

John bounded across craters to another vantage point, artillery still impacting terrifyingly close. He continued passing commands through Covey. An incoming shell exploded nearby, knocking him down and slicing a piece of meat from his left shoulder. John pulled himself up, still grasping the radio handset, and glanced at his shoulder. *"Not too much bleeding. Good."*

"Covey Five One Eight . . ." And so the morning went. John, blown up the day before, blown up and wounded again this morning, continued working flights of jets, using whatever Covey aircraft appeared overhead. In between, he directed teams of Cobra gunships. At the same time, Hải employed the limited ARVN artillery and, along with Mễ, brought in VNAF A-1s and occasional A-37s, trying to knock down the antiaircraft threat around Charlie. They all waited anxiously for word from Skinny Hùng that he'd secured the LZ and had it ready for helos.

Besides the machine guns, other targets demanded attention, as well. In the early afternoon, 114 Company reported a hundred NVA soldiers moving in the open to their south. *Bold bastards,* John thought. He requested more air to punish them. The trio kept up the pressure throughout the day with as many airstrikes and artillery barrages as they could muster. They threw everything they could at every known and suspected enemy troop, antiaircraft, and artillery location. John Duffy also asked for another B-52 strike to obliterate the big 130mm guns still pounding Charlie from their protected positions miles to the southwest.

Captain Skinny Hùng had a hard fight in the saddle. He'd pushed two platoons onto the LZ through stiff resistance. A larger enemy force came out of the gully to meet him. The 112 Company struggled to hold, but slowly gave ground. A little after 2:00 p.m., the NVA moved around their flank, forcing Hùng to withdraw back inside Charlie 2. The LZ could not be retaken. Mễ grabbed a radio handset and put in two flights of Skyraiders on the saddle.

Major Lê Văn Mễ had one last idea for salvation. He summoned Lieutenant Thinh.

"Brother Thinh. I need you to take your 111 Company to the east. Those who can still fight. I know your numbers are small, but we have to do this. Find a good spot. Secure it. Establish a new LZ. We are running out of ammunition. We need water. We need food. We need medical supplies. We've got to get our wounded out."

Thinh displayed his normal paratrooper zeal. "Yes, sir. We'll get it done!"

Thinh was an outstanding junior leader in the battalion. Mễ recognized his potential. He was one of his favorites. That's why Mễ had argued so strongly with Bảo to have him assigned as company commander after Nguyễn Đức Dũng was killed in the Dambae operation in Cambodia. He didn't have the rank, but he was Mễ's choice. Company commanders were usually captains. Thinh was only a lieutenant. That didn't matter at all right now. Mễ felt good that he was leading 111 Company on this essential mission.

As Thinh turned to leave, Mễ added, "The NVA have been coming at us mostly from the north, the west, and the south. They're fixed on 113 Company to the north. We've pounded them on all sides. You should be good to the east. Fight through. There will be some place there that helicopters can land. Secure it so we can get choppers in."

Thinh gathered his company. They headed east at 2:45. Twenty minutes later, they were in contact.

Duffy put in more fighters and Cobra gunships around Charlie and in support of Thinh. Mễ and Hải worked VNAF and artillery. Enemy artillery continued its pounding. Charlie Hill trembled.

They'd underestimated the enemy strength to the east. Thinh found himself in serious trouble. A good-sized enemy force had him pinned down with heavy fire from small arms, machine guns, and recoilless rifles. A burst of rifle fire hit Thinh in the head, killing him instantly. Platoon leader Ba dashed to aid Thinh. A second burst killed him.

Thinh's shaken RTO called Mễ. "Zero Zero Seven, this is Four Zero One Alpha. Four Zero One is down, KIA. Mister Ba is down, KIA. Several soldiers KIA and others wounded. Over."

Shocked, Mễ asked, "Any officers left?"

The forward observer took the handset and transmitted. "I am. Lieutenant Nguyễn Văn Khánh, the FO."

Mễ issued his order. "You take command and bring the company back. I'll send reinforcements to assist."

Khánh assembled the company and moved the survivors toward Charlie 2, bringing their wounded and some of the dead with them. They left other bodies on the field, unable to reach them.

Meanwhile, Mễ directed Hải to organize a platoon from 114 Company and send them out to link up with 111 and assist.

Late in the afternoon, a .51-caliber scored a hit on an A-1. The pilot turned his crippled aircraft east in a wobbly, smoking descent. He flew about three miles before ejecting. The plane gyrated out of control and crashed. Mễ learned later that the pilot was rescued.

Covey radioed. "Dusty, if able, look to your southwest in ten minutes."

John Duffy did. He saw the distant muzzle flash of one of the 130 guns. *Son of a bitch.* An instant later, the ground erupted in a massive swath of explosions. *Goddamn. Got my B-52 strike!*

Hải worked the final set of A-1s for the day. He put them in on the gully. Skinny Hùng's experience on the saddle proved the NVA were still there in force. Hai wanted them gone. Number one rolled in with rockets. Intense antiaircraft fire greeted him. Vietnamese Air Force First Lieutenant Dương Huỳnh Kỳ followed next with napalm. He maneuvered his Skyraider low to most effectively skip his canisters onto the target. Multiple .51-caliber rounds tore into his airplane and smashed into the cockpit. The right wing clipped a tree, flipping the fighter onto its back and smashing it into the earth with a loud crash. Flames spewed, and black smoke billowed. No one saw a parachute. There just wasn't time.

Hải froze in horror. *We knew those guys. We drank with them in Pleiku. They come every day to save us. I salute you, brave pilot. I salute the life you gave, the death you died for us.*

At dusk, Hải saw the band of paratroopers returning from the east. He rushed to the far side of the trench line, waiting as the small group moved closer. He saw 114 Company soldiers mixed with the small band of 111 Company survivors. All appeared weary but in good order, carrying the wounded and dead. Mễ joined Hải. They looked for Lieutenant Khánh. They didn't see him. They didn't see any officers or sergeants from 111 Company. Mễ scanned the bodies. Looking down at one, he shuddered. It was Lieutenant Thinh. His beloved Lieutenant Thinh.

With emotion filling his voice, one of the paratroopers reported to Mễ. "Lots of NVA. We fought through and got to a good LZ site, then they hit us in force. Machine guns, mortars, and recoilless rifle. More than a hundred enemy. We fought hard but couldn't hold them. The NVA shot Lieutenant Thinh in the head. He's dead. They killed Mister Ba and Lieutenant Khánh and Sergeant Lung. Others are dead too. Many wounded."

The 111 Company was gone, destroyed in battle. Between yesterday's fight on Hill 960 and the excursion to secure a new LZ, the enemy had killed all the officers and sergeants and whittled the unit down to a handful of effective fighters.

Mễ placed those few still walking into the perimeter sector manned by Headquarters Company. Soldiers stacked the dead on the growing rows of corpses and carried the severely wounded to the medical aid station, where Doc Liệu tended them as best he could. Most medical supplies had run out. The badly wounded lay there, helpless and frustrated, dealing with the agony of their pain and the guilt of not being of further worth in battle.

Hải and Mễ found Duffy, still working airstrikes.

Mễ told him, "There be no new LZ. NVA hit 111 Company hard. Many casualty. Trung uý Thinh dead.† All officer and sergeant dead."

The news shocked Duffy, but he remained resolute.

"Okay, then we fight with what we've got. I'm going to rain airstrikes down on the bastards. Hải, will you do the same with the VNAF and arty?"

"Yes, Duffy."

"Good. Let's get to it. We've got some fighting to do."

Mễ reached through a cloud of despair and found yet more strength deep within. His paratroopers would fight. He would lead them. And Duffy would bring down hell from the heavens to make their enemies pay dearly for every move they tried to make on Charlie.

---

†*Trung uý* means "Lieutenant."

CHAPTER 14

Friday

April 14, 1972

Fighting continued through the night. From time to time, friendly artillery flares drifted across the dark sky, swaying beneath tiny parachutes, lighting sections of the battlefield beneath them. Shapes moved on the ground. Paratroopers took care. They fired only when they had sure targets well within range. Each man sighted carefully, breathed out, and pulled the trigger with an oh-so-steady squeeze. Ammunition had become frighteningly scarce. The North Vietnamese fired with much more abandon. They had ammo. They were being resupplied. The paratroopers were not.

Incoming artillery hit the camp at intervals through the night. Enemy patrols probed the perimeter defenses. Each was repulsed. One group of NVA soldiers slipped into the 11th Battalion's trench line. An aggressive paratrooper counterattack quickly eliminated them.

No one slept except the seriously wounded and dying. The 11th Airborne Battalion waited for the new day with dread anticipation, ready to fight on. The shelling fell silent toward dawn. The approaching day teased the paratroopers' psyche, creeping slowly, ever so slowly, from the east. A dull gray tinge stood stubbornly for what seemed forever, before finally yielding to the brilliance of the rising sun.

The new day began quietly enough. The artillery had stopped, and an eerie stillness settled over the land. The battlefield smoldered and smoked. The smell of explosives and burning wood filled the air. Dirty, bloodshot eyes peered through the silence, watching for the attacks that would surely come. The paratroopers on Charlie sensed this would be the day when one side would destroy the other. They were prepared, as their orders commanded, to fight to the death.

A heavy barrage of enemy shelling shattered the morning calm. Artillery, mortars, rockets, and recoilless rifles. The rain of explosions didn't stop. The battle for Charlie raged into its twelfth day.

Major Lê Văn Mễ stood stoically, the commander, the rock from which the paratroopers on Charlie drew their strength and their will to fight on. Putting his own miserable condition aside, he moved confidently through the defensive positions, exposing himself to enemy fire, and being a visible sign of courage and hope to all. He issued orders and directed artillery and VNAF airstrikes along with his deputy, Captain Đoàn Phương Hải.

Major John Joseph Duffy was busy, as well. Just as he'd done every day, he mustered all the air support he could get from any Covey forward air controller passing overhead. John heard a familiar voice as Rod Lennard, Covey 537, put in two flights of F-4s for him first thing that morning. As they had for days, the aircraft took heavy antiaircraft machine gun fire. That caused the pilots to release their bombs higher and jerk their aircraft violently to avoid being hit. The antiaircraft affected the slower VNAF airplanes even more. Not good. John tried to bring the strikes extremely close to friendly positions. That's where the enemy was, right there, readying their attack to wipe the airborne off the hill. The intense antiaircraft fire hampered close-in accurate bombing.

John shifted his focus back to those machine guns. He had to knock out as many as possible so that he could put precision airstrikes right in front of his brothers, bled badly in NVA attack after attack.

As he'd done so many times during the battle, John Duffy got up out of the trenches and braved exploding artillery to get a view of the enemy gun positions. He moved to the edge of the perimeter, radio on his back with its recognizable antenna high over his head. Enemy fire hit close by. He moved. More fire. He moved again. A North Vietnamese recoilless rifle shell exploded in the ground beside him. Fragments ripped into his left arm. He put pressure on the wound to slow the bleeding and then grabbed his radio handset as a flight of U.S. Army AH-1 Cobra attack helicopters checked in.

"Dusty Cyanide, this is Cougar Three Eight."

"Cougar Three Eight. Glad to have you on station. I've got enemy troop movement along the finger to the south, southeast of Charlie. Give me some runs there. A lot of fifty-one-cal fire in the area. If you see any, please engage."

The team of three Cobra gunships made several passes on the finger, expending all their ordnance. They headed to Kontum for more fuel and ammunition. Duffy watched them go. *What an awesome killing machine*, he thought. Cobras carried fifty-two rockets on their stubby wings with four thousand rounds of machine gun and three hundred rounds of grenades in their moveable nose turrets. A few mounted a deadly 20mm Vulcan Gatling gun with 950 high-explosive rounds.

The Cougar flight called as they departed, "We'll be back, Dusty."

Another Covey, 534, came on station and worked more strikes against the several machine guns John identified. Trouble was, when the fast jets dropped their big bombs close to the gun positions, they only quieted them for a time. Once the jets departed, the guns were soon back in operation. Only a direct hit really did the job. John concluded that Cobra helicopters were the best in putting ordnance right into the gun pits and silencing the weapons for good.

When Covey detected the flash of heavy artillery firing from several miles to the west, John encouraged him to put his next strikes there. The pounding artillery was taking its toll on lives and morale. No one knew where the next shell would hit.

Covey 537 returned to the battle to take over the close-in strikes, placing them mostly to the southwest. In the meantime, Hải and Mễ worked flights of VNAF A-1s against NVA formations moving on the finger and on the machine guns they saw firing. Hải continued to have his forward observers employ ARVN field artillery between airstrikes.

The 2nd Airborne Brigade hatched a plan for emergency resupply. A Huey approached Charlie from altitude. It flew high to minimize the risk from the antiaircraft machine guns. The paratroopers fixed their hopeful eyes on the drama above. Once over Charlie, streams of tracers stretched toward the chopper. The crew kicked out well-packed bundles of food, ammunition, and medical supplies. They missed the mark, landing outside the perimeter. The enemy got to them in a flash.

In extreme frustration, Mễ moved to a recoilless rifle and punished the thieves with several rounds. He glanced to his right and saw Doc Liệu on one knee, shooting a .45-caliber pistol in the same direction.

"What are you doing, Doc?"

Liệu turned his head toward Mễ, his iconic smile breaking the crust of grime covering his face; his uniform, hands, and arms stained in dried and drying blood. "I'm a doctor, not a chaplain. I've got no medical supplies left. Those assholes are taking our stuff. Fuck them."

In the midst of it all, a chicken ran through the melee, one of many that had been sent to supplement the food ration. The fighting on Charlie never gave the starving soldiers a chance to butcher and eat any of them.

Doc Liệu emptied all the rounds in the pistol and returned to tending patients.

Early afternoon another flight of Cobras checked in. Chief Warrant Officer Dan Jones flew lead. I piloted the second Cobra, flying on his wing.*

"Firebase Charlie, this is Panther One Three."

"Panther Lead, this is Dusty Cyanide. I have multiple targets for you. All fifty-one-caliber machine guns."

The crews knew the risk. Fifty-one-caliber machine guns seemed designed specifically to shoot down helicopters. They'd done plenty of damage over the past weeks.

Panther 13 calmly acknowledged, "Roger, Dusty Cyanide. We're inbound. Give us the positions when we get there."

The Cobras made several attacks on the enemy guns. Bullets streamed past their cockpits as the NVA gunners tried to bring them down. Attack helicopter pilots knew that rolling in on a .51 position was always dicey. Tracers came at them and missed by a few feet. Pilots tried to get rockets onto the machine guns before the enemy got lucky and blasted them out of the sky. The pilots held steady, focusing on controlling their helicopters, lining up the gun sights and shooting. The Panther 13 fire team took small-arms hits, but kept running at their targets again and again and again.

---

*Chief Warrant Officer, CW2, Dan Jones, flew the lead Cobra, call sign "Panther 13." I was "Panther 36." I flew his wing. I commanded the 3rd Platoon in the 361st Aerial Weapons Company out of Camp Holloway in Pleiku. Our call sign was "Pink Panther." Dan, the most seasoned pilot in my platoon, was within a couple of weeks of going home. He led the flight. We'd heard an urgent call for support at Firebase Charlie. Dan pointed our flight toward Rocket Ridge, and we coaxed as much speed as our Cobras would give.

John Duffy observed the shootout, taking it all in, commenting to himself. *They're coming out of the sun, going for the high gun first. That's good. Shit! Green and red tracers crossing in front of them. They're taking fire from everywhere. There, they punched off a salvo of rockets. Right on target. The gunners were surely blown up in that explosion. Wingman rolling in on the second gun. They're keeping at it. It's a dance of death. I love those guys. Badass Cobra pilots, so steady under such heavy fire. God, I'm glad I'm on the ground.*

The Panther lead radioed, "Dusty Cyanide, Panther One Three. Be advised, running low on fuel. Out of ammo. We're breaking station for rearm-refuel."

"Roger, One-Three. Four gun crews destroyed, four guns taken out. Good work. Hurry back!"

The pounding NVA artillery intensified later in the afternoon. John did a rough count and estimated three hundred rounds hit in a huge barrage around 3:00 p.m. That, in addition to incoming recoilless rifle fire and 82mm mortars. More artillery barrages hit a short time later—at least an additional four hundred rounds. The enemy was preparing for a major assault, there was no doubt.

Mễ needed all the battalion consolidated in one place. That was his only hope of holding Charlie. He called Big Hùng. "Four Zero Three. This is Zero Zero Seven. Withdraw from Charlie Three. Move to Charlie Two. Execute, now. I repeat, move to Charlie Two, now. Right now."

"Roger, Mê Linh. We will try."

Duffy moved around the hilltop working fast, directing jet fighters and the lethal Cobra attack helicopters. Always, the long antenna of his backpack radio swayed high above his head. Every time the enemy spotted it, they shot at him. He ran across the hilltop like a bounding hare, tempting death, but somehow staying half a step ahead of its grasp. The paratroopers looked in awe.

Hải shouted again and again, "Duffy, get down! You get killed, we in worse trouble. We all die."

Others joined in, "Duffy, *củi xuống!* Duffy, get down!"

John didn't hear. He was focused on his mission. *Get airstrikes on targets, kill the machine guns. Wreak death and destruction on the enemy. They're so close in front of the paratroopers. They're too fucking close.*

He ran to Mế. "Recommend you have artillery ready. The instant these jets pull off, you could put it on top of those .51-caliber machine gun positions that are firing. Use VT† fuse. Get them with airbursts while they are still standing at their guns."

The friendly artillery came quickly after the airstrike. The explosions just above the ground gave hope. That hope soon waned, dashed when the next aircraft arrived. Enemy tracers erupted once more after new crews emerged from the protective hollows they'd dug underground. They'd dragged the dead gunners away and taken their places.

Airstrikes continued. Other teams of Cobras worked. VNAF A-1 Skyraiders and U.S. jet fighters dropped more napalm and high-explosive bombs on the advancing enemy, as well. Even so, the NVA attack intensified, pressuring the South Vietnamese defenders. The enemy overran security outposts. They pushed into the perimeter of Charlie 2 itself.

Human waves of NVA came forward, shouting. "Surrender, you'll live. Fight back, you'll die!" But the paratroopers fought vigorously, picking the closest targets, aiming, shooting.

"Hold the trenches!"

"Don't fall back!"

"Fire! Shoot the guys over there."[1]

Chaos ruled the front. It became an inferno of smoke, dust, flame, and noise. The world convulsed in a crescendo of cracking gunfire, the deafening explosions of artillery, the whine of attacking aircraft, the thunderous boom of their bombs, and the sucking roar of the napalm they dropped. Paratroopers fought with all they had. They fought with grit and determination. They fought for their buddies and the pride of the 11th Airborne. They fought inspired by those Vietnamese paratroopers who had gone before, those who had sacrificed so much in historic battles of old. They fought until their bullets were gone. After that, they turned to grenades and knives. Many died swinging their empty rifles as clubs.[2]

The brave paratroopers withstood the onslaught with fierce determination. Still, their enemy pushed, taking patches of earth inch by inch, paying dearly for every small gain. Finally, the NVA overran Charlie's southwest

---

†VT, or variable time fuse, can be used to cause artillery rounds to explode several feet in the air, showering an exposed enemy with deadly shell fragments.

perimeter. They occupied much of the 114 Company's defensive positions and paused to catch their breath among the mingled dead of both sides.

Duffy got on the radio to Major Peter Kama at 2nd Brigade. "Cellar Five One, Cellar Five One. This is Dusty Cyanide. Prairie Fire, Prairie Fire, Prairie Fire. I am declaring a Prairie Fire emergency. We are being overrun."

John defaulted to a phrase familiar to him from his earlier Special Forces work behind enemy lines in Laos. "Prairie Fire" meant a Special Operations team was about to be overrun and all available assets were brought to bear. Peter Kama knew what John needed and translated the statement into words more commonly understood by conventional military forces. He declared a tactical emergency, or TAC-E, across all of II Corps. This required every available asset to be redirected to support the paratroopers on Firebase Charlie. John Duffy would now get everything flying in the skies over central South Vietnam. John, Mễ, and Hải got busier than they had ever been, working flight after flight of supporting aircraft.

Meanwhile, another team of Pink Panther gunships launched from Camp Holloway in response to the TAC-E. They'd been briefed on the deteriorating situation at Charlie. They knew the antiaircraft threat. Still, they spurred their helicopters toward Charlie to provide whatever support they could. The platoon leader, Captain Bob Gamber, led the flight. Captain John Mayes, the company operations officer, sat in his front seat as co-pilot/gunner. Lieutenant Ron Lewis flew as Bob's wingman, with Lieutenant Dave Messa in his front seat.

"Firebase Charlie, Panther Two Six, inbound with a flight of two. What can we do for you?"

"Panther, this is Dusty Cyanide. Our southwest perimeter is overrun. More NVA on the ridge to our west. Hit both areas. Hit them hard."

"Roger, Dusty. We're about five minutes out."

"Roger. Be advised we've got triple-A all around. I'll call those machine gun positions to you. Hit them too."

As he'd been doing all day, John Duffy moved about the hilltop, evaluating the situation, employing the Cobras on the most threatening enemy targets, adjusting their gun runs, and locating the zombielike antiaircraft machine guns that kept coming back to life. He'd directed strikes against the guns for days. They'd be hit, sometimes direct hits, obviously killed. Yet within minutes they spewed fire on attacking aircraft once more. *Absolutely unbelievable!* Duffy thought.

On their first run, the Panther 26 Cobras pounded the enemy on the southwest edge of Charlie. They came back around, this time lining up on the ridge. Bob Gamber unleashed the rest of his rockets. John Mayes sprayed mini-gun and thumped 40mm grenades onto the enemy soldiers who appeared to be maneuvering for yet another assault. Ron Lewis, just behind, adjusted his run to the source of a stream of .51-cal machine gun tracers coming from the west side of the ridge. Dave Messa bent over the tripod site in Ron's front seat, intently employing his turret weapons.

Wham! The helicopter lurched. A .51-caliber round tore through the nose, barely missed Dave's right shoulder, penetrated the back of his armor plated seat, and ripped through the rear cockpit. If Dave hadn't been leaning forward over the turret site, the round would have hit him in the face, killing him instantly.

Ron called on intercom, "I'm hit, I'm hit! You've got the aircraft."

Dave took the controls and turned the helicopter to the east.

"Two Six, Two Four. We've been hit. Back seat took a round. Headed to Vo Dinh. Need medevac."

"Roger, Two Four. Will follow you. Calling medevac."

The two Cobras landed at the 2nd Airborne Brigade's sandbagged operations bunker at Võ Định. Bob Gamber turned off the fuel, shutting his aircraft down. He scrambled from the cockpit with the rotor blades still turning, moved to Ron's helicopter, and pulled him from the back seat. Bob laid him down and tended to his wound. Bullet fragments had torn into his right leg. He'd lost some blood.

A UH-1 medical evacuation helicopter arrived. The crew put Ron on a stretcher. They offered Dave a ride.

"No thanks. I'll stay with my bird until we get it recovered."

The Huey lifted off and headed for the 67th Evac Hospital in Pleiku. Bob and John looked at Dave as they got back into their Cobra.

"You okay, here? We've got to get back to Holloway. It'll be dark soon."

"Sure, I'm fine."

Dave ended up spending the night, until he and his aircraft were recovered the next day. He got to eat Vietnamese Army rations and sleep in a bunker at Võ Định. A strange experience for an American aviator, but nothing compared to what the paratroopers endured atop Firebase Charlie.

On Charlie, the situation worsened as soon as Panther 26 flight departed. Late in the afternoon, the NVA pushed a fresh battalion into the battle in yet another human wave attack. The enemy came once more from the southwest and also advanced from the western ridge, climbing through the gully in large numbers, charging right into the flank of the defenders. Charlie began to crumble.

Hải continued to work VNAF A-1s. One of the strikes slowed the enemy for a time. Three Jupiter Squadron Skyraiders arrived ready for battle. Captain Bạch Diễn Sơn led the flight, his aircraft armed with rockets. Lieutenant Nguyễn Đình Xanh flew his wing, carrying four napalm bombs. Captain Vũ Văn Thanh was number three, with more rockets.

Captain Sơn rolled in, firing onto the ridge. Lieutenant Xanh slammed his stick hard to the side and hurtled toward the ground just behind him. Thanh followed, covering Xanh's flanks with rockets. Xanh shallowed his dive as he got close to the ground. He needed a level, low pass to get the best effect from his napalm. He let two canisters go and pulled up sharply, pushing the throttle to full power and heading for the sky.

Hải watched the gasoline mixture of the napalm bombs ignite in two huge fireballs, incinerating everything they touched. "Jupiter three one, good effect. Do it again. Same thing, but two hundred meters southeast of those bombs. Southwest corner of the hilltop. NVA battalion moving in the open."

The three Skyraiders maneuvered for another attack. The flight rolled in. Sơn again fired rockets to suppress the enemy. Xanh dove behind him, leveled his plane only a couple hundred feet above the ground, and dropped his last two napalm canisters right on target.

Xanh barely caught a glimpse of the tracers. He felt the bullets, though. He felt the .51-caliber rounds slamming into his right wing like a jackhammer. He looked out and saw smoke and hydraulic fluid spraying from ruptured lines. He turned east.

"Jupiter three one, this is three two, I'm hit. Right wing. Heading to Kontum."

Xanh climbed with difficulty, the controls stiff. He pointed the crippled Skyraider toward the airfield at Kontum City. Sơn and Thanh followed, one on each side. Two U.S. Army Huey helicopters headed toward them. He had an escort.

Thank God, Xanh thought as he saw the airfield in the distance. *I've made it.*

Everything changed in an instant. Smoke billowed from his wing. Flames erupted, racing toward the cockpit. They engulfed the engine. He lost control. *No time. No time.* Xanh reached between his legs and grabbed the handle on the Yankee ejection system. The extraction rocket fired, pulling him up by his shoulders, taking him well above the disintegrating airplane before his parachute opened. One of the American helicopters landed, the crew waiting for him before his feet hit the ground. Nguyễn Đình Xanh had skirted death one more time.[3]

—◆—

The enemy delayed only a short while before getting back up and continuing their assault. They were about to overrun the 11th Battalion.

"Dusty Cyanide, this is Cougar Three Eight. Inbound."

"Welcome back, Three Eight. Enemy advancing rapidly from the west and southwest. Battalion strength. Heaviest from southwest. Expend on that formation."

"Roger, Dusty. Will give 'em hell."

Cougar 38's heavy fire team of three Cobras came in from the northeast. They drew intense enemy antiaircraft fire, dropping to just above the trees to minimize their exposure. They flew past Duffy and Mễ, then continued right into the face of the attack.

Duffy commented, "What guts those guys have. Never seen anything like it. Right on the deck. Those crazy bastards are gonna kill themselves to save us. Goddamn heroes."

Each aircraft fired its entire ammunition load on one pass, pilots launching pairs of rockets as fast as their fingers could press the firing button, front-seat gunners working their turret weapons incessantly, raining death and destruction. They annihilated the breadth of the attacking formation. The enemy staggered. He stumbled. He fell. He pulled back, needing to regroup once again. The courage of those three Cobra crews stalled the NVA attack—for now. There was no doubt the resolute enemy would come again.

Mễ needed his other company. He'd ordered them to consolidate hours ago. Where were they?

He called 113 Company again. "Four Zero Three. What's your progress?"

Big Hùng responded, "We're trying. Lots of enemy around us."

Mễ sternly ordered, "Break through and get down here. Do it now. We need the battalion together."

"Roger."

Mễ frowned in frustration.

Hải used the temporary lull to move about and assess the situation. He ran quickly among the defenders, by then compressed into a much smaller circle. They had something over a hundred effective fighters left of the 471-man battalion. Hải moved from position to position, utilizing trenches as much as possible, but at times dashing into the open, from foxhole to foxhole. He spent a few minutes talking to each leader and spoke with paratroopers along the way, bolstering their will to fight by whatever means remained.

Hải finished his circuit and rejoined Mễ in the command post trench. Dusk settled in. Mễ called Duffy, who joined them there. Blood seeped from a gash in John's right shoulder. He'd been hit yet again by another shell fragment. Hải shook his head and began his report.

"We in bad shape. Many dead. More wounded. I count only little over one hundred still can fight. Most them hurt. Not much ammunition. Some have no ammo, even after take from dead. No way to stop next attack. Next attack end Eleventh Battalion."

Mễ looked straight into Hải's eyes for a time, studying him, digesting what he'd just said. He turned to Duffy, ready to speak, but paused. Both minds churned through options.

Hải spoke again. "Casualty high. Ammo run thin. Cannot stop VC. Most of battalion dead. We stay longer, all die. Should leave."

He leaned close to Mễ and spoke in Vietnamese. "Got to get the battalion off this fucking hill before the enemy comes at us again."

Mễ nodded and responded in English, "Yes. We order withdraw."

Duffy had a plan. He'd risk his life to try to save what was left of the battalion. It seemed insane, but it made perfect sense to him. "I will stay and try to delay the NVA. Maybe we'll get some more air in time to make a difference."

Mễ insisted, "I stay with you. We team. American and Vietnamese. We fight together."

John nodded, full of determined grit. John Duffy and Lê Văn Mễ would form a two-man rear guard to allow what was left of the battalion to break contact and escape. Two men against two enemy battalions. Mễ faced his operations officer with a look of resignation. "You lead the battalion off of Charlie, Hải. Major Duffy and I will delay as long as we can. We're your rear guard. Go about eight hundred meters northeast and wait for One One Three Company. I'll tell Big Hùng to move east until he finds you. One One Three is in good shape. They have ammo and only a few casualties. You'll be okay."

Hải saluted, responding smartly, "Yes, sir. We go." He rallied the surviving paratroopers. Those who could walk helped others who couldn't. Hai led the way off the hilltop toward the sanctuary of the jungle below.

Mễ made another call to Big Hùng, this time with new instructions.

"Four Zero Three. Change of mission. Do not come to Charlie Two. Instead, move one kilometer east, one thousand meters east, and we will link up there. We are abandoning Charlie now. We will meet you one thousand meters due east of Charlie Three."

"Roger, Mê Linh. Understand."

As dusk turned to darkness, a strange silence brought a chill. It was as if Mễ and Duffy were in the eye of a storm. The enemy had fallen back, for the moment. The artillery and mortars fell still. Their battalion had gone. There was no chatter on the radio. Not a sound on the hilltop, save the whimpers of the dying.

They sat alone on the edge of what had been Firebase Charlie, waiting warily for their enemy's next move, not doubting for a moment he would attack. It was dark. Suddenly the silence broke. Whistling projectiles hurled through the air. Incoming enemy artillery erupted across the hilltop. One shell burst not far to their front.

The explosion rocked them, the blast deafening in the night. For an instant, it lit their dirty, blood-smeared faces, their hollow eyes set in hopeless determination. A few more shells crashed around them, none as close as the first. Each blinding flash shone upon the corpses lying across the battlefield, gruesome evidence of the fight that had raged over the past days.

Hundreds lay dead over the hilltop outpost—the bodies of South Vietnamese paratroopers mixed with those of their determined North Vietnamese enemy. The hellacious battle had allowed the paratroopers to recover only some of their fallen comrades. They'd wrapped a number in plastic ponchos and placed them in trenches. That was a while ago, earlier in the fight, when there'd been time to render a modicum of respect. Later, they'd stacked other bodies in rows, as they were able. Most of the dead, though, were strewn where they'd been cut down in the last hours of combat—punctured, torn, dismembered, and shredded; grotesque reflections of their final, violent seconds of life.

The explosions stopped. The dark returned. Only the moans of the wounded pierced the silence of the night. The stench of death filled the nostrils of the last two men fighting. Smoke choked their lungs. They waited in anticipation. They heard orders shouted from across the field. They sensed movement as another attack wave swept toward them.

The American advisor leaned close to his Vietnamese counterpart and exclaimed, "Shit. Here they come again."

The reply, in broken but well-practiced English, was resolute. "I know. We fight. We fight more."

The enemy once again rose from the darkness, tearing through the night, coming at them as vague shapes, screaming and shooting, throwing grenades as they advanced closer, and closer still. Both John Duffy and Lê Văn Mě knew this was the final assault. Bullets whizzed by them. A grenade exploded, ripping a hole in Mě's chest. He gasped for air.

Duffy, already wounded several times himself, looked over his left shoulder. He nodded, satisfied, seeing the decimated force, all that was left of the once mighty 11th Airborne Battalion, escaping down the hillside.

John and Mễ were all that stood between the remnants of the battalion and their annihilation.

They'd been out of food for days. They had no water left in their canteens. Their ammunition was nearly gone. But still the American and his South Vietnamese comrade fought, and still the enemy came. There was no talk of surrender. No thought but to kill as many as they could before they were, themselves, cut down where they squatted on the edge of their abandoned positions.

Lê Văn Mễ strained to speak. "Fight, Duffy. Fight."

They battled with everything that remained in their hearts and souls, but the end of their road was only minutes away. They knew they were about to die.

John Duffy sensed his mortality as words welled in his soul.

Death's moment is near,
I can feel its flame.
Soon it will be here,
It seems strange no more.[4]

Duffy's radio crackled. "Dusty Cyanide, this is Panther One Three. Back with you."

Duffy looked at Mễ. "Hot damn!"

He grabbed his radio handset, "Roger, Panther. Welcome back."

"Dusty, we're inbound with rockets, forty mike-mike and mini-gun. Thought you might need a little more help."

Through the blackness, the Cobra crews saw fires and chaos on Charlie. They could only imagine the desperate situation on the ground. Their world remained so different from his. As they approached, all stayed quiet in the cocoon of their cockpits, save the reassuring sound of rotors churning the night air and the steady whine of the Lycoming turbine engine driving the blades. They only heard the chilling noise of battle in the background, when Duffy keyed his mic to talk.

Hải led the survivors farther off the hilltop. How much quieter the sounds became as he gained distance from the din of the battle raging behind them. He knew the sacrifice that was being made. He doubted he'd ever see Mễ and Duffy again.

Duffy radioed the Cobras. "Enemy broken through on the southwest. Charlie overrun. There are three prominent fires on the hilltop, one big and two small. The large one is on the southwest part of the base. You see one small fire a short distance north and another a hundred meters east of that. We are right on the north edge of that eastern small fire. Need you to shoot right in front of us, just to our west—but real close."

"Roger, Dusty. We've got 'em."

The Cobras rolled in firing.

Duffy adjusted their runs closer. The attacking enemy was about on top of him. He cut down several with his CAR-15. Mễ did the same with his M-16, but that didn't slow them a bit. The enemy, still charging, was just feet away as the Pink Panthers began another gun run. The head of the closest soldier exploded, hit by a 40mm grenade from one of the Cobras. His reflexes kept his legs moving for a step or two before he crumbled to the ground so close that blood and tissue splattered on Duffy and Mễ.

"Right there, Panther. Keep it up."

The Cobras kept it up. Duffy delighted in the hot shell casings raining down from above. After a number of attack runs, Duffy called, "Panther Lead, this is Dusty Cyanide. You have broken the enemy attack, for now. Hundreds of bodies on the field—maybe a thousand. But we cannot hold."

After a short break, he continued, "We are leaving Firebase Charlie, now. Stop them from following us. Whatever it takes. Put your stuff all over the hilltop, *now*."

The two ran for their lives, Mễ first, followed by Duffy. U.S. Army Special Forces Major John Joseph Duffy was the last to leave Firebase Charlie.

Another Cobra flight joined the team with Lieutenant Forrest Snyder in one of the front seats. That gave Panther 13 a heavy team of four aircraft. Forrest was the best gunner the Panthers had. The team fired everything they had at the hill that had been Firebase Charlie. They turned toward home. The flight picked its way through mountains and valleys below a worsening layer of scud clouds in the pitch black of night. What was left of the 11th Airborne Battalion moved toward the refuge of the valley below.

John and Mễ stumbled and fell through the darkness, moving swiftly in spite of their painful injuries. Once the North Vietnamese had taken the hill, the enemy advance halted, for the moment—the attackers too devastated to continue. The Cobras had saved the day.

The NVA scoured the hilltop, looking for the American advisor. They wanted to capture him, knowing he was the link to deadly U.S. air support. They didn't find him. But on the edge of the hill, they found a helmet with a major's leaf and the name *Lê Văn Mễ* scrawled on the inside headband.

Amazingly, Duffy and Mễ were still alive. They moved as quickly as their torn bodies allowed. After a couple hundred yards, they stopped and looked at each other, overwhelmed with a sudden rush of emotion, laughing in disbelief at their good fortune. Only then did they pause to assess their condition, Mễ with a hole in his chest and Duffy dealing with several wounds from the past days, his left arm still bleeding, his head buzzing from earlier concussions. Mễ felt for his helmet. It was gone, lost somewhere on Charlie. They chuckled again, Mễ's laugh cut short by a searing pain. He winced.

They started out again, Duffy making an urgent call on the move. "Any Covey, any Covey. This is Dusty Cyanide. We are withdrawing off Charlie. Two NVA battalions, in the open, on the hilltop. Request immediate diversion of a B-52 Arc Light strike to Charlie."

"This is Covey Five Three One. Stand by, Dusty."

Only a few minutes later, Covey transmitted, "Dusty, affirmative, 'Carbon Outlaw'[†] diverted Arc Light for your target. ETA, twenty minutes. You need five hundred meters distance. Be in defilade. Open your mouths and keep your heads down."

Duffy knew he was only a couple hundred yards off the hilltop. But he needed his enemy bloodied so they couldn't regroup and pursue.

"Roger, Covey. We will be over five hundred meters clear. Let the bombs fall."

They moved quickly, soon rejoining their battalion. Hải and Doc Liệu were shocked they were alive. They never expected to see either of them

---

[†]"Carbon Outlaw," the Air Force Direct Air Support Center (DASC), was collocated with the ARVN II Corps Headquarters in Pleiku, in communication with both the American senior advisor, John Paul Vann, and the 7th Air Force command post, "Blue Chip," at Tan Son Nhut Airbase in Saigon where a Strategic Air Command liaison officer sat. The system facilitated the diversion of in-flight B-52s. At this point in the war, Vann had broad authority for diverting Arc Light strikes as did his deputy, U.S. Army Brigadier General George Wear.

again. Tired, exhausted, and dragging their wounded, the battalion gained little ground, moving maybe another hundred yards before they heard the whistling bombs of death. Hundreds of 500- and 750-pound bombs demolished the NVA forces on Charlie.

The paratroopers hugged the earth. Duffy and Mễ lay prone under a tree that shook like a wet dog, showering them with leaves as the ground shuddered violently beneath them. Pieces of debris crashed close by. Floating residue of the earth-churning explosions drifted down around them. Close. Very close, but very necessary. The possibility of death, when weighed against its certainty, left them only one choice, and they'd taken it.

A dark cloud of smoke rose from the carnage of Charlie. John lamented, *Nothing could have survived. Two weeks of battle end in an NVA funeral pyre. Corpses sit as the victors atop their prize.*

Doc Liệu tended Mễ's chest wound. Mễ began spitting up blood. He turned toward Duffy, agony in his voice. "You commander now, Duffy. Must take command of battalion. You lead fight. Save paratroopers."

John, strong and confident in spite of his wounds and fatigue, reassured Mễ. "I'll get us out of here. You'll be okay. We'll be back in Saigon in a few days, drinking VSOP cognac at the Dragon Bar. The NVA are dead. They can't follow us."

With that, the big American led the South Vietnamese 11th Airborne Battalion into the black jungle, and down the mountain off Rocket Ridge.

CHAPTER 15

Saturday

April 15, 1972

In darkness, the paratroopers followed Major Duffy down the mountain-side. They carried those who couldn't walk. They struggled through the tangled jungle. Exhaustion numbed their senses. Even so, they still felt the pain that racked their bodies. Infected wounds screamed with every step. In spite of their misery, hope swelled in their hearts as they left the carnage of Charlie Hill ever farther behind.

The weary band heard the drone of a big AC-130 gunship lumber over-head. Its Gatling guns ripped into the already-devastated hilltop. Soldiers turned to each other, smiling, knowing the added pounding, on top of the B-52 strike, sealed the enemy's fate. There would be no pursuit. Images of food, drink, baths, and family began to dance in their heads. They were on their way home.

Boom! Boom! Boom!

"I-n-c-o-m-i-n-g!"

Everyone dropped to the ground. Rounds exploded on top of them. They'd come from the east. Friendly artillery. Who the hell had called friendly artillery on top of them? The explosions knocked Duffy down. He got up. Several dead and wounded lay just behind him. He called on the radio strapped to his back. "Cellar, Cellar, this is Dusty Cyanide. Check fire. Check fire. Immediately. Artillery is hitting us. Suspect friendly fire. Cease fire."

The shelling stopped. Duffy fumed with anger.

"Cellar, this is Dusty Cyanide. Who called that fire mission? Who authorized it?"

"Dusty, this is Cellar. No idea. Will check. Over."

Duffy barked into his handset, "No more. I have three killed and seven wounded. Tell them to clear all fire missions in this area with me."

"Roger, Dusty. Will do. Anything else?"

"Aside from blowing your brains out, no. Dusty Cyanide, out."

They left the dead and carried the newly injured as they continued their march toward freedom. They moved like zombies through the night.

The slope leveled and the jungle gave way to a field of tall grass and reeds just as dawn broke. Birds came alive with the morning sun. Their songs offered a reassuring melody. John halted their advance. They stood on the edge of a small valley. He made his way back to Mễ. Doc Liệu had bandaged Mễ's chest nicely. He walked unassisted. Pain still stung his every breath, but he felt better, his head clear.

"I take back command now, Duffy. Thank you for get us here."

"You're welcome, sir. The command is yours."

John told Mễ all that had happened through the night and gave his appraisal of the current situation. Mễ led the battalion forward to the location they'd picked to link up with 113. The company wasn't there.

The area sat beside a small stream. It made a good landing zone, big enough for several helicopters. Mễ set the paratroopers in a protective circle. Leaders rotated the men, allowing some to go to the stream, one small group at a time. They gulped water through parched lips and filled canteens. John washed his feet and checked his weapon and radio. He thought of food. *So hungry. God, it will be good to get out of here.*

Mễ got on the radio with 113 Company, checking their progress to the link-up point. There had been none. Duffy joined him just as he let go of the handset, frowning. "I talk Big Hùng. He say he on the move, but many enemy. I order him fight through. We wait see what happen."

Duffy uttered one word. "Damn."

Hải had been unable to communicate with Võ Định all night. Now he had the time to rig a long antenna to his radio. Success. He raised the 2nd Airborne Brigade command post.

"Red River, this is Zero Zero Six. We are off the mountain in a northeast direction from our old home. At the base of the ridge. I have about one hundred fifty. Many wounded. Request helicopter extraction. Over."

"Zero Zero Six, this is Red River. Negative. There are no helos available. Walk out. Over."

"This is Zero Zero Six. Roger, out."

Duffy saw Hải's disgust. "What's up?" he asked.

"No helicopter. We walk."

Mẽ was worried. The soldiers were tired and hungry, many injured. They only had a few rounds of ammunition among them. It would be tough, but after what they'd been through, they could gut out a five-mile march. First, though, he'd see if his advisor could help.

"Duffy, you can get U.S. helicopter for us?"

John nodded. "I'll try."

Before he could make the call, the enemy struck. *Ratta-tat-tat. Crack, crack. Boom! Boom!*

"Ambush!"

Machine gun and rifle fire snapped around them. Mortars exploded everywhere. Enemy soldiers attacked from the trees. Men dropped, wounded and dead. Many of the younger, green paratroopers, out of ammunition and at their wits' end, broke and ran, mowed down in their tracks. The NVA 320th Division commander had positioned a fresh force east of Charlie to cut off any withdrawal. The 2nd Battalion from the 48th Regiment was waiting in concealed positions. They hit the paratroopers hard.[1]

John Duffy raised his weapon and shouted, "Mê Linh. We need to break out of this. Gather all the men you can. I'll lead. You cover me and follow."

"Okay, Duffy. We no surrender. We fight to death."

John cocked his CAR-15, and firing a few well-placed rounds, led a desperate counterattack. Amazingly, they broke through the enemy and found refuge a couple of hundred yards north in trees along the stream.

Duffy puffed. "We made it. How many do we have?"

Mẽ counted. "Thirty-six. Plus you. Thirty-seven total. We have Captain Hải and Doc Liệu and others."

Mễ directed Hải, "Set a perimeter. Redistribute ammunition to be sure every soldier has at least some. This is where we'll make our stand."

Duffy's immediate thought was, *We need air. Need it now.*

He grabbed his handset to make the call. Nothing.

"Shit."

Mễ caught sight of his back. "Duffy, you take hit in radio. Big hole. It finished. You okay?"

Duffy—several times wounded, bloody, filthy, tired, head throbbing, body rife with pain—answered, "Yeah, I'm fine." He took the radio off his back and dropped it to the ground. He grabbed one of the two small aircrew survival radios he had clipped to his web gear, turned it on, and transmitted on the emergency frequency that all aircraft monitored.

"Any aircraft, any aircraft, this is Dusty Cyanide. Tactical emergency."

U.S. Air Force Captain Jim Higgins, a forward air controller on his way back to Pleiku from supporting a special operation near the Cambodian border, heard the call. His fuel was low, but he responded, "Dusty Cyanide, this is Covey Five Five Five."

"Covey, Dusty Cyanide. We withdrew off Charlie last night. I'm northeast, off the hill, in a small valley. Just ambushed. Many killed. We broke out. Need helicopter extraction. I have thirty-seven, three seven pax. Several wounded. Need four helos."

"Roger, Dusty. Stand by. I'll see what I can rustle up."

Mễ pulled John's right sleeve and pointed down the valley. A hundred yards away, scores of NVA moved toward them, advancing slowly through the brush and reeds, searching.

John spoke softly to Mễ. "They know we got away. They're looking for us. Some are coming up the streambed. They'll see us soon. Pass word to hold fire until they're on top of us. I'll get us some air support."

Duffy brought the small survival radio to his lips again. "Covey, this is Dusty Cyanide. Estimated enemy company moving toward us. Less than one hundred yards south and closing. Need air support. No fast movers. Too close. Request Cobras or Skyraiders."

"Roger. I've got a handle on a flight of U.S. Skyraiders. I'll get them here shortly. Look up. I should be somewhere overhead. If you see me, give me a shiny."

John pulled his signal mirror from his pocket and held it to reflect a beam of sunlight toward the small spotter plane.

"Dusty. I've got your shiny. Have your position."

"Roger, Covey. I am on the south edge of friendlies. Give me air one hundred meters south my position. Will adjust."

Duffy added, "There are other friendlies farther south, possibly mixed with enemy. Take care."

"Dusty, I've got eyes on confirmed NVA just south of you. That's what I'll hit."

Captain Higgins rolled in and fired a white phosphorous rocket.

"That's it, Covey. Your Willie Pete is spot-on."

Higgins put in a pair of American Skyraiders based in Nakhon Phanom, Thailand. He'd had them on his special operation mission, and they had enough fuel and ordnance to help out for a time before heading home. He followed their strike with a pair of VNAF Jupiter A-1s. The strafing, bombs, and napalm demolished the enemy.

"Dusty, got lots of bodies. No movement. Looks like we've stopped 'em cold. We took machine gun and B-40 rocket fire from the hills to your east. Hit them too. I've got another VNAF flight coming in just to be sure, and I'm working your helicopter lift package."

Major Mike Gibbs commanded B Troop, 7/17 Cavalry Squadron based at Camp Holloway. That morning, he piloted a UH-1 Huey helicopter, leading a squadron mission north of Kontum. He heard the radio chatter on the emergency "guard" frequency. It had gotten the attention of his entire crew.

Specialist Dallas Nihsen manned the left side M-60 machine gun. Nihsen earned the spot on the commander's bird by being the best helicopter crew chief in the troop. He was a great young man, enthusiastic and always eager on combat missions. Another soldier served as the door-gunner on the right side.[2]

Nihsen transmitted on intercom, "Sir, we need to go help those guys."

Gibbs keyed his mic and glanced to the right, catching the eye of his copilot, twenty-one-year-old, Warrant Officer One (WO1) Dennis Watson, as he transmitted.

"Covey Five Five Five, this is Embalmer Six. I've got Hueys and Cobra guns. Can we be of any help?"

"Embalmer Six, this is Covey Triple Nickel. Affirmative. I've got thirty-seven friendlies for extraction at the base of Rocket Ridge. They were over-run on Firebase Charlie last night. One U.S. and thirty-six ARVN. Likely a hot LZ."

"Roger. I've got four Hueys and two Cobra guns. Lift ships' call sign is 'Pallbearer.' Cobras are 'Undertaker.'"

"Thanks, Embalmer. I'm working a flight of A-1s. Will be ready when you get here. Break. Pallbearer Lead, this is Triple Nickel."

"Roger. We're headed off the red ball [Route 14] toward your location."

"Dusty Cyanide is on this push, and he's got thirty-seven people, most of them wounded. There's ground fire all around him. You're gonna have to work it for yourselves. I don't know if you're gonna want to go in there. We've been working the ridgelines around here. We've received B-40s and light-caliber fire."

"Roger. Listen, my Undertakers should be up this push, also. Maybe you could give them where the bad guys are."

Covey made contact with Undertaker 22, Chief Warrant Officer Richard Barron. Being low on fuel, Covey turned the mission over to Barron after giving him a detailed description of the situation and the friendly and enemy locations.

Barron called Duffy on the aviation emergency frequency. "Dusty Cyanide, this is Undertaker 22. Inbound to your location. Will need a shiny on arrival. I have four Hueys for extraction. Need you on the first bird out."

"Undertaker, Dusty. I've got my shiny ready. Negative on extraction. I will not be on the first bird out. I will be on the last. My seriously wounded coming out first."

Barron arrived overhead just as the last VNAF airstrike finished up. On pullout, one of the Skyraiders climbed smack in front of his Cobra, close enough that Richard saw the pilot in the cockpit, grinning. He confirmed Duffy's location and set up for the rescue.

"Dusty, Undertaker 22."

"Undertaker 22, this is Dusty, over."

"I got my slicks out here. They're setting up for single ships. When I get them around, pop smoke."

The Cobras fired on targets identified by Duffy. Barron's Cobra was one of the few that mounted a 20mm Vulcan cannon on one wing. It was devastating. He directed the Hueys in, one at a time, from north to south. As the lift helicopters landed, a Cobra flew on each side, firing to keep the enemy's heads down. Pallbearer lead came first. Duffy threw a smoke canister and took over final control.

"Got you in sight. About three hundred feet, three hundred feet. Down, down, down. Okay, my troops are moving out, troops moving out."

Once the Huey lifted off, Duffy's position came under fire, and they heard another enemy element approaching from the south. John directed a deadly Cobra strike as he and Mễ led the remaining survivors northward to get farther from their pursuers. Sniper rounds hit around them. In a few minutes, the next Huey came in; a couple of minutes later, the third. The routine was the same every time: smoke canister, directions to the ground, Cobras shooting, load up, and lift off. John and Mễ led the remaining paratroopers farther north up the small valley for the final pickup.

Embalmer 6 came in, the last of the four rescue helicopters. Gibbs descended on approach as the enemy closed in on the remaining paratroopers. The NVA shouted. Mễ translated, "Surrender, you live. Resist, you die. Major Lê Văn Mễ, you surrender."

Mễ shook his head in bewilderment. "They must find my helmet on Charlie and tell these guys. Or they capture paratrooper and find my name."

Duffy radioed, "Cobra, Cobra. They're twenty-five meters away. They're in that wood line. Go get 'em."

"Roger, Dusty. We're inbound. Keep your heads down."

The Cobras laid waste. Embalmer 6 called short final. The enemy opened up with small arms and machine gun fire. A B-40 streaked past. The Huey pulled up and turned sharply to the left, climbing. The right-side door gunner reported a jam in his machine gun. He was out of action. No more protective fire on the right side.

More enemy pressed in on Duffy and Mễ. They moved their group as fast as they could go. Undertaker 22 kept track of them.

"Dusty, you still on the LZ or moving away from it?"

"We're moving to the November."

"Roger, I'll be in with 20mm."

"Still got small arms. We've moved another hundred meters. We're gonna stop here. We got five people left. Over."

Embalmer 6 began another approach. Duffy popped his last smoke.

Gibbs transmitted, "I've got yellow smoke."

Duffy warned, "Still got small-arms fire. Still got small-arms fire. Automatic rifles."

Undertaker added, "Still drawing small arms fire from the tree line down there. Across the trees at your twelve are the friendlies and bad guys are in the trees."

Embalmer 6 continued his approach. Duffy guided him down to the ground. The last five members of the 11th Airborne Battalion scrambled aboard.

"Go! Go!" Duffy shouted.

He stood on the landing strut, firing his CAR-15 and helping the others in. An NVA soldier ran toward the helicopter, his arm cocked, ready to throw a grenade. Duffy cut him down. Lieutenant Long climbed in followed by Corporal Long, Captain Hải, and Major Mẽ.

Crack! A round blasted through the cockpit. *Crack!* Another passed just behind Dennis Watson's head. It hit Dallas Nihsen in the back as he fired his door gun, protecting the crew. He pushed his intercom button. "Hey, hit." Watson looked back. Their eyes held for a moment, then Nihsen's closed.

With everyone on board, Duffy gave the other door gunner a thumbs-up, and the young man hollered on intercom, "Go! Go! Go! Go! Get outta here!"

Bullets riddled the chopper as it lifted. At a hundred feet, one smashed into Hải's right foot. He fell backward out of the helicopter. John Duffy, still standing on the landing skid, grabbed hold of his web gear just as he slid by, stopping his fall and certain death. With help from Mẽ, he pulled Hải back in. Mẽ rendered aid. Duffy looked across the helicopter and saw Dallas Nihsen hanging out the other side, held by his safety tether.

John climbed in and moved over to Dallas, pulling him back inside. He patched the wound in Nihsen's back with a plastic sealer and bandage. He turned him over. Dallas had a much larger hole where the bullet exited his chest. It was bad. The wound bubbled. The bullet had hit his lung. John started patching and sealing the hole when the bubbles quit. Dallas stopped breathing. John tried mouth-to-mouth. Nothing. Dallas Nihsen died in John Duffy's arms.

Mike Gibbs flew directly to the medical aid station in Kontum, landing at the MACV helipad. Dennis Watson got out and helped put Dallas on a waiting stretcher. He walked reverently beside him into the aid station, where a medical officer made the official pronouncement of death. Dennis was devastated.

Medics also carried Đoàn Phương Hải inside, where his treatment and long road to recovery began. Duffy declined the offer of medical attention. Dennis returned to the helicopter, visibly shaken. Major Gibbs put him in the front seat of a Cobra for a ride back to Camp Holloway. The Cobra pilot took Watson's seat in the Huey, and Gibbs departed on the short flight north to Võ Định to deliver the others to 2nd Brigade.

John studied Mễ en route. He thought of what they'd been through together over the past months, of the battles fought, of the desperate ordeal at Charlie, of soldiers lost, and of what they'd all endured in holding the enemy at bay for two weeks. Mễ impressed him as a fearless leader, as a principled man, as a friend. John looked at his CAR-15 carbine and remembered the words Jim Butler had uttered when he gave it to him: *Just be sure you pass this along to another brave warrior when you leave.* He leaned forward and handed it to Mễ.

"Only a warrior has rights to this gun. I give it to you."

Mễ's eyes teared. He took the gun and said, "I honor this gun as warrior. Will fight for country I love. Will fight with courage and now with gun of hero."[3]

The helicopter landed at Võ Định. The 2nd Airborne Brigade commander, Colonel Lịch, went out to meet them. Major Peter Kama walked with him. Lieutenant "Buddha" Griswold followed, just behind. Four haggard, filthy, bloodied paratroopers got off the Huey. Mễ and John followed

Colonel Lịch and Major Kama into the command bunker. Lieutenant Griswold remained. He stood alone. He hadn't moved. He stared at the helicopter, stunned by what he saw, aghast at the amount of blood all over the seats, the floor, the bulkheads, the struts, and the skids. Bullet holes were everywhere. "My God. It looks like a slaughterhouse," he muttered to himself, before turning and following the others inside.

It had been five days since the enemy began their final all-out assault against Charlie. Five days of some of the most intense combat ever fought. Five days in hell, consigned to death, but committed to fighting with valor to the end. Indeed, it had been less than two weeks since the 11th Battalion, fresh from its duty in Saigon, had occupied Firebase Charlie on Easter Sunday. But that was a lifetime ago. Their world had changed. It was different from how it had been, and it would never be the same, for any of them, ever again.

CHAPTER 16

Aftermath

SEN SAT AT HOME IN SAIGON, LISTENING TO THE RADIO. THE NEWS on the commercial stations was bad; the pronouncements on the underground communist Radio Hanoi, worse. She'd listened to reports of enemy advances for days. Now she heard of terrible fighting in the highlands and setbacks along a ridgeline northwest of Kontum City. On its propaganda-filled station, North Vietnam claimed the annihilation of the elite South Vietnamese 11th Airborne Battalion, destroying it atop Charlie Hill, killing or capturing every paratrooper there. Sen's heart sank. Tears stained the letter she held in her hands, the one she'd received from Mẽ only days before, promising to come safely back to her, to return to her arms.

❦

Inside the bunker at Võ Định, someone handed Mẽ a canteen. He took several gulps and gave it to John. They passed it back and forth, quenching their raging thirst. Blood seeped from the bandage on Mẽ's chest. It still pained him to breathe. But he wanted to debrief before getting treated. John felt the same. His many wounds hurt, but none threatened his life. He'd bandaged most himself. Doc Liệu had also tended him during the battle. Further treatment could wait. Peter offered him coffee. He took it, and sat, holding the cup in both hands, sipping the warm brew and recounting all that had happened as Peter and Buddha took careful notes. Mẽ did the same with Colonel Lịch and the brigade staff. They were soon joined by General Ngô Dzu, the II Corps commander. The arduous debriefing ritual had begun.

Sen heard a loud knock. She moved slowly, undid the latch, and cautiously opened the door. Confirming her worst fear, a uniformed paratroop officer stood before her, surely to deliver the news of her husband's death. Her expression filled with dread. She searched his eyes.

He smiled. "He's okay. Mễ is okay. He is alive."

Sen wept in relief. She went to her children, held them tight, and gave thanks to all that was sacred.

Mễ and John would be queried at every level of command. The ARVN tried to point an accusing finger toward Mễ, the commander who had suffered defeat at Firebase Charlie. John wouldn't have it. He sang Mễ's praise as the hero of the battle, taking over on the death of Lieutenant Colonel Bảo, inflicting horrendous casualties on the enemy, and when ammunition was nearly exhausted, partnering with his American advisor to act as the rear guard, allowing the withdrawal of the surviving members of the battalion. In the end, the United States awarded Mễ the Silver Star for his courageous actions on Charlie, and Vietnam confirmed him as the new commander of the 11th Airborne Battalion and honored him with the Republic of Vietnam's highest award for valor, the Cross of Gallantry with Palm.

After briefing Peter Kama, Duffy flew by helicopter to Pleiku. He'd only been rescued from the jungle that morning. How suddenly his world had changed. He'd been delivered from hell. Duffy found a room with a cot, took off his boots and socks, lay down, covered his eyes with his socks, and slept for ten hours. A knock woke him early the next morning.

"Major Duffy, clean up and meet General Wear for breakfast in the officers' mess."

John took a shower and dusted off his ragged uniform as best he could before going to breakfast with Brigadier General George Wear. Wear served as the senior U.S. military commander in II Corps, and deputy to the civilian senior advisor for the region, John Paul Vann.

Duffy debriefed General Wear as they ate together. Their conversation continued long after breakfast, lasting a couple of hours. John found the general's keenest interest to be the B-52 strikes that he had called in, possibly closer to friendly troops than ever before, and in the enemy's use of the 130mm artillery guns. Duffy took time to credit the Cobra attack helicopters with saving his butt, called the Vietnamese Air Force fearless in their strike missions, and cited the valor of the rescue helicopters that had plucked the survivors from the jungle under intense fire. He asked that his thanks be conveyed to the B-52 crews if that was at all possible.

The Regional Assistance Group staff officers seated around the table gawked at John.

"What's up?" he asked.

One of them spoke. "Sorry. It's like seeing a ghost. We thought you were dead. The reports coming in during the battle left no doubt you were going to be killed. No one expected you to survive."

General Wear ordered John to the medical aid station, where he received his first proper hygienic medical care. The medics cleaned his wounds, stitched some closed, and applied sterile bandages. The deepest shell fragments remained, though, to be removed at the more capable 3rd Field Hospital in Saigon.

Major Duffy remained in Pleiku for a second day in order to provide further debriefing details to the Regional Assistance Group intelligence officer and the Air Force liaison officer. He emphasized the importance of air support as the single most critical element in the paratroopers' ability to hold off a ten-to-one superior enemy force for as long as they did.

That same day, he boarded a C-130 cargo plane for a flight to Tân Sơn Nhứt Airbase in Saigon. He caught a cab to his BOQ,* a short distance outside the airbase gate. He'd kept this room in Saigon throughout this tour of duty. He cleaned up, grabbed a clean uniform from his closet, went downstairs to the dining room, ate a steak dinner, drank a beer, returned to his room, and collapsed into bed.

Peter Kama had asked him to brief General Fred Weyand, Peter's old boss and now the commanding general of all U.S. forces in Vietnam. John

---

*BOQ: Bachelor Officers' Quarters provide lodging for officers unaccompanied by a spouse or other family members.

arrived at the general's office to find him gone on a field visit. Duffy prepared a summary of his experience and recommendations with the help of General Weyand's administrative officer. He emphasized the same points he had made to Brigadier General Wear.

He left the report for delivery to the commanding general and headed to the 3rd Field Hospital, the most capable medical facility in Vietnam. A nurse weighed him. He'd lost twelve pounds in the two weeks he'd been on Charlie Hill. She moved him to a treatment room. Doctors cleaned and redressed all his wounds. They removed shrapnel embedded deeply in the left side of his face. They left the smaller pieces in his scalp in place, advising that they'd work their way out in a couple of weeks. They did.

In the days ahead, Duffy wrote and submitted award recommendations for those he felt deserving of medals for their heroism on Charlie. That included paratroopers as well as those who had courageously supported from the air. He also typed his official after-action report and presented it to the new senior U.S. advisor to the ARVN Airborne Division, Colonel Robert Hyatt, who was presently advising the war effort from his office on Tân Sơn Nhứt.

His official duties ended, Duffy spent his time reading and relaxing, and taking in much of Saigon's culture while he awaited orders for his travel back to the United States. He set his hand to poetry again, as well. He crafted a poem about the sacrifices of the 11th Airborne Battalion at Firebase Charlie. It would be the first of a series of poems that would occupy him for the rest of his years.[1]

Peter Kama submitted Major Duffy for the Medal of Honor for his conspicuous gallantry on Charlie Hill above and beyond the call of duty. The army downgraded the award to the nation's second-highest recognition of heroism, the Distinguished Service Cross. It appeared to be an expedient action for a military service consumed with rapidly disengaging from a long and unpopular war.[†]

[†]The army did not favorably support any Medal of Honor recommendations during the period of the most intense combat of the Vietnam War, the 1972 Easter Offensive. The last Vietnam War Medal of Honor presented to a member of the United States Army was for action on August 7, 1971, nearly eight months before the start of the North Vietnamese spring offensive.

The 2nd Brigade medical company at Võ Định treated Mễ's wounds before he shepherded the surviving 11th Battalion paratroopers back to Saigon and their garrison at Red Hat Hill. There, they went to work preparing for further action. The wounded received additional medical treatment, and most quickly returned to duty. The more seriously injured endured weeks or months of hospitalization and recovery. Some eventually rejoined the army. Others passed from memory as disabled veterans.

Doctors couldn't do much for Captain Đoàn Phương Hải at the medical aid station in Kontum. That's where the rescue helicopter had dropped him. A bullet had smashed into his right foot and ankle, breaking several bones. They could only stabilize him there. The next day, April 16, a plane flew him back to Saigon, to the Đỗ Vinh hospital, a capable one-hundred-bed facility exclusively for Vietnamese airborne patients. Seven months and several surgeries later, his wounds had healed somewhat, and Hải returned to limited staff duty at the Airborne Division headquarters. His foot and ankle never healed right. He'd limp badly the rest of his life. He spent the remainder of the war as a desk-bound staff officer in Saigon, rising to the rank of major.

After landing at Tân Sơn Nhứt Airbase in Saigon, Mễ headed directly home for a day of rest before returning to duty to begin rebuilding his battalion. He approached his house, excited and anxious at the same time. He could only imagine the anguish he'd put his family through.

He opened the door and hollered, "Hello! I'm home."

Sen came running, crying with joy. The children followed, screaming excitedly. They all hugged.

"Don't go back. Don't ever go back," Sen pleaded, knowing the impossibility of what she asked.

"I have to."

Mễ, Sen, and the kids spent a special afternoon and evening together, feeling closer to each other than ever before. The next morning, Mễ returned to Red Hat Hill for intensive re-manning, reequipping, and training. He'd come home only infrequently after that. He had much to do.

197

Over the days ahead, Mễ heard, sadly, that the enemy had captured Captain Big Hùng and his 113 Company, *in toto*. They'd apparently not gotten far off their position that Friday night when they ran into an overwhelming enemy force. He also found that Captain Nguyễn Tấn Nho, the 110 Company commander, had also been captured along with some of his troops.

But there was good news, as well. It turned out that a few other paratroopers had escaped the trap at the base of Charlie and avoided capture. Mễ learned that at the same time he, Hải, and Duffy had rallied the soldiers around them to break out of the NVA ambush, Lieutenant Nguyễn Văn Lập, the 114 Company artillery officer, had led a handful of paratroopers in a desperate dash into the jungle. As Lập evaded the enemy, he encountered other small groups of survivors who joined him. They all swore an oath to escape or die. If they encountered an enemy force, they'd fight to the death. They would not be captured. Three days later, Lập and his band of twenty-six found their way to Diên Bình, well north of Võ Định along Route 14. Many suffered serious wounds. Nuns from a nearby Catholic convent treated their injuries before trucks arrived to transport them to Pleiku for a flight back to Saigon. There, they received further treatment. Those fit for duty returned to the re-forming battalion at Red Hat Hill.

A few other small groups had also escaped the slaughter, avoided capture, and made their way to friendly lines. Among their numbers were the 112 Company commander, Captain Skinny Hùng, and Lieutenant Phan Cảnh Cho, the 114 Company commander, as well as Lieutenant Đinh Viết Trinh, a platoon leader from 112 Company who would replace his fallen leader as the new company commander.

On April 27, South Vietnam's Joint General Staff withdrew the ARVN 2nd Airborne from the Highlands. The brigade returned to Saigon to prepare for their next deployment to bolster I Corps in the desperate battles taking place just below the DMZ. The fight in the Central Highlands continued without them. But they had done their duty.

The battle at Charlie had denied the North Vietnamese a rapid advance into Kontum City. It stopped them cold for two weeks. It blunted their advance from the west and deprived them of free access down Route 14 from the north. The fight critically depleted the NVA's prestigious 320th Division in lives, ammunition, and critical leaders lost. It inflicted horrific casualties, destroying at least two combat battalions and badly bloodying others.[2]

It took time for the North Vietnamese Army to lick its wounds and reconstitute units, time the South Vietnamese used to bolster their defensive posture, relocate an additional infantry division, and prepare for one of the greatest battles of the Vietnam War, the Battle of Kontum. Because of the 11th Airborne Battalion's stand at Firebase Charlie, the North Vietnamese had to alter their plan and delay their advance. Though more ground would be lost to the enemy in the weeks ahead—including the rest of Rocket Ridge and the 22nd ARVN Division's base at Tân Cảnh/Đắk Tô—South Vietnam gained the time necessary to prepare to defend the provincial capital city, Kontum. They'd ultimately win the decisive battle to save it and turn the tide of North Vietnam's Easter Offensive in central South Vietnam.[3]

The sacrifices made in the battle for Charlie inspired the South Vietnamese population. Radio and television stations broadcast the story again and again for months. In death, the 11th Airborne Battalion's commander, Nguyễn Đình Bảo, became a national hero. The army promoted him to full colonel, posthumously. Huge banners with his image hung in Saigon. Soldiers and citizens marched in parades in his honor. The book *Mùa Hè Đỏ Lửa*, containing a detailed account of the battle, turned into a Vietnamese bestseller, and a song about the battalion's fight, *"Người Ở Lại Charlie,"* quickly became one of the most popular tunes in South Vietnam. It remains so among the expatriate Vietnamese community today.[4]

Before John Duffy flew home on April 30, he drove out to Red Hat Hill and visited the 11th Airborne during their training. As he stood with Mễ, the pair looked like two old gladiators, battered by their bouts in the arena, yet hardened—proud and resolute and ready to fight again. That night, Duffy hosted a party for the officers at their favorite watering hole, the always-notorious Dragon Bar in Saigon. They drank and reminisced. John ordered bottles of Martell cognac late into the evening. He filled his and Mễ's glasses, then passed the bottles around.

Once everyone had poured some, John raised his glass high and shouted, "What does VSOP stand for?"

A crescendo of voices screamed back, "Very sexy, old paratrooper!"

⚬⚬⚬

On May 8, 1972, the reconstituted 11th Airborne Battalion flew north to Huế. They landed at the outlying Phu Bai Airfield and loaded trucks for the short drive into the city. There, they joined the rest of the 2nd Airborne Brigade, preparing to reinforce I Corps and stop the NVA divisions sweeping the region. New raw recruits filled much of the 11th Battalion's ranks. Mễ had worked hard, though, building on the proud airborne heritage and the 11th's heroic reputation, to forge them into a powerful fighting force. He'd done it in a little over two weeks. They were ready for battle once again, this time with a new American advisor, Captain Gail Woodrow "Woody" Furrow, another Special Forces officer.

The situation in I Corps was bleak. The North Vietnamese invasion had begun with an artillery bombardment on March 30. A ground assault followed the next morning. The enemy came from the north and the west, attacking with two divisions across the Demilitarized Zone (DMZ), and launching another division across the Laotian border. Within days, two more enemy divisions followed from the north and one more from the west.[5]

The NVA immediately put the South Vietnamese defenders on their heels, rapidly gaining territory. Civilian refugees poured south, seeking sanctuary from their communist "liberators." On April 29, the NVA laid into a convoy fleeing toward Huế along Highway 1. They slaughtered thousands, the vast majority of whom were civilians. They left the bodies, mostly old men, women, and children, rotting where they'd cut them down along the roadway, in fields, or still packed into the vehicles from which they could not escape.[6]

By the opening days of May, the North Vietnamese had captured Quảng Trị City and controlled South Vietnam's entire northern province. They prepared to move on Huế and take the old imperial capital, delivering a devastating blow to the South. The new I Corps commander, Lieutenant General Ngô Quang Trưởng, replaced weak leaders, reorganized forces, and repositioned them. He also asked for help. In response, the Joint General Staff sent in the 2nd Airborne Brigade. They arrived just in time.[7]

General Trưởng immediately dispatched the airborne brigade to reinforce the defensive line at the Mỹ Chánh River, only twenty miles northwest of Huế. As they waited to enter the action, Mễ and his new executive officer, Major Nguyễn Văn Thành, along with the new S-3, Captain Nguyễn Đức Tâm,[†] coined a motto for the battalion: "Dual Swords Regaining the Frontier" (*Song Kiếm Trấn Ải*). The slogan helped motivate the paratroopers, already eager for the opportunity to avenge the deaths of so many brothers on Charlie.

Four days later, with an attached platoon of armored personnel carriers, Mễ led the 11th Battalion on a search-and-destroy mission, thrusting westward from Highway 1, along the southern bank of the river. They found their foe, lots of them. The battalion battled units from the NVA 325th Division that countered their advance with heavy artillery bombardments, including salvos from the big 130mm guns. The 11th endured ground attacks, small-arms fire, and machine guns. They even suffered an attack by three enemy tanks. The paratroopers were right back in the thick of it, right where they wanted to be.[8]

With effective artillery and air support, and the spirited fighting of the paratroopers, the 11th Airborne prevailed, defeating the enemy along the way. The 2nd and 7th airborne battalions followed, holding the south bank of the Mỹ Chánh. The 11th halted its advance at the foothills, holding the western sector of the line. During the battle, B-40 rocket-propelled grenade fragments tore into Mễ. Battalion medics moved him to the rear, where an ambulance evacuated him to the Phu Bai military field hospital for treatment. He didn't stay long. He wangled his way out of the hospital in a few days and returned to his command, ready to dirty his clean bandages.

The Joint General Staff soon added more combat power to I Corps. The 3rd Airborne Brigade showed up on May 22, along with the Airborne Division headquarters. The 1st Airborne Brigade began arriving in late May, but its final battalion, the 6th, wouldn't get on the ground until June

---

[†]The same Nguyễn Đức Tâm who had introduced Mễ and Sen in Saigon ten years earlier.

25, completing the deployment of Vietnam's entire Airborne Division to I Corps.[9]

In the meantime, the 11th Airborne Battalion fought at the spear point of one of the most decisive battles of the northern campaign. Intelligence indicated enemy preparation for a massive attack directly to the front of the battalion. Colonel Lịch, the 2nd Brigade commander, created a task force around the 11th Battalion. Mễ had the 11th minus 113 Company, which Lịch had previously detailed to provide security for brigade artillery units. In its place, Colonel Lịch assigned him two companies from the 3rd Airborne Battalion, which just arrived from the battle at An Loc. Lịch also strengthened him with armor from the ARVN 17th Cavalry Squadron. The squadron sent him twenty M-41 tanks, and a platoon of four armored personnel carriers (APCs). Additionally, he got a newly deployed TOW antitank missile system.[§]

The battle commenced early in the morning on June 2. Heavy enemy artillery rained from the sky. The paratroopers heard the sound of NVA tanks approaching. The task force forward observers went to work, unleashing their own artillery strikes against the communist firing positions within range and putting shells on top of the advancing tanks.

Mễ made the necessary adjustments as the battle unfolded, positioning himself to best influence the fight and issuing orders to maneuver his forces most effectively against their foe. Captain Furrow employed U.S. air and naval gunfire assets to support Mễ's scheme. Still, five NVA tanks crossed the river, heading straight for the center of the battalion. The 111 Company, alongside the two companies from the 3rd Battalion, countered with effective artillery fire and antitank weapons, destroying three tanks and capturing a fourth. An airstrike destroyed the fifth.

Mễ suspected his opponent had only scratched at him to gauge his reaction and determine his positions. He expected much more to come. Sure enough, at dawn the next day, the NVA launched a massive armor assault with its 204th Tank Regiment. T-54 tanks and PT-76 armored

---

[§]TOW: Tube-launched, optically tracked, wire guided missile. These were new to the Vietnam War. They'd been rapidly deployed from the United States in response to the North Vietnamese use of tanks in their Easter Offensive. Major Peter Kama, still the 2nd Airborne Brigade senior advisor, argued strongly for ARVN soldiers to be trained in using the ground-mounted version of the system. These crews had only been qualified with the TOW missile just days before.

vehicles rolled forward. Hundreds of infantry soldiers followed. The enemy formation hit the task force and mayhem ensued.

TOW missiles knocked out the lead tanks. Mễ's own tanks aimed their cannons carefully and destroyed others. Paratroopers shot their shoulder-fired LAW antitank rockets to finish any that got closer. An enemy tank exploded, hurling its turret into the air. Paratroopers cheered. Excitement mounted as the battle raged. Mễ's soldiers killed and disabled more tanks in rapid succession. American fire support and VNAF A-1 Skyraiders, along with artillery, once again supported the task force with devastating effect. Holding the carbine John Duffy had given him tightly in hand, Mễ moved to the front and ordered a counterattack, stopping the enemy infantry in their tracks and driving them into a rout.

The battle ended at noon on June 3 with the enemy retreating northward back across the Mỹ Chánh. Two days of fighting cost the North twenty-four tanks destroyed and a battalion slaughtered (six to seven hundred soldiers killed). The 11th Battalion task force lost two tanks, twelve paratroopers killed in action, and twenty wounded. The Joint General Staff cited the 11th Airborne Battalion as having destroyed the most North Vietnamese tanks of any unit during the Easter Offensive. They'd stopped the North Vietnamese threat against Huế and set the conditions to retake Quảng Trị.[10]

Because of his leadership and courage in battle, the army awarded Mễ his second Cross of Gallantry with Palm—the highest award for heroism that his country could bestow.

The 2nd Brigade's reconnaissance company later counted 119 enemy tanks destroyed across the brigade's entire front. The Mỹ Chánh tank battle became the watershed event of the campaign. The enemy's offensive culminated. They'd lost their momentum. The attackers fell back and became defenders.[11]

On June 28, 1972, I Corps launched Lam Son 72 to retake Quảng Trị and to secure Huế's western and southern approaches at the same time. The Airborne Division crossed the Mỹ Chánh River and attacked northward along the west side of Highway QL1, Vietnam's major north-south roadway. The Marine Division paralleled along the east side of the highway.

The 3rd Airborne brigade seized the bridgehead on the north side of the Mỹ Chánh. On July 2, the 2nd Airborne Brigade launched the main attack, inserting the 9th and 11th Battalions by helicopter six miles south of Quảng Trị City and marching the 7th Battalion to join them. Colonel Lịch put the 11th Battalion at the center of his brigade, flanked by the 9th and 7th. He augmented Mê by attaching an M-48 tank company, armored personnel carrier platoon, two Special Forces companies, and one local infantry battalion. The combined force attacked northward toward La Vang Basilica a little over a mile south of the city center.

The Marine Division continued its attack along the east side of QL1. The ARVN 1st Infantry Division focused its operations west of Huế to pin down North Vietnamese forces there. The 1st Ranger Brigade conducted supporting operations as required. Three South Vietnamese divisions fought six from the North. Still, the South Vietnamese drove forward with tenacity, bravery, and powerful U.S. air and naval gunfire support.[12]

On July 4, 1972, as the campaign regained territory and threatened a chokehold around Quảng Trị City, the NVA massed for a counterattack. Major Peter Kama, still the U.S. senior advisor with the 2nd Airborne Brigade, faced a large enemy force directly to the brigade's front. He needed to bloody the bastards. He used his direct communications with General Weyand to request the diversion of B-52 strikes.[§] A phone call from the general to the 7th Air Force commander did the trick. Word came back to Kama that the strike should arrive in four hours.

Major Kama had a table set with a white tablecloth and glasses. Colonel Lịch, his staff, and the brigade's American advisors assembled around the table for lunch. Peter broke out cans of Coca-Cola and a couple of bottles of VSOP along with some precious cubes of ice. The B-52s hit precisely at noon. The ground shook, pummeling the NVA. With cognac and Coke, all raised their glasses high as Peter Kama toasted.

"Here's to your great fight toward victory. Happy Fourth of July!"

Hard fighting continued. The brigade pressed forward with the 11th Battalion still in the lead. They defeated NVA forces and retook La Vang Basilica on July 6. The paratroopers drove the enemy back handily to the

---

§General Weyand had moved from deputy to become the MACV commander on June 30, taking over from General Creighton W. Abrams, who advanced to become the army chief of staff in Washington.

edge of the city. Their foe dug in as the contest for downtown turned into a brutal, slow, house-to-house struggle.

The battalion attacked westward to seize the bridge across the Thạch Hãn River in order to block the North Vietnamese reinforcement of the city. Mẽ put Captain Hoàng Ngọc Hùng's 112 Company in the lead. A tough clash ensued. On July 22, Captain Hùng, Skinny Hùng, survivor of the fight on Charlie Hill, was cut down and died only a hundred yards from his family home in the town where he'd been born.

The assault on the city's fortified citadel brought back memories of the battle for Huế during Tết 1968. Hard fighting raged, but the airborne forces, reinforced with elements of the ARVN 1st Ranger Brigade, prevailed. They took the citadel on July 23 at a cost, suffering high casualties. Mẽ had sent his 111th Company, under its new commander, First Lieutenant Đinh Viết Trinh, another Charlie Hill veteran, to augment the 5th Airborne Battalion for the Citadel attack. The remainder of the 11th, along with the 6th and 9th airborne battalions, continued fighting in the southern part of Quảng Trị City, supporting the Citadel operation by tying down NVA forces there.

A friendly fire incident ruined the day. An errant 500-pound bomb killed forty-five paratroopers and wounded nearly one hundred. A timely enemy counterattack took the prize away. The Citadel, so painfully taken, was quickly lost. The airborne force fell back, nearly spent. The Vietnamese marines took over the brunt of the fighting in the city on July 26, and they would assume the bulk of the casualties going forward.[13]

Fierce fighting raged on for nearly two more months.

On September 16, more than eleven weeks into the battle, the marines finally drove the NVA from the Citadel and raised the Republic of Vietnam flag. Major Lê Văn Mẽ turned to his American advisor and smiled broadly. Captain Woody Furrow looked at him and declared, "There you go. You've won. You've won the war!"

EPILOGUE

THE VICTORY AT QUẢNG TRỊ GAVE THE SOUTH VIETNAMESE ARMED forces a most glorious moment. They had taken the full burden of the ground war from the Americans and had soundly defeated their North Vietnamese foe in the largest offensive of the war—admittedly with hefty American air support. They'd beaten the NVA on all three axes of the Easter Offensive: An Lộc, Kontum, and now Quảng Trị.

For Lê Văn Mẽ, the triumph marked the high point of his military career. It brought the greatest glory the 11th Airborne Battalion had known. It also gave the paratroopers a taste of sweet revenge. Under Mẽ's leadership, the battalion went from near-annihilation on Charlie Hill, to emerge as a powerful fighting machine once again, playing a key role in South Vietnam's final great victory of the war. The army rewarded Mẽ by promoting him to lieutenant colonel ahead of his peers, and assigning him as the G-3 (Operations and Training Officer) on the Airborne Division staff in Saigon. He sat atop the world: victorious, elevated to a high-level staff position, and enjoying the luxury of spending time with his family.

The situation stabilized between the opposing forces for a time. The ARVN pushed their adversary out of all major urban areas, but the enemy still controlled broad swaths of rural countryside. Positions changed very little over the months ahead. On January 27, 1973, the belligerents signed the Paris Peace Accords with naïve hopes for a stable future. Then their world began to crumble.[1]

Watergate consumed the Nixon administration. That opened the door for the U.S. Congress to pass the Case-Church Amendment in June 1973, ending American involvement in the Vietnam War. The legislation did, however, allow military equipment, ammunition, fuel, and economic support to continue. Nixon resigned in August, turning the presidency over to Gerald Ford. The American people had tired of the long war. Their elected officials represented that view. When the communists blatantly violated the provisions of the peace accords and South Vietnam looked to the United States for help, Congress cut funding.[2]

North Vietnam took that as a signal to launch an all-out campaign in 1975, knowing the United States had abandoned its longtime ally. The operation went swiftly. South Vietnam had scarce funds, few replacement parts, and little fuel or ammunition. Their morale sank. Forces fell back before well-equipped and supplied NVA divisions. The VNAF abandoned flyable fighter aircraft as they evacuated air bases because there was no aviation fuel. Artillery battalions ran short of ammunition. The situation rapidly disintegrated until Saigon finally fell to the communists on April 30, 1975.[3]

The United States paid a high price fighting to preserve the freedom of the Republic of Vietnam: 58,328 Americans killed, more than 300,000 wounded, many of those physically and mentally maimed for life, and more than 1,500 still missing in action. Vietnam suffered horrendously. Estimates vary from source to source, but most put ARVN losses at over 250,000 men killed. The whole of Vietnam saw more than two million soldiers and civilians killed, and untold millions wounded.[4]

But what of those who fought at Firebase Charlie? What has become of the gallant warriors, those who gave so much in defense of Charlie Hill, who showed such extraordinary valor, only to have their victory squandered and ultimately suffer national defeat at the hands of their enemy?

John Duffy flew home from Vietnam on August 30, 1972. He worked out of Fort Devens, Massachusetts, as advisor to an Army Reserve Special Forces company. Additionally, he became advisor to a reserve component battalion and brigade, each normally a full-time position. He volunteered to return for a fourth tour of duty in Southeast Asia in June 1973. The army assigned him to the U.S. Support Activities Group, located on the Royal Thai Air Force Base at Nakhon Phanom, Thailand. There, he joined the team advising the Cambodian armed forces in their fight against communist insurgents and helping to coordinate the U.S. air operations that still continued in Laos and Cambodia.

When that mission ended in August, Duffy managed a transfer to the Joint Casualty Resolution Center (JCRC), located on the same base. That organization formed out of MACV-SOG assets as that command disbanded. JCRC teams scoured jungle sites, searching for remains, to determine the status of those American service members listed as missing in action, an undertaking that evolved over the years and continues today, globally, as the Department of Defense POW/MIA Accounting Agency. John Duffy led one of those teams with missions into Laos, Cambodia, and back into South Vietnam. His immediate boss and launch site commander was Lieutenant Colonel Charlie Beckwith, who later went on to found Delta Force. Major John Duffy made his final flight home from Southeast Asia on May 28, 1974.

After retiring from the army in 1976, Duffy became the president of a publishing company and later the founder and president of an investment firm. All the while, he continued reading and writing poetry. He created a website of his poems* and has written six poetry books, including *The Battle for "Charlie."* Indeed, John Duffy had been given the nickname "Du Fu" by his Vietnamese comrades during the battle of Charlie, Du Fu being a noted Chinese warrior-poet whose name was not far from the Vietnamese pronunciation of "Duffy."

Major Duffy is one of the most highly decorated officers from the Vietnam War. Major Peter Kama, his superior, submitted him for the Medal of Honor for his actions on Charlie Hill. The army downgraded the award to a Distinguished Service Cross, the nation's second-highest award for heroism. Major Kama never let go of his belief that Duffy deserved the Medal of Honor. He resubmitted the award in 2012. After years of bureaucratic delays, the Department of the Army convened a board of officers to reconsider the merits of the case in 2017. John Duffy awaits a decision.

His other numerous awards include the Soldier's Medal, four Bronze Stars with one "Valor" device, eight Purple Hearts for wounds received in action, seven Air Medals with six "Valor" devices, three Army Commendation Medals with one "Valor" device, and the Republic of Vietnam's highest valor award, the Cross of Gallantry with Palm, plus two more with Silver Stars. His unit awards include four Presidential Unit Citations, the

---

*Visit www.epoetryworld.com.

Valorous Unit Award, the Meritorious Unit Commendation, and the Vietnamese Gallantry Cross Unit Citation. He also earned the Combat Infantryman Badge (CIB) and the Master Parachutist Badge.

Today, John Duffy lives happily in retirement with the love of his life, Mary, in the seaside community of Santa Cruz, California, about thirty miles south of San Jose.

Mê Van Le (Lê Văn Mê) stood in the Airborne Division's operations center, radio mic in one hand and telephone in the other, the day before the fall of Saigon. The lieutenant colonel dutifully directed counterattacks against the advancing enemy, as he'd done for days with almost no sleep. With his country's collapse imminent, and the headquarters nearly abandoned, Mê decided to take a much-needed break. He jumped in his army jeep and headed home for lunch. At the security gate, a colonel told him the Airborne Division commander had quit. He advised him to go straight to the Saigon Harbor and escape the country before it was too late. Mê sped home, collected his seven-months' pregnant wife and the children, along with his brother and sister-in-law, and headed to the harbor with hopes of getting aboard a fleeing boat. Sen only had time to pack one red suitcase, quickly stuffing it with clothes, documents, and money—Republic of Vietnam currency that would soon be worthless.

Mê's parents and four sisters had been living with the family in Saigon since their village near Huế had fallen to the North Vietnamese Army.[†] It had been their ancestral home for five generations. They loved Vietnam. They wouldn't leave. They chose to remain and deal with whatever might come. Mê saw no choice. He couldn't stay. He'd be killed and his family murdered or terrorized. His father bid a tearful farewell to the sons he'd never see again. Sen never had the chance to say good-bye to her parents, her brother, or her three younger sisters. They, too, remained in Vietnam.

Mê drove through mass confusion, his CAR-15 in hand, pistol holstered on his hip, and a rocket launcher within reach. Panic gripped the city. People filled the streets, some moving with purpose, others frozen in fear. Chaos reigned. Terrified civilians reached out for the jeep as it made its way through the crowds. Mê's heart wept that it had all come to this.

[†] Mê had four surviving sisters at the end of the war. Of his eight siblings, two boys had died in childhood, and his older sister passed away in 1970.

The family arrived at the harbor to find it empty. All boats had gone. Mễ turned the jeep and headed for the naval base. As darkness fell, explosions rattled the night. Mễ drove through the madness, arriving to find a broken ship tied to the dock, sailors feverishly working a repair.

Desperate people mobbed the gangway. It became impassable. Mễ looked to the sailors on deck. He identified himself as a paratroop officer. With a nod, they threw marine cargo nets over the side. With the help of his brother, Đáo, he sent Sen and his sister-in-law, Mạch, both pregnant, climbing the perilous, wobbly netting to join other military families already on board. He followed with his six-year-old son, Vũ, clinging to his back. He repeated the feat with his four-year-old daughter, Quyên, and three-year-old Phương. All the while, he heard screams from others falling off, some crashing back onto the dock, a few splashing into the water as the ship strained its lines, moving to and fro from the pier. Weighted down with their worldly possessions, they sank straightaway to the bottom.

After his family boarded, the sailors completed enough repairs for the ship to get underway with one engine. They warily snaked their way down the Saigon River toward the ocean. The next morning, April 30, 1975, the radio broadcast that South Vietnam had surrendered. The North Vietnamese occupied the capital city later that day, ending decades of warfare, but not the suffering of the freedom-loving South Vietnamese.

Conditions on the open sea became desperate. The refugees consumed the last of the food and water. They sailed for days, death's breath ever closer, until a U.S. Navy ship from 7th Fleet found them and provided provisions.

After many more days at sea, they arrived at Subic Bay in the Philippines. Before disembarking, the navy ordered the refugees to surrender their weapons and change out of their uniforms. They all stood proudly on the deck and sang the Republic of Vietnam national anthem. Mễ stripped off his airborne fatigues and donned civilian clothes. He grasped his beloved CAR-15, the gift from John Duffy. As he held it, so many thoughts, so many memories and flashes of battles raced through his mind. He'd fought hard, but he had lost his country. Tears welled, but he capped his emotion and threw the weapon as far as he could into the sea, watching it splash and disappear. Mễ stepped off the ship with his family, having no idea what the future might hold.

The navy loaded their passengers directly onto a civilian cargo ship, the *Greenleaf*. It sailed to Guam and their first home outside the borders of Vietnam—a hastily constructed refugee camp. There they received food, clothing, shelter, and showers while being processed for onward movement. An administrator stamped Mễ's file for resettlement in the United States. A clerk issued everyone identification documents. A new persona appeared. Lê Văn Mễ became Me Van Le, the westernized version of his name.[†] Lieutenant Colonel Mễ transformed, in that instant, into Mr. Le.

Upon their arrival in the United States, the family spent time in a refugee camp at Fort Chaffee, Arkansas, before finding church sponsorship and resettlement in Warsaw, Missouri. While at Fort Chaffee, Sen gave birth to a son, whom they named Ozark in honor of the nearby Ozark Mountains.

In Warsaw, Me worked as a part-time janitor and also took college classes in electronics. He hitchhiked the twenty-five miles to campus or bummed rides from parishioners in the church or fellow students when he could. Sen devoted herself to raising their four children. They both wanted more. After saving every penny for eleven months, they traded a gifted used Barracuda for a used Chevy Vega station wagon, loaded the kids and their few possessions, and headed west with $400 and twenty-four cans of Valvoline oil.

The Le family made their way to San Jose, California, initially camping out with a friend in his apartment. Armed with thirty-four college semester hours in electronics, Me went in search of work. He found it with Memorex, as a research and development technician. The family moved into a one-bedroom apartment. Me enrolled in night classes at San Jose City College to complete his associate of science (AS) degree. He continued his evening educational pursuits, ultimately receiving his bachelor of science in electrical engineering (BSEE) from Northwestern Polytechnic University.

[†] Like many Asian cultures, Vietnamese place the surname first and the given name last. The name tags on their military uniforms always showed the given, or first name. This might seem a bit awkward, but it was not at all. Large numbers of Vietnamese share the same family names, so there would be many Nguyens, Trans, and Les in any given unit, many times more than Smiths and Joneses in the West.

Sen took accounting classes in a government-sponsored program under the Comprehensive Employment and Training Act (CETA) and landed a job at National Cash Register (NCR) in their accounting department. She continued night classes at San Jose Community College. They saved money. In a month, they moved into public housing. In two years, they bought a three-bedroom single-family home in San Jose's North Valley.

Over the years, Me and his family prospered, along with the Vietnamese community that developed in San Jose. They all became American citizens. Me held a number of positions with various high-tech firms in Silicon Valley. He retired as the senior manager of research and development for Samsung Information Systems, America. In his twenty-eight-year professional career in the United States, he contributed significantly to his field. He holds seven U.S. patents related to the design and development of computer hard drives.

The Le children have succeeded, as well. Their older son, Vu, earned a degree in mechanical engineering from San Jose State University and works with a high-tech company in Silicon Valley. Daughter Quyen received a bachelor of arts from the University of California, Berkeley, a master of arts in social work from Columbia University, and a law degree from the University of California, Davis. She is the director of data and evaluation at the East Bay Asian Youth Center (EBAYC) in Oakland, California. Daughter Phuong finished her bachelor of arts at UCLA and completed a master of arts at the University of Michigan. She became a journalist with the Associated Press, and lives in Seattle, Washington. Ozark earned his bachelor of arts at the University of California, San Diego, and a master of arts in communications at San Jose State University. He is an administrator with the San Jose Holiday Inn franchise. All continue to excel in their professions and the care of their families.

Today, Me and Sen enjoy retirement and frequent visits from their children and grandchildren.[5]

Hai Doan (Đoàn Phương Hải) still worked as a staff officer in the Airborne Division headquarters when Saigon fell. As the city crumbled, Hải drove home and loaded his wife, Qui, and their five-year-old daughter and three-year-old son into his jeep. He headed straight for the naval base, weaving his way through the mass of humanity filling the streets. He got to the base and ran toward the nearest ship he saw. He got onboard with his family only to find the ship inoperable. A uniformed naval officer told him repairs were ongoing and not to worry, they'd soon be underway. Hải took his family belowdecks and found space in a small room crowded with other refugees. Once the engine started and they sensed movement, the family fell fast asleep.

The next day, walking the deck as the ship rolled on the open sea, Hai saw a familiar face. He walked as quickly as his not yet-seaworthy legs would allow.

"Mễ! Mễ! Is that you?"

The two comrades reunited with a tearful hug. They'd stay together to the Philippines and onward, on the same ship to Guam. From there, they went their separate ways, Mễ to Fort Chaffee, Arkansas, and Hải to Dallas, Texas, where he found employment with the DuPont Company.

In 1978, Hải moved his family to San Jose, California, joining his friend Mễ in the rapidly growing Vietnamese community there. After graduating from Bay Valley Technical Institute, he worked for several electronics companies in the area, moving up through the positions of technician, engineer, and manager. All the while, he enjoyed reading and writing articles for many Vietnamese-language magazines. He retired in 2004 and moved to Sunnyvale, California, to be close to his two children and four grandchildren. He has published two books, *Horizon of the Sea* and *Remember the Old Soldier*, and is the editor of *Đa Hiệu* magazine.

Hai's wife, Qui, worked for Apple Computers for twenty-nine years in their import/export department, retiring in 2015. His daughter, Katherine, went on to college at the University of Texas, earning an MBA. His son, Tony, graduated with a bachelor of science from San Jose State University.

Lieu To (Doctor Tô Phạm Liệu) continued as the battalion surgeon for the 11th Airborne following the battle at Firebase Charlie. He once again treated battlefield trauma throughout the Quảng Trị counteroffensive. He even got wounded once himself. After the ARVN victory, he moved to the Brigade's 2nd Medical Company. Later, he served at the Airborne Division's Đỗ Vinh Hospital in Saigon.

As South Vietnam imploded in early 1975, Liệu met on occasion with his brother, Thái, an officer in the ARVN 18th Division. They'd get together at their mother's house, just outside the city. The two soon began talking about escape should South Vietnam fall. Lieu did not include his wife and children in the plans. They had separated some months earlier, and she had no desire to go with him or to allow their two daughters and son to do so, either.

On April 29, the brothers met at their mother's house. They made their decision. At 7:00 p.m. that night, Thái jumped onto his motorcycle, with Liệu following close behind in an army jeep. They drove to the navy headquarters, where they found two sorry-looking vessels still tied to a pier. They pressed into the crowd at the gangway trying to get onboard. The brothers separated in the mayhem. Liệu made it onto the ship, only to learn the engines wouldn't start.

He shouted back onto the dock to his brother, "It's broken. Go to the other boat."

Before he could push his way through the mob to get off the ship, a hopeful crewmember told him that repairs were underway. He decided to stay put. In several hours, they steamed down the river. The next morning, he heard the radio broadcast South Vietnam's surrender. The news demoralized everyone. Even the gregarious Doctor Liệu fought back tears, knowing his nation's years of bloodshed and sacrifice had come to naught. He soon found something to raise his spirits, though. He ran into his old friends Mễ and Hải onboard. They had escaped with their families. He had not. Still, he smiled broadly.

Upon arrival in Subic Bay, Philippines, the refugees transferred to the cargo ship, *Greenleaf*, for the transit to Guam. Liệu delighted in finding his brother, Thái, already aboard. In the refugee camp on Guam, Doctor Tô Phạm Liệu's identity changed to Mr. Lieu To to accommodate the Western name order.

Lieu flew to the United States on May 10, over a week before his brother. He was processed through Camp Pendleton, California, where he quickly found work at the base medical facility helping refugees. The state of South Dakota recruited him as a potential physician. They sponsored his move to the town of Pierre, where he worked for the state's Department of

Health. There he successfully passed the examinations required for licensing as a medical doctor in the United States.

He practiced medicine in South Dakota for several years, but he found the winters brutal. He moved to Wichita, Kansas, in 1981, then to Denver, Colorado, a few years later. The weather was better, but still too cold. He uprooted again, landing in Houston, Texas, with a position at the Veterans Administration Hospital. In 1987, he transferred to the VA Hospital in Alexandria, Louisiana. He loved it there. He'd finally found a place he could call home.

Lieu sponsored his wife and three children to come to the United States. They settled in San Diego, living with his mother. They formally divorced shortly afterward. Lieu traveled to California frequently to spend time with the children and hosted them on visits to Louisiana. He met his second wife, Thuy, shortly after his arrival in Alexandria. They remained happily married and had three children.

Like so many Vietnam War refugees, Lieu To and his family found success in America through hard work and study. All Lieu's children finished college and are successful in their careers. Some followed their father's footsteps into medicine. Of his six children, one finished an MA and two earned their PhD. Two daughters became medical doctors, one specializing in internal medicine and the other in opthalmology.

Sadly, Lieu To died of liver cancer on September 29, 1997. He was just fifty-six years old. His family scattered his ashes over the sea, off the California coast, where the waters of the Pacific Ocean also wash onto the shores of his native Vietnam.

Lap Nguyen (Nguyễn Văn Lập), the critically important artillery forward observer during the Charlie battle, fared far worse than those who were able to get out of Vietnam when Saigon fell. He'd fought the final battles of the war as the 3rd Airborne Brigade Fire Support Officer, coordinating the artillery fire planning for the brigade. In the last days, he commanded an artillery unit to be set up in Cộng Hòa stadium, close to downtown Saigon. He missed the evacuations on April 29 and 30. He stood by dutifully, ready to fire his guns until word finally reached him that South Vietnam had surrendered. He went home to await his fate.

The new government ordered all former ARVN soldiers to register within three days. Lập did so. A month later, the government ordered him to report for ten days of reeducation training. He did so. He spent the next six years in communist Vietnam's notorious reeducation camps.

In fact, those camps were crudely fashioned prisons, often in remote jungle areas of the country. Lập's "educators" beat, interrogated, and indoctrinated him. He suffered long hours at forced labor to the point of exhaustion. When sick and vulnerable, they forced him to write confessions of war crimes. They held him inside a compound surrounded by a wall made of logs and bamboo. There, he slept in one of several small huts, crammed with other detainees.

After his confinement, his wife, Trọng, moved back to her hometown of Long Khánh, forty-five miles east of Saigon. She struggled to survive, raising three young daughters without a father. All the while, she suffered discrimination from local communist authorities as the wife of an officer in the defeated South Vietnamese army. In a good year, she got permission to visit Lập once every three months, bringing some food and a bit of medicine. That was in a good year. Most often, the time between visits exceeded that interval by a lot. Meanwhile, men got sick, and many died. Lập faced death again and again, but somehow survived.[6]

The government released Lập in 1981. He went home and immediately began exploring ways he could escape. He found no good options and struggled over the years that followed. He worked as a field hand while Trọng traded goods at the local market, making what money she could. He had to report to the local police once a week and account for his activities. He couldn't travel, not even to visit his mother in Saigon, without getting government permission. The family faced tough, and sometimes desperate, times. Still, hoping for a better life ahead, Trọng gave birth to a son in 1986.

Finally, when the United States and the Socialist Republic of Vietnam initiated the jointly agreed Humanitarian Operation (HO) program in 1989, Lập applied. The program offered resettlement in the United States to former reeducation inmates. Four years later, in December 1993, he moved his family to Southern California. Just over a year later, Trọng delivered their fifth child, a daughter they named Jane, a natural-born U.S. citizen.

Mr. Lap Nguyen studied for six years at Santa Anna College and Golden West College while working as a welder and automotive repair technician. He went on to work as a reporter for local Vietnamese-language media. In 2003, he moved his family to Dallas, Texas, for a similar press opportunity there. All five of his children attended college in the United States, earned their bachelor degrees, and embarked on successful careers in the greater Dallas area. Lap now lives happily in retirement with his wife and enjoys time with his children and grandchildren when he is not turning in an occasional story as a part-time reporter. Life is good but for the ache in his heart for the Vietnam that he once knew and defended so bravely.

REUNION

Ever since the collapse of South Vietnam, John Duffy wondered what had happened to Me and his family. He'd asked, but always hit dead-ends. He came to assume that Me had probably died in one of the final battles of the war, or that he'd been captured and executed by the communists after their victory.

On occasion, John would relate the incredible story of the fight on Charlie Hill. He'd speak of his special bond with a Vietnamese paratroop officer named Me. He told the story to a friend living in the nearby town of Los Gatos, California. In early 1981, that friend shared the account with a Vietnamese shop owner in town.

"Unbelievable!" she exclaimed. "Me is alive! He was my neighbor. His family lived in my same apartment complex in San Jose. I know where he is now."

The next day, John Duffy showed up at Me's home with a bottle of Martell VSOP cognac. The moment went beyond words as they opened their arms and embraced. Broad smiles broke through the tears. Their friendship has remained steadfast ever since, and their families have grown close. Their numbers increased after Me told Duffy that Hai Doan also lived in San Jose. The trio continue to get together frequently, and always on the Fourth of July. Three thankful Americans, bound as brothers by the specters of war, sharing a gratitude and love of life that few will ever know.

APPENDIX 1

Lessons Learned

LESSONS FROM CHARLIE

1. Vietnamese soldiers, properly trained and competently led, were effective fighters. ARVN Marines and Rangers were among the best in the world, and the ARVN airborne ranked squarely with the best of the best.

2. B-52 strikes provided extraordinary close air support, as close as three hundred meters to friendly forces.

3. U.S. advisors contributed most effectively in battle by delivering accurate, timely, and devastating fire support (American tactical air, helicopter gunships, and artillery)—not by telling experienced combat leaders how to fight.

4. Friendly artillery must be able to match the range of the opposing enemy artillery.

5. Airborne and other elite light forces should be used in offensive operations, not digging in and defending a fixed piece of terrain.

6. Effective communications are essential.

APPENDIX 2

Key Personnel

11TH AIRBORNE BATTALION

Position	Rank/Name	Nickname	Call Sign
Commander	LTC Nguyễn Đình Bảo	Grey Tiger/ *Anh Năm*	008
U.S. Senior Advisor	MAJ John Duffy	Đỗ Phủ (Du Fu)	Dusty Cyanide
Executive Officer	MAJ Lê Văn Mễ	Mê Linh	007
S-3, Operations	CPT Đoàn Phương Hải	Hải Khều	006
Surgeon	CPT Tô Phạm Liệu	Doc	
HQ Company CO	CPT Nguyễn Tấn Nho		405
111 Company CO	1LT Nguyễn Văn Thinh		401
112 Company CO	CPT Hoàng Ngọc Hùng	Skinny Hùng	402
113 Company CO	CPT Phạm Đức Hùng	Big Hùng	403
114 Company CO	1LT Phan Cảnh Cho		404
Forward Observer	1LT Nguyễn Văn Lập		314

2ND AIRBORNE BRIGADE

Position	Rank/Name	Call Sign
Commander	COL Trần Quốc Lịch	
U.S. Senior Advisor	MAJ Peter Kama	Cellar 51
Deputy U.S. Advisor	1LT Terry Griswold	Cellar 55

II CORPS

Position	Rank/Name	Call Sign
Commander	GEN Ngô Dzu	
U.S. Senior Advisor	Mr. John Paul Vann	Rogue's Gallery
Deputy U.S. Senior Advisor/ Commander U.S. Forces	BG George Wear	

GEN: General
BG: Brigadier General
COL: Colonel
LTC: Lieutenant Colonel
MAJ: Major
CPT: Captain
1LT: First Lieutenant

Historical Note: The ARVN Airborne

The ARVN Airborne (*Mũ đỏ*)

In the commentary on the performance of Vietnam's military during the war, almost nothing is heard of the forgotten South Vietnamese airborne. The army of South Vietnam generally receives mixed reviews. Many cite units that performed badly under poor and corrupt leadership. Only a few give accolades to units that conducted themselves well and honorably. However, there can be no question that the Republic of Vietnam's airborne units fought aggressively, with courage and tenacity, throughout the war, and that they easily ranked among the world's finest combat forces.[1]

The story of the 11th Airborne Battalion's fight on Charlie Hill sits within that larger context of South Vietnam's proud paratroop heritage. The 11th was but one of many battalions that made up the ARVN Airborne Division, the country's strategic reserve, the most elite force in the nation. Every paratrooper volunteered, and each was filled with a sense of service beyond self, of an overwhelming pride, of being one in a brotherhood devoted to the ideal of "death before dishonor." That conviction had come to them from France. Their heritage, their comradeship, their fighting spirit—all drew directly from the French, from France's airborne units dispatched to Vietnam after the Second World War.[2]

During the war, Japanese forces occupied French Indochina, which included the modern states of Laos, Cambodia, and Vietnam. With the defeat of Japan and its ouster from the region at the end of the war, France sought to regain its Southeast Asian colony. Their immediate challenge was to wrest control from Hồ Chí Minh and his Việt Minh fighters who had proclaimed Vietnamese independence as the "Democratic Republic of Vietnam" under their governance. France deployed military forces in late 1945 and early 1946 to seize the reins of government and to quash the growing communist insurgency that followed. In 1946, the introduction of two French airborne battalions gave them increased flexibility. Other parachute battalions would follow. French commanders soon decided that adding indigenous paratroopers to those battalions would further enhance that mobile strike capability. By 1947, the French began training select Vietnamese candidates to form the core of an indigenous parachute force to augment their own.[3]

Early graduates of the program formed the 1st Indochinese Parachute Company (*Compagnie Indochinoise Parachutiste—CIP*). On January 1, 1948, the company joined the French airborne command as an operational unit, adopting the distinctive French paratroop uniforms and red berets. Other Vietnamese parachute companies emerged in the months that followed. The French Foreign Legion created two companies (*Compagnie Indochinoise Parachutiste Légion Étrangère—CIPLE*). In every case, however, the companies had French officers and noncommissioned officers as cadre. They led the units and served as role models for their Vietnamese understudies. The companies soon saw action, fighting as integral parts of French parachute battalions. On August 13, 1948, a Vietnamese airborne company made the first combat parachute jump to conduct a strike operation. Ultimately, fourteen Vietnamese airborne companies formed.[4]

Vietnam's fledgling airborne force fought with valor throughout the remaining years of French control, often taking heavy casualties, always demonstrating magnificent courage. In 1949, the French created a "State of Vietnam" that was to join the French Union as an "associated state," but still under tight French control. In fashioning the state, they began to stand up a Vietnamese National Army in 1951. As part of that effort, they formed the 1st Vietnamese Parachute Battalion (*Tiểu Đoàn Nhảy Dù 1*). By 1953, Vietnam boasted four battalions. Like the companies, French officers and NCOs filled the top positions—that is, until the activation of another battalion in 1954. That battalion was led by the very best, specially selected, Vietnamese paratroop leaders. Vietnamese parachute units, of various size, joined in eighty-six combat jumps from 1948 to 1954.[5]

The Vietnamese airborne played an important role in the decisive battle of Điện Biên Phủ. The battle resulted in the resounding defeat of French forces and led directly to their withdrawal from Vietnam. Nonetheless, the Vietnamese airborne fought bravely and cemented its reputation as the premier force in the land. The 5th Vietnamese Parachute Battalion jumped into the valley of Điện Biên Phủ on November 22, 1953, as part of Operation Castor, the largest airborne drop since World War II. The 5th joined five French parachute battalions that had parachuted in over the previous two days. Each of those had its own indigenous Vietnamese parachute company. The force pushed through a series of hard-fought engagements to secure an airfield and surrounding positions for what would become a major French military base.[6]

With their mission complete, the 5th Vietnamese Parachute Battalion was flown out just after Christmas, only to return when the communist strangle hold on Điện Biên Phủ threatened the annihilation of the defending garrison. At 2:45 p.m. on March 14, 1954, the 5th Battalion jumped back in from only 600 feet to minimize exposure to the intense enemy fire. They immediately joined the fight. The battalion fought courageously for weeks but was destroyed in the meatgrinder of the final days as the communist Việt Minh overran the defenders and brought the battle to an end on May 7, 1954. The six Vietnamese airborne companies fighting in the French parachute battalions perished, as well.[7]

In their sacrifice at Điện Biên Phủ and the years of hard-fought battles leading up to it, Vietnamese paratroopers emerged as legendary warriors, their courage and tenacity in battle extolled across the land. After the battle, and with peace negotiations underway in Geneva, Switzerland, the few airborne survivors of the battle moved to Saigon, where they resurrected the 5th Vietnamese Parachute Battalion. The remaining Vietnamese parachute battalions joined them to form a Vietnamese Airborne Group, prepared to serve the nation—whatever that soon-to-be independent country might become.[8]

The 1954 Geneva Conference had opened in Switzerland in April to address the conflicts in Korea and Indochina. Discussions turned to Vietnam on May 8, the day after the battle at Điện Biên Phủ ended. The talks concluded with the 1954 Geneva Accords announced on July 21. One of the provisions divided Vietnam at its waist, along the 17th parallel. The agreement granted Ho Chi Minh and his communist Việt Minh dominance of the north, and the existing State of Vietnam, control of the south. Unification elections were to be held in two years. Those never happened. [9]

The communists again proclaimed the Democratic Republic of Vietnam, this time just in the northern half. In the south, the rump State of Vietnam became the Republic of Vietnam. Now there were two Vietnams: communist North Vietnam, and the imperfectly democratic South Vietnam. Hundreds of thousands of refugees fled the North, seeking freedom in the South, where a strongly anticommunist government took hold. The Vietnamese National Army became the Army of the Republic of Vietnam, the ARVN. In 1959, the Vietnamese Airborne Group became the ARVN Airborne Brigade, which expanded to become the Airborne Division on December 1, 1965. The United States, already deeply involved even before the departure of France, began bombing North Vietnam after two American destroyers were reportedly attacked in the Tonkin Gulf in early August 1964. U.S. Marines landed ashore at Da Nang in the South on March 8, 1965. American forces plunged into an escalating war in Vietnam. [10]

The Airborne Division consisted of eight airborne infantry battalions, three airborne artillery battalions, and three reconnaissance companies organized under three brigade headquarters. The 11th Airborne Battalion stood up on December 1, 1967, bringing the division total to nine airborne infantry battalions. The division was also home to airborne support, signal, medical, and engineer battalions, as well as the Airborne Training Center at Tân Sơn Nhứt Airbase in Saigon. The habitual battalion alignments are:

REPUBLIC OF VIETNAM AIRBORNE DIVISION[11]			
1st Airborne Brigade	2nd Airborne Brigade	3rd Airborne Brigade	Division Troops
1st Airborne Battalion	5th Airborne Battalion	2nd Airborne Battalion	ABN Signal Battalion*
8th Airborne Battalion	7th Airborne Battalion	3rd Airborne Battalion	ABN Support Battalion*
9th Airborne Battalion	11th Airborne Battalion	6th Airborne Battalion	ABN Medical Battalion*
1st ABN Artillery Bn	2nd ABN Artillery Bn	3rd ABN Artillery Bn	ABN Engineer Battalion*
1st ABN Recon Company	2nd ABN Recon Company	3rd ABN Recon Company	ABN Training Center

Routinely placed one company under the operational control of each of the brigades.

The all-volunteer Airborne Division fought gallantly throughout what became known as the "Second Indochina War," America's "Vietnam War." Much of that heroism is captured in the accounts of John Duffy, Lê Văn Mễ, and others described in this book. The airborne continued to make combat jumps. Eight of the Division's nine airborne battalions received the coveted U.S. Presidential Unit Citation, as did all three of the airborne brigades. The Presidential Unit Citation is awarded by the president of the United States to a select few American units for extraordinary heroism in combat, and even more infrequently to exceptional units from allied nations.[12]

The ARVN airborne was key in all major combat operations through the end of the war, including the 1968 Tet Offensive, the 1970 Cambodia Campaign, Operation Lam Sơn 719, and the three decisive battles of the 1972 Easter Offensive: An Lộc, Kontum, and Quảng Trị. They fought nobly in the final days as South Vietnam collapsed in 1975, their sacrificial blood staining the land and draining the life from their formations. Some paratroop battalions, down to 20 percent, still stood fast, making last stands against the crushing North Vietnamese onslaught. The 11th Airborne Battalion fought as part of the 2nd Airborne Brigade defending Phan Rang, 160 miles up the coast from Saigon. They were led by Major Nguyễn Văn Thành, who had replaced Lê Văn Mễ as commander. The battalion was savagely attacked on April 17. They suffered heavy casualties, and Major Thành was captured. Few survived, and fewer still were able to evade capture themselves while making the arduous trek back to Red Hat Hill. There, they worked diligently to reconstitute the battalion in the final days of the war.[13]*

At the end of it all, the remnants of the 1st Airborne Brigade joined the 18th ARVN Infantry Division and others at Xuân Lộc for the final major battle of the Vietnam War—less than fifty miles northeast of Saigon. The defenders fought one of the most determined, heroic engagements of the war, but were crushed in the end by overwhelming force. When the town fell on April 21, airborne forces battled to delay the NVA, allowing other surviving ARVN soldiers to withdraw toward Saigon and Vũng Tàu. Scattered skirmishes continued until Saigon fell to the communists a little over a week later, on April 30, 1975. It was over.[14]

Barry McCaffrey is a retired four-star general who led an army division in the 1991 Gulf War, commanded U.S. Southern Command in Panama, and later served as the director of the Office of National Drug Control Policy, the "Drug Czar" of the United States. He is a noted national security analyst and appears frequently on NBC News. In 1966 and 1967, he was a young paratroop lieutenant in Vietnam, part of Advisory Team 162, serving as an assistant battalion advisor in the South Vietnamese Airborne Division. Here is his take, looking back from 2017:

> *The Vietnamese Airborne forces served throughout the Vietnam Conflict as the National Strategic Reserve. By 1967, at peak strength,*

---

*The Joint General Staff had stood up a fourth airborne brigade in early 1975, consisting of the newly created 12th, 14th, and 15th Battalions. Experienced cadre transferred to the battalions from other units while new recruits filled the ranks. The brigade fought defensive battles around Saigon and neighboring Long Bình and Bien Hoa. A fifth airborne brigade was created on paper in the waning days. It never became anything more than that.

more than 13,000 paratroopers were formed into nine [airborne] infantry battalions, three artillery battalions, and division troops. Battalion combat teams staged by parachute assault or helicopter insertion from Tan Son Nhut Airbase in Saigon as reinforcements to the major battles of the war. Throughout the endless war, the parachute forces were constantly committed to fight wherever the action was most dangerous.

The long years of bloodshed took their steady toll on these brave soldiers. In the final desperate struggles of 1975, the Airborne Division was expended and bled to death in the horrific battles of Phuoc Tuy Province in the Central Highlands and Xuan Loc. These courageous Vietnamese airborne soldiers fought to the very end. Their spirit and tradition lived on long after the war. For years after the downfall of the Saigon government, refugees spoke of surviving groups of ARVN paratroopers fighting an unsupported guerilla war in the mountainous jungles of the Central Highlands.

The bravery of the Vietnamese Airborne soldiers is also a reflection of the matching courage and professionalism of US Advisory Team 162 (ABN) and the Red Hat USAF forward air controllers who served with their Vietnamese counterparts as liaison officers, fire support coordinators, trainers, friends, and occasionally as advisors.

These American Red Hat advisors were an elite group selected from the many US airborne sergeants and officers who volunteered to serve with the Vietnamese Airborne Division. Most of the advisors were young but experienced American sergeants and captains with four extra months of training in the Vietnamese language and the Ft. Bragg MATA [Military Advisor Training Academy] course. They were a bit different from other American paratroopers—a touch of the romantic, and ear for the soldier poetry of Rudyard Kipling, and a sense of adventure which led them to volunteer to live and fight with a foreign unit of shock troops. Many of these American advisor volunteers paid with their lives. The casualty rates among these Red Hat Co Van My [American advisors] were enormous in numbers of killed and maimed. Many of those who survived would go on to prominent positions in the American Army. BG Herb

Lloyd, a legend of the Vietnam War; COL Jack Jacobs (Medal of Honor), MG Mike Davison, MG John Herrling, MG Joe Kinzer, MG Guy Meloy, MG Leroy Suddath, MG Bern Loeffki, BG John LeMoyne, BG Arvid West, General Jim Lindsay, who retired as the Special Operations Command Commander; and General Norman Schwarzkopf, the US commander in Desert Storm, are examples of the many dedicated and courageous advisors who served with the Vietnamese [airborne units].[15]

Author's Note

THIS IS THE STORY OF ONE OF THE GREATEST BATTLES OF THE VIETnam War and those brave warriors who fought there. It is a true story based on investigation into original source documents and a myriad of other reference materials, as well as my own experience flying a Cobra attack helicopter in support of the 11th Airborne Battalion on the final day of the fight. The research also entailed many hours of interviews with participants, extending over a period of years. The dialogue had to be reconstructed. This was done according to the best recollections of those involved. It is faithful to the conversations that actually took place. The story is as factual and true to the events as possible. Even so, there are surely some errors that may be found. For those, I apologize and can only promise that I will accept all criticism in the spirit of correcting those mistakes in any future editions of this book that might be published.

I am grateful to John Duffy, Me Van Le, and Hai Phuong Doan for sharing the details of their lives and the fight at Firebase Charlie. I spent hours reading and rereading John Duffy's poetry that captures the emotion of the battle so well. His captivating verses are presented online and are a must for anyone truly wanting to feel this battle in their hearts (www.epoetryworld.com).

I must also express my appreciation to Tom McKenna and Jack Heslin for setting the larger historical context for the Battle of Firebase Charlie—Tom in his book *Kontum: The Battle to Save South Vietnam*, and Jack for his marvelous website, which presents a collection of impressive firsthand accounts of the fights that made up the larger, encompassing Battle of Kontum (www.thebattleofkontum.com).

Glossary

AAA. Antiaircraft artillery. See *Weapons*.

Arc Light. B-52 strike normally consisting of three of the heavy bombers.

ARVN. Army of the Republic of Vietnam (South Vietnamese Army).

C-ration. A small box of canned food items. The standard army ration at the time.

Democratic Republic of Vietnam. See *DRV*.

DMZ. Demilitarized Zone. The area within five kilometers either side of a line roughly approximating the 17th Parallel, dividing North and South Vietnam.

DRV. Democratic Republic of Vietnam. Communist North Vietnam.

DZ. Drop zone for parachute drops of personnel, equipment, or supplies.

FAC. Forward Air Controller.

Firebase. A position, stripped of vegetation, fortified with trenches, bunkers, coiled razor wire, and land mines, defended by a force ranging from platoon to battalion that often conduct combat operations outside the firebase perimeter. Artillery units often positioned their cannons on firebases.

FO. Forward Observer. Artillery officer who emplaces artillery strikes and naval gunfire in support of ground combat operations. Normally assigned with companies and battalions.

LRP Rations. Long-Range Patrol rations. Freeze-dried meals weighing only eleven ounces.

LZ. Helicopter landing zone.

MACV-SOG. Military Assistance Command Vietnam, Studies and Observation Group. The MACV special operations command that ran highly classified, covert special operations across the borders into Laos and Cambodia.

Military aircraft:

- A-1E, "Skyraider." Korean War era, single-engine, propeller driving attack airplane operated by both U.S. and Republic of Vietnam Air Forces.
- A-37, "Dragonfly." Small jet-powered attack airplane used by the Republic of Vietnam Air Force.
- AC-47, "Spooky" ("Puff the Magic Dragon"). C-47 (DC-3) propeller-driven cargo airplane converted into a gunship. Developed early in the war by the United States and later operated by the Republic of Vietnam Air Force.
- AC-130, "Spectre." U.S. Air Force four-engine, turboprop, cargo aircraft converted into a massive, capable gunship.
- AH-1G, "Cobra." U.S. Army attack helicopter.
- B-52. Boeing Stratofortress heavy bomber, capable of carrying loads of up to 108 500- and 750-pound bombs.
- F-4, "Phantom." U.S. Air Force, Navy, and Marine all-purpose jet fighter-bomber. Used in both air-to-air combat and ground-attack missions.
- H-3. Twin-engine, all-weather helicopter used by the U.S. Air Force for special operations insertions and search and rescue.
- HH-53. A more capable follow-on to the H-3. Known famously as the "Jolly Green Giant."
- Huey (see UH-1).

- L-19/O-1 "Bird Dog." Light, single-engine, propeller-driven, two-seat observation airplane.
- O-2, "Skymaster." Twin-engine, push-pull, propeller-driven, observation airplane used by U.S. Air Force forward air controllers.
- OV-10, "Bronco." Twin turbo-prop, two-seat observation airplane used by U.S. Air Force forward air controllers.
- Spectre (see AC-130).
- UH-1, "Huey." U.S. and the Republic of Vietnam Air Force utility helicopter used for troop movement and resupply. Capacity up to twelve soldiers or over 3,000 pounds of cargo. The workhorse helicopter of the Vietnam War.

Military formations:

- Squad. Eight to twelve men led by a sergeant.
- Platoon. Twenty to forty men led by a lieutenant and/or platoon sergeant.
- Company. Seventy to one hundred men led by a captain.
- Battalion. Four hundred to seven hundred men led by a lieutenant colonel.
- Brigade/Regiment. Two to five battalions led by a colonel.
- Division. Multiple brigades/regiments with artillery, engineer, and logistical support (sometimes armor). Eight thousand to twelve thousand men led by a major general.
- Corps. Several combat divisions, along with supporting artillery, engineer, intelligence, and logistics commands, often with separate combat brigades and regiments also assigned. In Vietnam, the four army corps were located in fixed areas of geographic responsibility.

NLF. National Liberation Front. The communist political organization established by North Vietnam inside South Vietnam that conducted Viet Cong military and terror operations.

NVA. North Vietnamese Army.

P-38. Small, keychain-sized, military can opener.

PAVN. Peoples' Army of Vietnam (North Vietnam). Synonymous with NVA.

Poncho liner. A lightweight military blanket made of quilted nylon with a polyester fill.

Republic of Vietnam. America's ally, South Vietnam.

RT. Reconnaissance Team, or Recon Team associated with MACV-SOG.

RTO. Radio-Telephone Operator.

Small Arms. Smaller-caliber rifles and pistols carried by individuals.

Tri-Border. The region where the borders of South Vietnam, Laos, and Cambodia come together.

VC. Việt Cộng, which translates to Vietnamese Communist. The term refers to the irregular guerrilla forces drawn from the local population inside South Vietnam, often led by cadre from North Vietnam. However, many often used the term *VC* indiscriminately to refer to regular North Vietnamese Army forces as well as the southern-based guerrillas.

VNAF. Vietnamese Air Force (South Vietnam's air force).

Weapons.

- South Vietnam.
  - Armor.
    - APC. Armored Personnel Carrier. Lightly armored tracked vehicle capable of carrying up to eleven soldiers.
    - M-41. Korean War era American light tank with a 76mm main gun.
    - M-48. American main battle tank with a 90mm main gun.

- Artillery and Mortars.

  - 60mm Mortar. Lightweight, high-firing angle weapon with a range of 3,800 yards. Crew able to fire up to twenty rounds per minute. Normally deployed at company level.

  - 81mm Mortar. Medium-weight, high-firing angle weapon with a range of 6,500 yards. Normally in a battalion weapons platoon.

  - 105mm Howitzer. Fires a 33-pound high-explosive projectile up to seven miles.

  - 155mm Howitzer. Fires a 100-pound high-explosive projectile up to nine miles.

- Claymore mine. Directional, command-detonated, antipersonnel mine with an effective and devastating firing range of fifty meters.

- CAR-15. Colt Automatic Rifle, Model number 15. MACV-SOG preferred the short-barreled "Commando" carbine version of the weapon. Fires 5.56mm x 45mm ammunition. 7.5 pounds.

- "Forty-five." A .45-caliber semiautomatic pistol. Carried principally by officers and tank crewmen.

- LAW. Light Antitank Weapon. 66mm, shoulder-fired, antitank rocket-propelled grenade with a range of 220 yards.

- M-1 "Garand" Rifle. 7.62mm x 63mm (30.06-caliber) semiautomatic rifle. World War II–era rifle that served as the primary individual weapon of South Vietnamese forces in the early years of American involvement in the war. 11.6 pounds

- M-16 Rifle. 5.56mm x 45mm automatic rifle. U.S. infantry weapon beginning in 1965. Issued to the South Vietnamese airborne starting in 1967, then the ARVN infantry in following years. 7.5 pounds.

- M-60 Machine Gun. 7.62mm lightweight machine gun used by both the U.S. forces and the Army of the Republic of Vietnam.

- ○ M-79. Handheld 40mm grenade launcher.
- ○ Recoilless Rifle. 90mm, shoulder-fired, antitank/antipersonnel weapon, firing a projectile while allowing propellant gases to escape from the rear, thus eliminating any recoil.
- North Vietnam
  - ○ AK-47. The principal individual weapon of the North Vietnamese Army. 7.62mm x 39mm automatic rifle manufactured by the Soviet Union and China.
  - ○ AAA, or Triple A. Antiaircraft artillery. Any of the various antiaircraft weapons ranging from the .51-caliber antiaircraft machine gun through the 14.5mm double- and four-barreled guns, to the 23mm twin-barreled and 37mm guns used inside the boundaries of South Vietnam.
  - ○ Armor.
    - ▪ PT-76. Soviet-manufactured amphibious light tank with a 76.2mm main gun.
    - ▪ T-54. Soviet-manufactured main battle tank with a 100mm main gun.
  - ○ Artillery and mortars.
    - ▪ Mortars. Various caliber, short-range, high-firing angle weapons from 60mm through 107mm.
    - ▪ 122mm rocket. Three- to seven-kilometer-range rocket with devastating high-explosive fragmentation warhead. Utilized the Soviet-built single-round "Grad" launcher, though often fired less accurately from bamboo-launching apparatus crafted on sight.
    - ▪ 130mm gun. Soviet-manufactured, vehicle-towed field gun, firing a 73-pound projectile as far as seventeen miles, significantly farther than any South Vietnamese artillery.
  - ○ B-40. A shoulder-fired, 40mm, rocket-propelled grenade with a range out to 200 yards.

○ Recoilless Rifle. A weapon that fires a projectile while allowing propellant gases to escape from the rear of the weapon, thus reducing or eliminating recoil. The NVA utilized 57mm, 73mm, and 75mm recoilless rifles with devastating effect. Most often crewed by two or more soldiers and fired on a machine gun mount, achieving a range of several hundred yards.

Notes

Chapter 2

1. Ben Kiernan, *Viet Nam: A History from the Earliest Times to the Present* (New York: Oxford University Press, 2017), 194–97, 291.
2. Hugh Connelly, "The First Operation Hickory (Operation Hickory—Belt Tight—Beau Charger—Lam Son 54)." Summarized from source materials. 1967. Accessed at: http://www.amtrac.org/pdf_files/1atbn/OpHick01.pdf, 6 June 2018; 1st Battalion, 4th Marines, "Operation Lam Son 54." Accessed at: http://1stbn4thmarines.net/operations/history-folder/lam_son_54.htm, 6 June 2018.
3. James Willbanks, *The Tet Offensive: A Concise History* (New York: Columbia University Press, 2006), 15–18.
4. Ibid., 30.
5. Ibid., 43–52.

Chapter 3

1. For more on these two crises, see Alex von Tunzelann, *Blood & Sand: Suez, Hungary, and Sixteen Days of Crisis That Changed the World* (New York: Simon & Schuster, 2001).
2. See, for example, *New York Times*, August 4 and 5, 1964 (New York: Times Publishing), 1. Accessed at: https://timesmachine.nytimes.com/timesmachine/1964/08/05/issue.html, 28 January 2021.
3. For more on Rudolf Hess and Spandau prison, see Eugene K. Bird, *Loneliest Man in the World* (London: Martin Secker and Warburg, 1974).

Chapter 4

1. John Prados and Ray W. Stubbe, *Valley of Decision: The Siege of Khe Sanh* (New York: Houghton Mifflin, 1991), 55, 73–75.
2. Ibid., 94–98.
3. For an understanding of the Phoenix Program, see Mark Moyar, *Phoenix and the Birds of Prey: The CIA's Secret Campaign to Destroy the Viet Cong* (Annapolis, MD: Naval Institute Press, 1997).
4. John L. Plaster, *SOG: The Secret Wars of America's Commandos in Vietnam* (New York: Simon & Schuster, 1997), provides a full description of MACV-SOG and the secret cross-border operations.

CHAPTER 5

1. Gordon L. Rottman, *Khe Sanh 1967–1968: Marines battle for Vietnam's vital hilltop base* (New York: Osprey Publishing, 2005), 85–89. Jack Shulimson et al., *U.S. Marines in Vietnam: The Defining Year 1968* (Washington, D.C.: Headquarters U.S. Marine Corps, 1997), 283–90.

2. Ibid. For details of the fight at Lang Vei, see William R. Phillips, *Night of the Silver Stars: The Battle of Lang Vei* (Annapolis, MD: Naval Institute Press, 1997).

3. David Burns Sigler, *Vietnam Battle Chronology: U.S. Army and Marine Corps Combat Operations, 1965–1973* (Jefferson, NC: McFarland & Company, 1992), 72. Spencer Tucker, ed., *Encyclopedia of the Vietnam War: A Political, Social, and Military History*, Vol. 1 (Santa Barbara, CA: ABC-CLIO, 1998), 340. Rottman, 88.

4. Willard Pearson, *The War in the Northern Provinces 1966–1968* (Washington, D.C.: Department of the Army, 1991), 89–92.

5. Henry Kissinger, *Ending the Vietnam War: A History of America's Involvement in and Extraction from the Vietnam War* (New York: Simon &Schuster, 2003), 81–82. Richard Nixon, *First Annual Report to the Congress on United States Foreign Policy for the 1970s*, February 18, 1970, 68–76.

6. "President Nixon's Speech on Cambodia," delivered on national television on April 30, 1970.

7. Ibid. John M. Shaw, *The Cambodian Campaign: The 1970 Offensive and the Vietnam War* (Lawrence, KS: University of Kansas Press, 2005), 58–60, 158.

8. Shaw, 63–79.

9. Ibid., 158, 162.

10. James W. Willbanks, *A Raid Too Far: Operation Lam Son 719 and Vietnamization in Laos* (College Station: Texas A&M University Press, 2014), 27, 28–29, 35.

11. Ibid., 36–51.

12. Ibid., 73–74, 93, 96, 118–19.

13. Phan Nhật Nam, *A Vietnam War Epilogue: Phan Nhat Nam's Voice as a Soldier* (Westminster, CA: Thu Vien Viet Nam Toan Cau Publishing, 2013), 57–60.

CHAPTER 6

1. "Recommendation for awarding the Valorous Unit Award to the Vietnamese Airborne Division and the Airborne Division Assistance Team for actions during the period September 28–November 8, 1971," Long Bình, Republic of Vietnam, July 8, 1972; Vietnam Service Awards, Record Group 472-VNA -MACV, Box 29; National Archives Building, Washington, DC.

2. Ibid. Military Assistance Command, Vietnam (MACV) General Order #532, 19 February 1972.

3. Ha Mai Viet, *Steel and Blood: South Vietnamese Armor and the War for Southeast Asia* (Annapolis, MD: Naval Institute Press, 2008), 56–67.

4. For a summary of intelligence reporting on the enemy buildup, see U.S. Military Assistance Command, Vietnam (MACV), *1971 Command History,* Volume II (April 25, 1972) C1-C27, and *Command History, January 1972–March 1973*, Volume II (July 15, 1973) J1, K1.

CHAPTER 7

1. *MACV Command History, 1972–1973*, Volume II, Annex K, "Kontum: The NVA Buildup" (Saigon: Military Assistance Command, Vietnam, 15 July 1973), K2-K4. Peter A. Liebchen, "Kontum: Battle for the Central Highlands, 30 March–10 June 1972," *Project CHECO Reports* (Hickam AFB, HI: Headquarters, U.S. Pacific Air Force, October 1972), 1–6. Lynn Carlson, interview by author, Scottsdale, AZ, 29 April 2019.
2. *MACV Command History*, op. cit.
3. Ibid.
4. Byron E. Hukee, *USAF and VNAF A-1 Skyraider Units of the Vietnam War* (Oxford, UK: Osprey, 2013), 8–12.
5. For more information on these fascinating tribal minorities, see Gerald Cannon Hickey, *Sons of the Mountains* and *Free in the Forest* (New Haven, CT: Yale University Press, 1982), Oscar Salemink, *The Ethnography of Vietnam's Central Highlanders* (Honolulu: University of Hawaii Press, 2003), and Howard Sochurek, "Viet Nam's Montagnards: Caught in the Jaws of a War," *National Geographic*, 133, no. 4 (April 1968), 443–87.

CHAPTER 8

1. Noted at the time by Major Duffy and later written down. Included on John Duffy's website, *E-Poetry World* at www.epoetryworld.com.
2. For more on Captain James Butler and the action he saw with RT Python, see John Duffy's poem, "Captain Butler's Flag" at *E-Poetry World* and Mike Perry's "When Recon Team Python Ruled the Valley of Death," 22 June 2014, *Special Operations* website: https://specialoperations.com/29027/recon-team-python-ruled-valley-death/.

CHAPTER 9

1. Lynn Carlson interview. Dan Jones interview. Central Intelligence Agency declassified "Intelligence Memorandum," 4 April 1972 (LOC-HAK-559-30-13-4), 2–3.
2. Ibid. For a detailed account of this fight, see Jack Heslin, "Firebase Delta," *The Battle of Kontum* website: https://www.thebattleofkontum.com/memories/54.html.
3. Ibid.
4. The text of this letter can be found on John Duffy's website, *E-Poetry World*, at www.epoetryworld.com.
5. See Bernard B. Fall, *Hell in a Very Small Place: The Siege of Dien Bien Phu* (New York: Harper & Row, 1967).
6. Noted at the time by Major Duffy and later written down. Included on *E-Poetry World* at www.epoetryworld.com.

CHAPTER 10

1. For additional details about the southern prong of the offensive, see James H. Willbanks, *The Battle of An Loc* (Bloomington: Indiana University Press, 2005).

Chapter 11

1. Đặng Vũ Hiệp, *Ký ức tây Nguyên* (*Highland Memories*) (Hanoi: People's Army Press, 2012), 238, 237–39.
2. This tragic battle is presented in detail by Bernard B. Fall in his book, *Street Without Joy* (Mechanicsburg, PA: Stackpole Books, 1964). See also Kirk A. Luedeke, "Death on the Highway: The Destruction of Groupement Mobile 100," *Armor Magazine* (January–February 2001), 22–29.
3. Some credit the 1968 Tết Offensive as the largest enemy campaign of the war. This was not so. The 1972 Easter Offensive was much larger in scope and scale. Thomas P. McKenna notes in his book, *Kontum: The Battle to Save South Vietnam* (Lexington: University Press of Kentucky, 2011), "Unlike the Communist attacks during Tet 1968, an uprising in which the lightly armed VC led the charge, for the Ester Offensive of early 1972 the North Vietnamese had 15 combat divisions, including 2 VC divisions manned mainly by North Vietnamese. They would leave only one division in North Vietnam to defend the North and to serve as a reserve. The other 14 divisions would be committed outside the country. Two were already in Laos and Cambodia, and the other 12 divisions totaling 150,000 men were available to attack South Vietnam. This would be the largest military offensive and across-the-border invasion anywhere in the world since the fall of 1950, when the Communist Chinese People's Liberation Army attacked across the Yalu River into South Korea" (p. 60). See also John G. Heslin's website, *The Battle of Kontum*, http://www.thebattleofkontum.com.

Chapter 12

1. Đặng Vũ Hiệp. *Ký ức tây Nguyên* (*Highland Memories*) (Hanoi: People's Army Press, 2012), 237.
2. Remembered verbatim by John Duffy and included as the poem "The Commander's Burial," http://www.epoetryworld.com.
3. Phan Nhat Nam, *A Vietnam War Epilogue* (Westminster, CA: Thu Vien Viet Nam Toan Cau Publishing, 2013), 39–42.
4. Hiệp, 238. Nguyễn Trọng Luân, "Trận Đồi Charlie" ("The Battle of Charlie), http://chientruongvietnam.com/2018/08/02/tham-lai-cao-diem-1015-doi-sac-ly-tran-doi-charlie/, August 2, 2018.
5. Norman Birzer and Peter Mersky, *US Navy A-7 Corsair II Units in the Vietnam War* (Oxford, UK: Osprey Publishing, 2004), 83.
6. Hiệp, 237–38. Luân, op. cit.

Chapter 14

1. Informed by the accounts of Phan Nhat Nam in his book, *The Red Flames of Summer* (Do Vu Trading Corporation, 2015). The book is based on the author's interviews with survivors immediately following the Battle of Firebase Charlie.
2. Ibid.
3. Three and a half weeks later, Lieutenant Nguyễn Đình Xanh was shot down again on another airstrike just eleven miles south of Charlie. Shortly after he hit the ground, he was captured by enemy soldiers. On that same day, May 9, 1972, I was shot down in my Cobra

gunship twelve miles northwest of Charlie and captured after evading the enemy for three days. Xanh and I ended up in the same jungle prison camp and spent time together being force-marched up the Ho Chi Minh Trail to North Vietnam. See my book *Through the Valley: My Captivity in Vietnam* for details.

4. John J. Duffy, "Death's Breath," E-Poetry World website at https://epoetryworld.com/page.php?groupingID=miscellaneous5.

CHAPTER 15

1. Đặng Vũ Hiệp. *Ký ức tây Nguyên* (*Highland Memories*) (Hanoi: People's Army Press, 2012), 239.

2. The radio calls that follow are derived from extracts of an audio recording of the mission made by Dennis Watson. A transcript of that recording is available on the "Battle of Kontum" website at https://www.thebattleofkontum.com/audio/WatsonDuffy.html.

3. Remembered verbatim by John Duffy and included in the poem, "Warrior's Gun," http://www.epoetryworld.com.

CHAPTER 16

1. See the online poetry collection of John Duffy at www.epoetryworld.com.

2. Thomas P. McKenna, *Kontum: The Battle to Save South Vietnam* (Lexington: The University Press of Kentucky, 2011), 116. Nguyen Trong Luan, "Trận Đồi Charlie" ("The Battle of Charlie). http://chientruongvietnam.com/2018/08/02/tham-lai-cao-diem-1015-doi-sac-ly-tran-doi-charlie/, August 2, 2018.

3. Ibid. Ngo Quang Truong, "The Easter Offensive of 1972," *Indochina Monographs* (Washington, D.C.: U.S. Army Center of Military History, 1980), 85. Peter Kama interview, February 13, 2018.

4. Phan Nhat Nam, *Mùa Hè Đỏ Lửa (Fiery Red Summer)* (Westminster, CA: Nha Xuat Ban Song, 2015 [originally published in Vietnam, 1972]). "Người Ở Lại Charlie" ("Those Who Stayed at Charlie"), song written by Tran Thien Thanh, 1972.

5. Dale Andrade, *Trial by Fire: The 1972 Easter Offensive, America's Last Vietnam Battle* (New York: Hippocrene Books, 1995), 45–176, 222.

6. Van Nguyen-Marshall, "Appeasing the Spirits Along the 'Highway of Horror': Civic Life in Wartime Republic of Vietnam," *War & Society*, 20, no. 20 (April 2018): 6–9. Peter Kama interview, February 13, 2018.

7. Andrade, *Trial by Fire*, 168–89. Truong, 50–57.

8. Tin Trong Vo and Huu Vien Nguyen, "11th Airborne Battalion: My Chanh River Tank Battle," extracted and translated from *Binh Chủng Nhảy Dù 20 năm Chiến Sự (Paratroopers in 20 Years of War)* (published by the authors, 2000), 2–3, ISBN 9781629881669.

9. Truong, 60. John D. Howard, *First In, Last Out: An American Paratrooper in Vietnam with the 101st and Vietnamese Airborne* (Guilford, CT: Stackpole Books, 2017), 166.

10. Tin Trong Vo, and Huu Vien Nguyen. "11th Airborne Battalion: My Chanh River Tank Battle," extracted and translated from *Binh Chủng Nhảy Dù 20 năm Chiến Sự (Paratroopers in 20 Years of War)*. Published by the authors, 2000.

11. Peter Kama interview, February 13, 2018.

12. Truong, 64–66.
13. Truong, 67–70. Howard, 180.

EPILOGUE

1. Ngo Quang Truong, "The Easter Offensive of 1972," *Indochina Monographs* (Washington, D.C.: U.S. Army Center of Military History, 1980), 74–75. Henry Kissinger, *Ending the Vietnam War: A History of America's Involvement in and Extraction from the Vietnam War* (New York: Simon &Schuster, 2003), 429–30.
2. Kissinger, 486–87, 505–13. James H. Willbanks. *Abandoning Vietnam: How America Left and South Vietnam Lost Its War* (Lawrence: University Press of Kansas Press, 2004), 217–18, 229–31.
3. Cao Van Vien, *The Final Collapse* (Washington, D.C.: U.S. Army Center for Military History, 1985), 46–55.
4. For example, see Charles Hirschman et al., "Vietnamese Casualties During the War: A New Estimate," *Population and Development Review*, 21, no. 4 (December 1995): 783–812, and Rudolf J. Rummel, "The Vietnamese War State," chapter 6 in *Genocide and Mass Murder Since 1900* (New York: LIT Verlag), 1998.
5. For a detailed account of the Le Family's escape from Vietnam and resettlement in the United States, see Phuong Le, "A Daughter's Journey: One Family's Passage from Vietnam," *Seattle Post-Intelligencer*, March 6–9, 2000.
6. For a detailed, firsthand account of life as a prisoner in the communist reeducation camps, see Hoa Minh Troung, *The Dark Journey: Inside the Reeducation Camps of Vietcong* (Durham, CT: Eloquent Books, 2010).

APPENDIX 3

1. Barry R. McCaffrey, "The Forgotten South Vietnamese Airborne," *New York Times*, 8 August 2017.
2. Ibid. Michael Martin, ed., *Angels in Red Hats: Paratroopers of the Second Indochina War* (Louisville, KY: Harmony House, 1995), 11, 23.
3. Bernard B. Fall, *Street Without Joy* (Mechanicsburg, PA: Stackpole Books, 1964), 26–28. Martin, *Angels*, 24
4. Martin, *Angels*, 24. Gordon Rottman, *Vietnam Airborne* (London: Osprey Publishing, 1990), 23.
5. Martin, *Angels*, 23. Rottman, *Airborne*, 23.
6. Bernard B. Fall, *Hell in a Very Small Place: The Siege of Dien Bien Phu* (New York: Harper & Row, 1964), 17. Martin Windrow, *The Last Valley: Dien Bien Phu and the French Defeat in Vietnam* (Boston, MA: Da Capo Press, 2004), 248–49.
7. Fall, *Hell*, 150–51. Windrow, *Last Valley*, 327, 393, 536. Martin, *Angels*, 34–36. Rottman, *Airborne*, 23–24.
8. Martin, *Angels*, 23, 39.
9. Frederik Logevall, *Embers of War: The Fall of an Empire and the Making of America's Vietnam* (New York: Random House, 2013), 599–607, 653–57. Stanley Karnow, *Vietnam: A History* (New York: Penguin Books, 1983), 204.

10. Rottman, *Airborne*, 24–25. Martin, *Angels*, 35. John Prados, "The Numbers Game: How Many Vietnamese Fled the South in 1954," *VVA Veteran*, Jan/Feb 2005. Karnow, *Vietnam*, 366–72, 415–19.

11. Le Van Me telephone conversation with the author, March 23, 2020. Rottman, *Airborne*, 27.

12. Martin, *Angels*, 39–40.

13. Martin, *Angels*, 40–43. Le Van Me conversation.

14. Martin, *Angels*, 43. James H. Willbanks, *Abandoning Vietnam: How American Left and South Vietnam Lost Its War* (Lawrence: University of Kansas Press, 2014), 264–67. George J. Veith and Merle L. Pribbenow, "Fighting Is an Art: The Army of Vietnam's Defense of Xuan Loc, 9–21 April 1975," *Journal of Military History*, 68, no. 1, January 2004, 163–213.

15. Martin, *Angels*, 11–12.

Sources

Primary Sources
Interviews

Archambault, Raoul, 57th Aviation Company

Barron, Richard, B Troop, 7/17 Cavalry Squadron

Carlson, Lynn, 361st Aviation Company

Doan, Hai Phuong, ARVN 11th Airborne Battalion

Duffy, John Joseph, MACV Advisory Team 162, U.S. advisor to the ARVN 11th Airborne Battalion

Gamber, Robert, 361st Aviation Company

Higgins, Jim, 20th Tactical Air Support Squadron

Jones, Daniel, 361st Aviation Company

Kama, Peter J., MACV Advisory Team 162, U.S. Advisor to the ARVN 2nd Airborne Brigade

Le, Me Van, ARVN 11th Airborne Battalion

Lennard, William, 20th Tactical Air Support Squadron

Mayes, John, 361st Aviation Company

Messa, David, 361st Aviation Company

Nguyen, Lap Van, ARVN 11th Airborne Battalion

Nguyen, Nho Tan, ARVN 11th Airborne Battalion

Nguyen, Xanh Dinh, VNAF 530th Fighter Squadron

Rogers, Curtis, TDY to MACV Advisory Team 162, U.S. advisor at Firebase Yankee

Smith, Jim, Stars & Stripes reporter

Snyder, Forrest, 361st Aviation Company

To, Dung Thai, ARVN 18th Division (brother of Dr. Lieu Pham To, 11th Airborne Bn)

Truong, An Minh, VNAF 530th Fighter Squadron

Watson, Dennis, B Troop, 7/17th Cavalry

Documents
Central Intelligence Agency. "Intelligence Memorandum," 4 April 1972 (LOC-HAK-559-30-13-4), accessed at: https://www.cia.gov/readingroom/docs/LOC-HAK-559-30-13-4.pdf.
Duffy, John Joseph. Logbook kept by Major Duffy during the battle.

Books and Articles
Duffy, John Joseph. *The Battle for "Charlie."* Create Space, 2014.
Heslin, Jack. "Firebase Delta," *The Battle of Kontum* website, https://www.thebattleofkontum.com/memories/54.html.
Hiep, Dang Vu. *Ký ức tây Nguyên* (*Highland Memories*). Hanoi: People's Army Press, 2012.
Le, Phuong. "A Daughter's Journey: One Family's Passage from Vietnam," *Seattle Post-Intelligencer*, March 6–9, 2000.
Luan, Nguyen Trong. "Trận Đồi Charlie" ("The Battle of Charlie"), accessed August 2, 1018, http://chientruongvietnam.com/2018/08/02/tham-lai-cao-diem-1015-doi-sac-ly-tran-doi-charlie/.
Nixon, Richard. *First Annual Report to the Congress on United States Foreign Policy for the 1970s*, February 18, 1970.
———. "President Nixon's Speech on Cambodia," delivered on national television on April 30, 1970.
Troung, Hoa Minh. *The Dark Journey: Inside the Reeducation Camps of Vietcong*. Durham, CT: Eloquent Books, 2010.
U.S. Military Assistance Command Vietnam (MACV). *1971 Command History*, Volume II. April 25, 1972.
———. *Command History, January 1972–March 1973*, Volume II, July 15, 1973.
———. "Recommendation for awarding the Valorous Unit Award to the Vietnamese Airborne Division and the Airborne Division Assistance Team for actions during the

period September 28–November 8, 1971," Long Bình, Republic of Vietnam, July 8, 1972; *Vietnam Service Awards*, Record Group 472–VNA–MACV, Box 29; National Archives Building, College Park, MD.

Audio

Watson, Dennis and Mike Gibbs. Cockpit voice recording during extraction of 11th Airborne Battalion survivors, April 15, 1972, accessed January 24, 2018, https://www.thebattleofkontum.com/audio/index.html.

Video

Doan, Hai Phuong. "Máu Lửa Charlie" ("Blood and Fire on 'Charlie'"). Autobiographical documentary video. Paris: Red Hat Lam San 719, 2015.

Websites

Duffy, John Joseph. *E-Poetry World*. The battle described through the poetry of the American advisor on the ground, along with a collection of related witness statements and other primary source documents. www.epoetryworld.com.

Heslin, Jack. *The Battle of Kontum*. A collection of firsthand accounts by battle participants. www.thebattleofkontum.com.

SECONDARY SOURCES

1st Battalion, 4th Marines, "Operation Lam Son 54," accessed June 6, 2018, http://1stbn4th marines.net/operations/history-folder/lam_son_54.htm.

"1972 Vietnam Counteroffensive," Chapter 7, RB 100-2, vol. 1, *Selected Readings in Tactics*. Fort Leavenworth, KS: US Army Command and General Staff College, 1974.

Andrade, Dale. *Trial by Fire: The 1972 Easter Offensive, America's Last Vietnam Battle*. New York: Hippocrene Books, 1995.

Bird, Eugene K. *Loneliest Man in the World*. London: Martin Secker and Warburg, 1974.

Birzer, Norman and Peter Mersky. *US Navy A-7 Corsair II Units in the Vietnam War*. Oxford, UK: Osprey Publishing, 2004.

Conboy, Kenneth and Kenneth Bowra. *The NVA and Viet Cong*. London, UK: Osprey Publishing, 1991.

Connelly, Hugh. "The First Operation Hickory (Operation Hickory—Belt Tight—Beau Charger—Lam Son 54)." Summarized from source materials. 1967, accessed June 6, 2018, http://www.amtrac.org/pdf_files/1atbn/OpHick01.pdf.

Correll, John T. "Arc Light," *Air Force Magazine*, January 2009.

Fall, Bernard B. *Hell in a Very Small Place: The Siege of Dien Bien Phu*. New York: Harper & Row, 1967.

———. *Street Without Joy*. Mechanicsburg, PA: Stackpole Books, 1964.

Hartsook, Elizabeth H. and Stuart Slade, *Air War: Vietnam Plans and Operations, 1969–1975*. Fort Pierce, FL: Defense Lion Publications, 2013.

Hastings, Max. *Vietnam: An Epic Tragedy, 1945–1975*. New York: HarperCollins, 2018.

Hickey, Gerald Cannon. *Free in the Forest*. New Haven, CT: Yale University Press, 1982.

———. *Sons of the Mountains*. New Haven, CT: Yale University Press, 1982.

Hirschman, Charles et al. "Vietnamese Casualties During the War: A New Estimate," *Population and Development Review*, 21, no. 4 (December 1995): 783–812, accessed November 21, 2019, https://faculty.washington.edu/charles/new%20PUBS/A77.pdf.

Howard, John D. *First In, Last Out: An American Paratrooper in Vietnam with the 101st and Vietnamese Airborne*. Guilford, CT: Stackpole Books, 2017.

Hukee, Byron E. *USAF and VNAF A-1 Skyraider Units of the Vietnam War*. Oxford, UK: Osprey 2013.

Karnow, Stanley. *Vietnam: A History*. New York: Penguin Books, 1983.

Kiernan, Ben. *Viet Nam: A History from the Earliest Times to the Present*. New York: Oxford University Press, 2017.

King, Seth S. "Malayan Jungle Schools Fighters," *New York Times*, May 3, 1964, accessed June 6, 2018, http://www.nytimes.com/1964/05/03/malayan-jungle-schools-fighters.html.

Kissinger, Henry. *Ending the Vietnam War: A History of America's Involvement in and Extraction from the Vietnam War*. New York: Simon &Schuster, 2003.

Liebchen, Peter A. "Kontum: Battle for the Central Highlands, 30 March–10 June 1972," *Project CHECO Reports*. Hickam AFB, HI: Headquarters, U.S. Pacific Air Force, October 1972, accessed October 7, 2017, https://apps.dtic.mil/dtic/tr/fulltext/u2/a487009.pdf.

Logevall, Frederik. *Embers of War: The Fall of an Empire and the Making of America's Vietnam*. New York: Random House, 2013.

Luedeke, Kirk A. "Death on the Highway: The Destruction of Groupement Mobile 100," *Armor Magazine*, January–February 2001, 22–29.

Martin, Michael, ed. *Angels in Red Hats: Paratroopers of the Second Indochina War*. Prospect, KY: Harmony House, 1995.

McCaffrey, Barry R. "The Forgotten South Vietnamese Airborne," *New York Times*, August 8, 2017, accessed March 15, 2020, https://www.nytimes.com/2017/08/08/opinion/south-vietnam-airborne.html#story-continues-3.

McKenna, Thomas P. *Kontum: The Battle to Save South Vietnam*. Lexington: University Press of Kentucky, 2011.

Moyar, Mark. *Phoenix and the Birds of Prey: The CIA's Secret Campaign to Destroy the Viet Cong*. Annapolis, MD: Naval Institute Press, 1997.

Nam, Phan Nhat. *Mùa Hè Đỏ Lửa (Red Flames of Summer)*. Westminster, CA: Nhà Xuất Bản Sống, 2015.

———. *A Vietnam War Epilogue*. Westminster, CA: Thu Vien Viet Nam Toan Cau Publishing, 2013.

Nguyen-Marshall, Van. "Appeasing the Spirits Along the 'Highway of Horror': Civic Life in Wartime Republic of Vietnam," *War & Society*, 20, no. 20 (April 2018): 1–17, accessed November 20, 2019, http://www.viet-studies.net/kinhte/HighwayofHorror_W&S.pdf.

Pacific Stars and Stripes, 28, nos. 113, 114, April 17 and 24, 1972, accessed March 3, 2018, https://www.thebattleofkontum.com/stars/.

Pearson, William. *The War in the Northern Provinces 1966–1968*. Washington, D.C.: Department of the Army, 1991.

Perry, Mike. "When Recon Team Python Ruled the Valley of Death," 22 June 2014, *Special Operations* webpage, accessed June 28, 2018, https://specialoperations.com/29027/recon-team-python-ruled-valley-death/.

Phillips, William R. *Night of the Silver Stars: The Battle of Lang Vei*. Annapolis, MD: Naval Institute Press, 1997.

Plaster, John L. *SOG: The Secret Wars of America's Commandos in Vietnam*. New York: Simon & Schuster, 1997.

Prados, John. "The Numbers Game: How Many Vietnamese Fled the South in 1954," *The VVA Veteran*, January/February 2005, accessed March 20, 2020, https://web.archive.org/web/20060527190340/http://www.vva.org/TheVeteran/2005_01/feature_numbersGame.htm.

Prados, John and Ray W. Stubbe. *Valley of Decision: The Siege of Khe Sanh*. New York: Houghton Mifflin, 1991.

Rottman, Gordon L. *Army of the Republic of Vietnam, 1955–1975*. Oxford, UK: Osprey Publishing, 2010.

——. *Khe Sanh 1967–1968: Marines battle for Vietnam's vital hilltop base*. New York: Osprey Publishing, 2005.

——. *Vietnam Airborne*. London: Osprey Publishing, 1990.

Rummel, Rudolf J. "The Vietnamese War State." Chapter 6 in *Statistics of Democide: Genocide and Mass Murder Since 1900*. New York: LIT Verlag, 1998, accessed November 21, 2019, https://www.hawaii.edu/powerkills/SOD.CHAP6.HTM.

Salemink, Oscar. *The Ethnography of Vietnam's Central Highlanders*. Honolulu: University of Hawaii Press, 2003.

Shaw, John M. *The Cambodian Campaign: The 1970 Offensive and the Vietnam War*. Lawrence: University of Kansas Press, 2005.

Shulimson, Jack et al. *U.S. Marines in Vietnam: The Defining Year 1968*. Washington, D.C.: Headquarters U.S. Marine Corps, 1997.

Sigler, David Burns. *Vietnam Battle Chronology: U.S. Army and Marine Corps Combat Operations, 1965–1973*. Jefferson, NC: McFarland & Company, 1992.

Sochurek, Howard. "Viet Nam's Montagnards: Caught in the Jaws of a War," *National Geographic*, 133, no. 4, April 1968.

Truong, Ngo Quang. "The Easter Offensive of 1972," *Indochina Monographs*. Washington, D.C.: U.S. Army Center of Military History, 1980.

Tucker, Spencer, ed., *Encyclopedia of the Vietnam War: A Political, Social, and Military History*, Vol. 1. Santa Barbara, CA: ABC-CLIO, 1998.

von Tunzelann, Alex. *Blood & Sand: Suez, Hungary, and Sixteen Days of Crisis That Changed the World*. New York: Simon & Schuster, 2001.

Veith, George J. and Merle L. Pribbenow. "Fighting Is an Art: The Army of Vietnam's Defense of Xuan Loc, 9–21 April 1975," *Journal of Military History*, 68, no. 1, January 2004.

Vien, Cao Van. *The Final Collapse*. Washington, D.C.: U.S. Army Center for Military History, 1985.

Viet, Ha Mai. *Steel and Blood: South Vietnamese Armor and the War for Southeast Asia.* Annapolis, MD: Naval Institute Press, 2008.

Vo, Tin Trong, and Huu Vien Nguyen. "11th Airborne Battalion: My Chanh River Tank Battle," extracted and translated from *Binh Chủng Nhảy Dù 20 năm Chiến Sự (Paratroopers in 20 Years of War).* Published by the authors, 2000. ISBN 978-1629881669.

Vu Hiep, Dang. *Ký úc tây Nguyên (Highland Memories).* Hanoi: People's Army Press, 2012.

Willbanks, James. *Abandoning Vietnam: How America Left and South Vietnam Lost Its War.* Lawrence: University Press of Kansas, 2004.

———. *The Battle of An Loc.* Bloomington, IN: Indiana University Press, 2005.

———. *A Raid Too Far: Operation Lam Son 719 and Vietnamization in Laos.* College Station, TX: Texas A&M University Press, 2014.

———. *The Tet Offensive: A Concise History.* New York: Columbia University Press, 2006.

Windrow, Martin. *The Last Valley: Dien Bien Phu and the French Defeat in Vietnam.* Boston, MA: De Capo Press, 2004.

INDEX

American Forces Vietnam Network (AFVN), 100

An Lộc, fighting in region of, 121, 127, 137, 202, 207, 227

Arc Light strikes, 119, 133, 176

Army of the Republic of Vietnam (ARVN), 18, 57, 80, 98, 207; An Lộc garrison, 127; Bảo consulting with, 99; in Cambodia, 59, 62, 76–77, 81; at Charlie Hill, 112, 123, 155, 163; Eleventh Airborne Battalion, joint task force with, 79; elite status of unit, 11; enemy attacks on, 186; historical note, 223–28; Hyatt as senior U.S. advisor to, 196; I Corps, dispatching brigade to, 19; at Kontum Province, 65, 87–88; Lam Son 719 thrust into Laos, 63–64, 109; lessons learned regarding, 219; Mễ, accusatory attitude towards, 194; post-Charlie activity, 199, 202, 204, 208; post-war fate of former soldiers, 214–13, 217; at Rocket Ridge, 97; Tận Sơn Nhứt Airbase headquarters, 74; Tết offensive, response to, 20; war losses, 208; withdrawal from highlands, 198

Bạch Diễn Sơn (Bach Dien Son), 169–68

Bảo. *See* Nguyễn Đình Bảo

Barron, Richard, 186–85

Beckwith, Charlie, 209

Big Hùng. *See* Phạm Đức Hùng

Blue Dragon Bar, 83, 177, 199

Bru peoples, 43–46, 47, 91

Butler, James, 109–8, 189

Carlson, Lynn, 111

Case-Church Amendment (1973), 207

Charlie Hill: 130-millimeter guns, enemy use of, 117–16, 134, 195; battle-space map, *103*; battle to the end, beginning of, 121–21; Charlie Two, defense of, 112, 113, 114–14, 120; Duffy preparations for battle, 100, 106, 109–8; Eleventh Airborne Battalion efforts, *105*, 111, 112, 127, 141–40, 148, 161, 170, 171, 173, 177, 188, 190, 193, 196, 199, 223; friendly fire upon, 181–80; initial helicopter assault, 101–2, *104*; legacy of, 207; lessons learned from Charlie, 219; Mễ, deciding to give up Charlie 1, 146–45; North Vietnamese activity, 97–98, 133, 135–34, 141, 143–43, 156, 161–68, 174, 198; Task Force Mễ, 112–14; veterans of, 205, 208–16; withdrawal from, 172, 175–75, 181–88

Church, John, 19

Civilian Irregular Defense Groups (CIDG), 44–45, 46, 48

Claymore antipersonnel mines, 61, 100, 141, 237

combat operations: Operation 72, 203; Operation A Shau, 58–59, 109; Operation Castor, 225; Operation Citadel, 205; Operation Dambae, 79–81, 156; Operation Delaware/ Lam Sơn 216, 58; Operation Eagle 800, 17; Operation Hickory, 18; Operation Lam Sơn 72, 203; Operation Lam Sơn (Lam Son) 719, 63–64, 93, 109, 227; Operation Núi Bà Đen (Nui Ba Den), 80; Operation Pegasus/Lam Sơn 207A, 57–58; Operation Tiến Giang (Tien Giang) 54, 13; Operation Toàn Thắng (Toan Thang) 2-71, 77–78

Compagnie Indochinoise Parachutiste (CIP), 224

Cooper-Church Amendment, 63

C-Rations, 100, 233

Crenshaw, William, 48

Đàm Vú Hiệp (Dam Vu Hiep), 145

Delta Firebase, 94, 111–10, 114, 116

Demilitarized Zone (DMZ), 5, 18, 44, 63, 82, 90, 97, 127, 198, 200, 233

Điên Biên Phủ (Dien Bien Phu), battle of, 136, 225, 226

Đinh Viết Trinh (Dinh Viet Trinh), 198, 205

Đoàn Phương Hải (Doan Phuong Hai), 81, 93, 118, 135, 174, 221; Bảo as commander of, 67, 68, 79, 102, 104, 143, 144; Big Hùng, communicating with, 151, 153; Duffy, interactions with, 91, 102, 117, 121, 127, 129, 165, 167; injuries, sustaining, 188–87, 197; Kontum travel orders, 80, 84, 92; Mế, as deputy to, 65, 157, 162, 171, 172, 184; NVA ambushes and, 147, 198; radio operations, maintaining, 106, 109, 111, 123, 133, 182–81; in second

helicopter at Firebase Charlie assault, 99, 101; Vietnam, escaping with family, 213–12, 215; VNAF, working with, 77, 100, 119, 122, 142, 155, 156, 158, 163, 169

Duffy, Inge, 42, 50; family and, 32–33, 49; at Fort Bragg, 35, 36; in Germany, 29–30, 37, 41

Duffy, John: Bad Tolz assignment, 29–31; Berlin assignment, 36–37; Cambodia, forbidden from entering, 79; Charlie Hill airpower, coordinating, 115–21, 127–27, 133–35, 142–46, 151–50, 162–65, 170; childhood and adolescence, 25–27; continuing studies, 49–50; debriefing after Charlie Hill, 193, 194–95; with Fifth Airborne Battalion, 80–81; first enlistment, 27–28; Fort Bragg assignment, 33–34, 35, 36; Fort Sherman training, 41–42; in Kontum Province, 88, 90–94; Lang Vei assignment, 43–47, 48; Mế and, 4, 67, 75–76, 83–84, 136, 171, 173–72, 199, 211; Medal of Honor, consideration for, 196, 209; in the Mike Force, 47–48; at Operation Toan Thang 2-71, 77–78; post-war activities, 208–8, 212–11; rear guard, 173–75; recovery from arm injuries, 31–32; at Red Hat Hill, 75, 81, 199; retreat from Charlie Hill, 172–75, 181–88; Rocket Ridge action, 97–102, 104, 106–8; SOG missions, 51–54, 73–74; wounded, 46, 78, 145–46, 154–55, 162, 184

Dương Huỳnh Kỳ (Duong Huynh Ky), 157

Easter Offensive (1972), 199, 203, 207, 227, 244n3

Eighth Airborne Battalion, 57, 227

Eleventh Airborne Battalion, *105*, 221, **227**; "Dual Swords Regaining the Frontier" slogan, 201. *See also under* Charlie Hill

Fifth Airborne Battalion, 59, 62, 80, 81, 205, 227

Firebase Charlie. *See* Charlie Hill

Firebase Delta, *89*, 94, 111–12, 114, 116, 129

First Airborne Brigade, 63, 127, 201–202, 227, 228

Fleet, Robert, 35

French Indochina, 136, 223–22, 226

Furrow, Gail Woodrow, 200, 202

Gamber, Robert, 167–66

Geneva Convention, 50, 136, 225–24

Gibbs, Mike, 185, 187, 188, 189

Green Berets, 34, 92; Duffy as a Green Beret, 31, 42, 75–76; at Lang Vei village, 45, 47–48; SOGs, working with, 50–51, 74

Griswold, Terry (Buddha), 189–88, 193, 222

Gulf of Tonkin attack, 35

Hải. *See* Đoàn Phương Hải

Hess, Rudolf, 36–37

Higgins, Jim, 184–83

Hitler, Adolf, 31, 36

Hoàng Ngọc Hùng (Hoang Ngoc Hung), 101, 112–11, 120, 153, 155, 198, 205, 221

Hồ Chí Minh (Ho Chi Minh), 136, 224, 226

Ho Chi Minh Trail, 51, 58, 63, 245n3

Humanitarian Operation (HO) program, 217

Hyatt, Robert, 196

II Corps, 88, *89*, 98, 167, 193, 194, 222

Isler, Jack, 51

Joint Casualty Resolution Center (JCRC), 209

Jones, Daniel, 164

Kama, Peter J., 93, 146, 190; as 2nd Airborne Bridage advisor, 119, 189, 204, 222; B-52 strikes, arranging, 128, 129; debriefings, assisting with, 193, 194, 195; Medal of Honor, submitting Duffy for, 196, 209; Prairie Fire call from Duffy, receiving, 167; Rocket Ridge, giving background on, 94, 97–98

Kennedy, John F., 10–11

Khe Sanh base, 5, 19, 42–43, 44, 57–58, 63

Khuất Duy Tiến (Khuat Duy Tien), 141

Kontum Province, 136, 163; Battle of Kontum, 199, 207, 227; Central Highlands location, 5, 65, *89*; ground convoy to, 88, 90–91; Kontum City, 92, 93, 170, 193, 198–97; medical aid in, 134, 189, 197; orders to proceed to, 84, 87; Rocket Ridge as key to defense of, 94, 98

Lập. *See* Nguyễn Văn Lập

Lavine, Skip, 65–66, 69

Le Duc Dat (Colonel Dat), 97

Lê Lợi (Le Loi), 18

Lennard, Ron, 116–15, 162

Lê Văn Mẽ (Le Van Me), 19, 111, 157, 198, 218; advanced infantry course, attending, 62–63; air strikes, directing, 118, 119, 120, 121; Bảo and, 66, 68, 77, 104, 106, 109, 112, 114, 116; at Charlie Hill, 116–17, 121–20, 127, 129, 133, 135, 142–41;

as commander, 144–46, 153, 155–56,
162, 163–65, 171–75, 182–82,
187–88, 202–205; Duffy and, 4,
67, 75–76, 83–84, 99, 136, 173–72,
199, 203, 211; Dũng, replacing
with Thinh, 81–82; early life, 9–10;
Eleventh Battalion and, 64–65, 69,
197, 200–204, 207, 221, 228; escape
from Vietnam, 210–11, 214, 215;
heroism of, 187, 189, 194, 203, 227;
injuries, sustaining, 4, 17, 173–72,
201; Kontum, traveling to, 84, 88, 90;
Lịch, working with, 64, 84, 93–94;
marriage and family, 14–15, 20–21,
60, 83, 115, 193, 194, 197; Nam,
under command of, 57–58; Ninety-
first Company, leading, 20; in One
Hundred Fourteenth Company,
78, 79, 113; promotions, 13, 18, 61,
207; Saigon duty, 16, 59; in Second
Platoon, 11–13
Lewis, Ron, 167, 168
Lịch. See Trần Quốc Lịch
Liệu. See Tô Phạm Liệu
LRP rations, 100, 234
Lưu Văn Đúng (Luu Van Dung), 147

Martell cognac, 21, 68, 83, 177, 199–98,
204, 218
Mayes, John, 167, 168
McCaffrey, Barry, 228–28
Mễ. See Lê Văn Mễ
Mekong River Delta, 5, 11, 42
Messa, Dave, 167, 168–67
Military Assistance Command Vietnam–
Studies and Observation Group
(MACV-SOG), 50–53, 73, 92, 109,
110, 209, 234
Montagnards (mountain people), 44,
91–92

Mosiello, Albert, 53–54
Mũ Đỏ (Mu Do), elite status of, 16

National Liberation Front (NLF), 19, 235
Ngô Dzu (Ngo Dzu), 88, 193, 222
Ngô Lệ Tỉnh (Ngo Le Tinh), 64–65, 66
Nguyễn Chí Hiếu (Nguyen Chi Hieu), 61,
80
Nguyễn Đinh Bảo (Nguyen Dinh Bao),
81, 111, 122, 144; Charlie, mission
to defend, 94, 113, 116, 123, 143;
as commander, 67, 104, 106–7,
117, 121, 221; death of, 144; Duffy,
working with, 75–76, 129, 133,
135; eye injury, sustaining, 78–79;
Kontum, orders to deploy to, 84, 90;
as a leader, 66, 93, 101, 134; national
hero, 199; orders, giving, 77, 99, 102,
112, 114, 128; recognition of military
duty, 83, 199; Red Hat Hill club,
establishing, 68, 69; "Spooky" gunship
assistance, assessment of, 118–17;
Thinh promotion, consulting with Mễ
on, 82, 156
Nguyễn Đình Xanh (Nguyen Dinh Xanh),
169–68, 244n3
Nguyễn Đức Cẩn (Nguyen Duc Can), 58
Nguyễn Đức Dũng (Nguyen Duc Dung),
81–82, 156
Nguyễn Đức Tâm (Nguyen Duc Tam),
201
Nguyễn Khoa Nam (Nguyen Khoa Nam),
57
Nguyễn Lô (Nguyen Lo), 14, 62–63
Nguyễn Tấn Nho (Nguyen Tan Nho), 198,
221
Nguyễn Thị Sen (Nguyen Thi Sen):
courtship and marriage, 14–15,
16–17, 20–21; departure from
Vietnam, 210–11; family and, 20–21,

60, 61, 83, 109, 115, 194; in Saigon, 16, 59, 62, 82, 129, 193, 197
Nguyễn Văn Khánh (Nguyen Van Khanh), 156, 157, 158
Nguyễn Văn Lập (Nguyen Van Lap), 113, 118, 135, 198, 216–16, 221
Nguyễn Văn Thành (Nguyen Van Thanh), 228
Nguyễn Văn The (Nguyen Van The), 145
Nguyễn Văn Thinh (Nguyen Van Thinh), 82, 141–40, 147, 155–56, 201, 221
Nihsen, Dallas, 185, 188–87
Ninth Airborne Battalion, 19, 20, 21, 205
Nixon, Richard, 59, 61–62, 207

P-38 can openers, 100
Paris Peace Accords, 207
Pezzelle, Roger, 74
Phạm Đức Hùng (Pham Duc Hung), 151, 198, 221; Bảo, working with, 102, 121; as Big Hùng, 101, 104, 122, 153; Mễ and, 165, 171–70, 182
Phan Cảnh Cho (Phan Canh Cho), 113, 117, 198, 221
POW/MIA Accounting Agency, 209
Presidential Unit Citation, 209, 227

Quảng Trị (Quang Tri) battles, 19, 121, 137, 200, 203–2, 205, 207, 214, 227

recoilless rifles, 141, 143, 145, 162, 164, 165; describing and defining, 238, 239; enemy use of, 113, 129, 134, 156, 157; as a heavier rifle, 100
Red Hat Hill, 67; Bảo and 11th Airborne club, 68; Duffy, first visit to, 75; as Eleventh Battalion garrison, 66, 69, 81, 197–97, 228
Reeder, William (author), 164
Rhadé peoples, 48, 91–92

Rocket Ridge, 97, 117, 186; air support, fog preventing, 115–14; Eleventh Airborne Battalion at, 106, 177; Kontum, as key to defense of, 94; North Vietnamese activity at, 98, 199

Sadler, John, 73–74
Saigon, fall of, 208
Sanders, William, 53
Schirach, Baldur von, 36
Second Airborne Battalion, 66, 111, 112
Second Airborne Brigade, 64, 202, 227; emergency resupply, plan for, 163; at Firebase Pace, 79; I Corps, reinforcing, 200, 201; in Kontum region, 66, 88; Lịch as commander of, 93–94, 189, 204, 222; Mễ, as operations officer for, 63; Peter Kama as advisor, 119; Phan Rang, defending, 228; Võ Định operations bunker, 104, 168, 182
Selassie, Haile, 34
Sen. See Nguyễn Thị Sen
Seventh Airborne Battalion, 20, 204
Shelton, William, 52
Sixth Airborne Battalion, 57–58, 201, 205, 227
Skinny Hùng. See Hoàng Ngọc Hùng
Smith, Mike, 19, 21
Smith, Pat, 92
Snyder, Forrest, 175
Speer, Albert, 36
Stallings, Franklin D., 43–45, 48

Tận Sơn Nhứt (Tan Son Nhut) Airbase, 67, 74, 88, 195, 196, 197, 226
Tết (Tet) Offensive (1968), 18–19, 49, 227, 244n3
Third Airborne Battalion, 11–12, 17, 18, 57–58, 94, 201, 202

Third Airborne Brigade, 57, 62, 79, 201, 204, 216, 227

Tô Phạm Liệu (To Pham Lieu), 90, 104, 193, 221; Bảo, tending to, 79, 144; as battalion surgeon, 78, 158, 176, 183; Mễ and, 65, 164, 177, 182; post-war activities, 214–14

Trấn Quốc Lịch (Tran Quoc Lich), 64, 111; Bảo, communicating with, 123; debriefings, assisting with, 190, 193; as Second Airborne Brigade commander, 93–94, 189, 202, 204, 222

Trigg, Dennis, 147

Trưởng Ngô Quang (Truong Ngo Quang), 200–99

Vann, John Paul, 98, 194, 222

Vaught, Jim, 74–75

Việt Minh (Viet Minh) fighters, 116, 136, 224, 225, 226

Vietnamization, 59, 62, 74

VSOP. See Martell cognac

Vũ Văn Thanh (Vu Van Thanh), 169

Watson, Dennis, 185, 188, 189

Wear, George, 194–93, 196, 222

Weyand, Frederick, 93, 195–94, 204

ABOUT THE AUTHOR

William Reeder is a training and leader development consultant living in the Pacific Northwest. He spends parts of each year in the education of NATO Special Operations Forces in various European locations. He was formerly an associate professor of social sciences and deputy director of the U.S. Army School of Advanced Military Studies at Fort Leavenworth, Kansas. He retired from the U.S. Army in 1995 as a colonel and subsequently earned a PhD in history and anthropology from Kansas State University. His military service included assignments in field artillery, cavalry, and aviation. He has extensive combat experience.

Reeder is a thirty-year Army veteran with two tours of duty in Vietnam, flying armed OV-1 Mohawk reconnaissance airplanes and AH-1 Cobra attack helicopters. He participated in deep reconnaissance and surveillance operations throughout Southeast Asia and supported the special operations missions of MACV-SOG (Military Assistance Command Vietnam, Studies and Observations Group). He has more than three thousand hours of flight time, including more than one thousand hours in combat. During his second combat tour, he was shot down and captured by the communist North Vietnamese, spending nearly a year as a prisoner of war.

Subsequent military assignments included various Army command and staff positions and a stint at the U.S. Air Force Academy. He commanded at all levels, platoon through brigade (including command of an AH-64 Apache attack helicopter squadron). His last assignment before retirement in 1995 was as the deputy chief of staff, de facto chief of staff, for the United States Southern Command in Panama.

His military awards and decorations include the Silver Star for gallantry, Valorous Unit Award, Defense Superior Service Medal, Legion of Merit, two Distinguished Flying Crosses, and three Bronze Star Medals, three Purple Hearts for wounds received in action, the POW Medal, Vietnamese Cross of Gallantry with Bronze Star, and numerous Air Medals (one with "V" device). In 1977, he was named Army Aviator of the Year, and he was inducted into the U.S. Army Aviation Hall of Fame in 2014. He was featured in the PBS documentary *The Helicopter Pilots of Vietnam*, as well as the "Attack Helicopters" episode of *Deadliest Tech* on the Military Channel. He has provided military commentary on CNN and the Discovery Channel.

Reeder is married to the former Melanie Lineker of Westminster, Maryland, who is also a retired Army colonel and recently retired from her postmilitary career as the director of manpower (N-1) for the U.S. Navy Northwest Region, headquartered at Bangor Submarine Base, Washington. They have four children and one grandchild.